LIGHTING THE
SHAKESPEAREAN STAGE

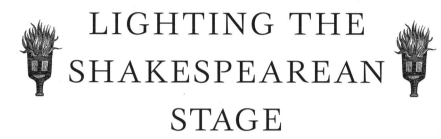

LIGHTING THE SHAKESPEAREAN STAGE

1567–1642

R. B. GRAVES

Southern Illinois University Press

Carbondale and Edwardsville

Library of Congress Cataloging-in-Publication Data
Graves, R. B., [DATE]
Lighting the Shakespearean stage, 1567–1642 / R. B. Graves.
p.   cm.
Includes bibliographical references and index.
1. Stage lighting—Great Britain—History—16th century.
2. Stage lighting—Great Britain—History—17th century. I. Title.
PN2091.E4G73 1999
792'.025—dc21   99-19002
ISBN 0-8093-2275-7 (cloth : alk. paper)   CIP

The paper used in this publication meets the minimum requirements
of American National Standard for Information Sciences—Permanence of
Paper for Printed Library Materials, ANSI Z39.48-1984. ∞

CONTENTS

v

Contents

FIGURES

Figures

PREFACE

Offered here is a survey of English theatrical lighting from the rise of professional acting troupes in London to the close of the playhouses by act of Parliament in 1642. This period—which, for convenience, I refer to as Shakespearean—saw plays performed in a variety of venues, each with its own kind of illumination, and it is one of my purposes to compare and contrast the effect of stage lighting in various playhouses and on different plays and audiences. In doing so, I have been under the obligation of presenting evidence from a number of primary sources, secondary works in theatrical history, and studies in such far-flung fields as psychophysics, architectural lighting, and the history of weather. I have tried to consolidate this evidence as much as possible, choosing the most representative examples, while bearing in mind that descriptions of one playhouse do not necessarily apply to others and that an effect achieved in one play may not have been achieved in others.

Wherever possible, I quote in the original spelling because the etymology of certain technical terms such as "lanthorne" is obscured by modernization. Similarly, pounds, shillings, and pence have been cited in their old forms where one pound equals twenty shillings and one shilling equals twelve pence. On the other hand, play titles, which were recorded in various forms, have been regularized in accordance with standard reference works, and old-style dates have been adjusted to conform with the modern practice of beginning the year on 1 January. Occasionally, I have found it useful to include diagrams to illustrate the directionality of light in the halls and amphitheaters, but these schematic drawings should in no sense be considered competent reconstructions of the playhouses or even adequate depictions of other important qualities of the illumination.

I am under many obligations for help received. Alan Dessen and the late S. Schoenbaum gave early counsel, while Michael Shapiro offered advice at a later stage when it was sorely needed. Andrew Gurr generously facilitated my research at the new Globe in Southwark, as did Michael Holden, Tiffany

Foster, and Kristin Dunstan. The editors of *Renaissance Drama*, *Shakespeare Quarterly*, and *Theatre Notebook* improved material originally published in those journals in different form, while Beverly Adamczyk checked many details, supported in part by a grant from the University of Illinois Graduate College Research Board. Don Llewellyn prepared several of the drawings, and the officers of the libraries and museums included in the captions graciously gave permission to reproduce photographs of material in their collections.

LIGHTING THE
SHAKESPEAREAN STAGE

1

LIGHT ON THE PLAY

I have . . . told twice over how many candles there are i'th' roome lighted, which I will set you downe to a snuffe precisely, because I love to give light to posteritie in the truth of things.

— *News from the New World* (1620)

WHEN THE PEDANTIC Chronicler of Ben Jonson's masque *News from the New World* boasts that he will tell how many candles lit its presentation at Whitehall, Jonson ridicules him just as scornfully as we should judge a modern critic who could think of nothing better than to count the number of spotlights at the latest Stratford Festival.[1] We feel that familiarity with the lighting practices of one's time makes such extravagance of detail unnecessary. And Jonson believed (or came to believe after a quarrel with his scene designer, Inigo Jones) that by dwelling on the physical aspects of stage production, the central dramatic concerns of language and meaning were ignored. But after nearly four centuries, our perspective is somewhat different, because the playtexts that have come down to us do not contain all the information we need to understand them. We are not always sure what such simple terms as "top," "above," and even "enter" mean; still less do we fully grasp how the physical environment affected the meaning of the actors' lines. The interest that attaches to early modern production arises from a desire to comprehend the theatrical environments that Jonson and his readers knew by heart but took for granted and failed to describe for us. Jonson could not have predicted that our stage investigation, far from directing attention away from the words he cherished, seeks to understand them in their fullest context.

It is over Jonson's objections, then, that I offer here very nearly what his Chronicler tells us he will pass down to us—a detailed description of the kinds of light and lighting instruments used in the theaters of early modern London. I trace the contrasting traditions of daylit "public" playhouses and candlelit "private" playhouses, describe the different techniques, and estimate their effect. My purpose is to provide a clearer picture than has heretofore been available of what plays acted by Shakespeare, Jonson, and their contemporaries looked like.

Although the chapters that follow count unrepentantly torches and tapers, candles and footcandles, Jonson nevertheless warns us of methodological problems in recreating a play by means of describing the physical circumstances of its original production. As an archaeological principle, we must acknowledge that all we can know of the past is the durable, but there is no assurance that the durable is the most significant part of a bygone society or drama. The worth of physical artifacts is not intrinsic but rather contingent upon the degree to which artisans embodied important functions of their culture in them and left us codes by which we can decipher those functions.

With the discovery in 1989 of the foundations of the Rose playhouse and the subsequent uncovering of a portion of the foundations of the second Globe, we can now base our study of performed drama on the durable remains of two important amphitheaters. Nevertheless, even the best reconstructions of these remains do not necessarily tell us how the original audiences interpreted their significance. Even if the second Globe stood today for our inspection, we must not forget that early modern playgoers may have construed its structure very differently from the way we might today. As Stephen Greenblatt points out in a wider context, "Anthropological interpretation must address itself less to the mechanics of custom and institution than to the interpretive constructions the members of a society apply to their experiences."[2]

Viewed as evidence, light in one sense may be characterized as the least permanent aspect of theatrical production. For the spectators at Shakespeare's Globe, light was indeed an ephemeral element of the play. The stage pictures they admired vanished as soon as they were realized, inexorably mingling with the next picture. These images can never be recaptured. Yet in another sense, light remains one of the most enduring elements in our reconstructions, because the daylight that illuminated the original Globe stage is the same daylight that we enjoy and have at our disposal to know and study. In daylight, we possess the actual "material" that Shakespeare and his contemporaries employed in their theater. When in his growing despair Lear pleads, for example, "O let me not be mad, not mad sweet Heauens" (F 918), we may miss one iconographic meaning of his prayer because we are not sure what the roof over the stage, or heavens, looked like.[3] But we know how the sky over the Globe could look and thus are able to interpret at least one connotation of Lear's entreaty in terms of its original theatrical setting. We can see him crying out, not in the gloom of many modern revivals, but under an open sky, a sky nevertheless unpredictable, by turns friendly or warm, stormy or menacing. Similarly, even as Othello vows revenge "by yond Marble Heauen" (F 2110)—another allusion to the heavens or to the ceiling of the Whitehall banqueting house painted "overheade wth Cloudes and other devices"[4]—Iago's prayer to "you euer-burning Lights aboue, / You Elements, that clip vs round about" (F 2114–16) speaks to a wider sphere of influence, one that we know as well as Jacobean playgoers, even if our understanding of it may still differ from theirs.

No one today needs proof that stage lighting influences an audience's response to a play. Yet, our stage lighting differs from Shakespeare's with respect to the means by which the influence is exerted, namely its susceptibility to artistic control. For it was only with the introduction of gas and electricity in the nineteenth century that stage illumination became a full-fledged theatrical art. Only when the intensity, color, extent, and direction of light fell to the direct and flexible control of dimmer boards and adjustable spotlights did the function of general illumination rise above questions of simple visibility and actively begin to manipulate the aesthetic experience of the audience.

But what of the older drama whose light admitted of little or no regulation? Did the ungovernable daylight at the Globe actively participate in defining the meaning of the drama? Can we say that the candlelight at Blackfriars significantly influenced either the performance or the perception of plays performed there? We must recognize the effect of such choices as the building of a "shadow" over the outdoor stage, the closing of window shutters for certain tragedies indoors, and the bringing on of property lights not just for the purpose of visibility or scenic decoration but to act as signs of what time and location the scene was supposed to take place. Few of us, however, would claim that these efforts are equivalent to the flexible and controllable illumination of the modern lighting designer.

But the assumption that an audience's response to theatrical illumination derives primarily from artists' intentions is only a century old. Stage illumination did not emerge fully as an expressive element in the theater until Adolphe Appia touted light in his influential *Die Musik und die Inscenierung* (Munich, 1899) as the means by which actors, scenery, and text could be welded together in union with the underlying "music" of a play in performance. Theater historians did not begin reconstructing the original circumstances of performance until late-nineteenth-century scientific archaeology had asserted that a culture's past could be understood by piecing together its man-made artifacts. The search for the Elizabethan stage began in earnest with the discovery of the famous Swan sketch in 1888 by Karl Gädertz, but it was inspired as much, I think, by the successful excavations of Heinrich Schliemann at Troy and Mycenae in the 1870s and of Sir Arthur Evans at Cnossos a few years later. Early Elizabethan-stage scholars worked in a climate of scientific progress, a confidence that a culture's inner life could be explained by what it had made of its physical surroundings.

But this archaeological perspective may ignore some of the special problems inherent in reconstructing not a city or culture but a work of art. For in the historical examination of the drama, we are obliged to consider not only the intention of the artisans (playwright and actor) as evinced by their remaining work (text and staging) but also the manner in which the work was viewed by their contemporaries (the audience). Archaeological models for theater research may thus not take an audience's response sufficiently into account, because there is no real analogy to an audience in the study of ancient societies. How most artists manipulated their materials is inherent in finished paintings, poems, or plays—in material evidence, that is, that we can still examine. But an audience's response leaves little behind for us to study, especially when, as Andrew Gurr's census of playgoers reveals, much of what an audience experiences during the performance is routinely left unsaid.[5]

Even so, an audience's response to stage lighting, however difficult to assess directly, may in turn affect the playwright's craft, because it is an article of faith among theater historians that dramatists generally write with an eye toward production and that expected performance conditions will affect the composition of the play. In 1948, for example, G. E. Bentley published his pioneer article "Shakespeare and the Blackfriars Theatre," in which he argued that the apparent change in tone of Shakespeare's late romances may be accounted for in part by conscious artistic decisions that the King's men made in anticipation of their acquisition of the small, artificially lit second Blackfriars in 1609 in addition to the large, open-air Globe.[6] Evidence of fewer seats, a smaller stage closer to wealthier patrons, and the splendor of the lighting was adduced to explain the presence of a more sophisticated audience requiring a shift in Shakespeare's thematic interests. A few years later, Alfred Harbage followed in Bentley's footsteps and in *Shakespeare and the Rival Traditions* (New York, 1952) painted a similar picture of two widely divergent kinds of drama intended for indoor and outdoor production. Both assumed that the physical structures of the different theaters determined in part the style and meaning of the dramas performed there. They believed that, despite the King's men's playing both indoors and outdoors, a discernible shift in theatrical style had been imposed on actors and playwrights by the configurations of the Jacobean hall playhouses and their more sophisticated audiences.

Forty years later, however, the picture is less clear. Although Ann Jennalie Cook has asserted that audiences at both kinds of playhouses were drawn largely from privileged members of society, Andrew Gurr has shown that, while there may have been a slight increase in the sophistication in the hall audiences, Shakespeare's audience remained diverse, and the King's company "did not radically alter its repertory when it moved to Blackfriars."[7] Equally important, researchers looking into staging practices at the public and private playhouses found little to differentiate them, and the current assessment of Bentley's and Harbage's work is that they overstated the case. Indeed, in an investigation of staging practices for plays written from 1599 to 1642, T. J. King concluded that the physical differences between public and private playhouses were less significant than had been thought. "Although these two kinds of playhouses differed in outward appearance," he announced, "analysis of 276 plays probably first acted by professionals in this period shows that there were no significant differences in the staging requirements of the various companies"[8]

But a glance at King's book reveals that his careful analysis cannot conclusively compare the effect of indoor and outdoor production, because he has restricted the kind of evidence that can influence the meaning of the drama. He decides that the public and private theaters must have been similar in *inward* appearance because he examines only facilities over which the actors had more or less full control. Thus, King may be correct in saying there were no major changes in staging, because to him staging means the tables and chairs, doors and partitions, balconies and traps, onstage. The titles of his chapters make this narrow conception of staging plain: "Entrances and Large Properties," "Above the Stage," "Doors and Hangings," and "Below the Stage." But these are the very facilities that one would *not* expect to change as the actors moved indoors. The troupes would bring the same tables and chairs they used outdoors with them. They would set up doors and traps in their familiar places and attempt to duplicate as much as possible the environment to which they were already accustomed. One imagines that the stages, stage properties, and tiring-house walls of the two playhouses resembled each other as much as possible so that the actors could avoid restaging their plays every time they migrated from the summer Globe to the winter Blackfriars or to court.

Contrasting with attempts to see plays as written for specific theaters and lighting arrangements are the admonitions of Clifford Leech, J. A. Lavin, and others that playwrights wrote less to turn a given theater to good account than to please themselves or, at the least, to follow the prevailing literary fashion.[9] Lavin goes so far as to deny that the King's men could have seen any aesthetic distinction between the Globe and Blackfriars and will allow their playwrights no accommodation to it. Lavin's insistence on the interchangeability of public and private playhouse repertory is well taken in regard to the King's men, but Lavin forgets that playwrights, particularly Caroline playwrights, tell us that they sometimes wrote with specific theaters in mind, including the Blackfriars. For example, John Webster participated in adapting a Blackfriars play, Marston's *The Malcontent*, to the resources available at a public theater in 1604, when he was called on "to abridge the not received custome of musicke" at the Globe.[10] In spite of their various conclusions, Bentley and Harbage, on the one hand, and King and Lavin, on the other, all assume that aesthetic differences between the theaters may be measured only by the intentions of the artists involved. To Bentley and Harbage, there *must* be differences, because they find the plays written for each kind of theater different. To King and Lavin, there cannot be any major differences, because the actors apparently took no account of them.

But there were important elements of production that the players could not bring with them or duplicate as they moved back and forth from one playhouse to another. Among these, the acoustics, the size of the playing space, and the lighting remained more or less dependent on the actual production site and allowed little or no modification to suit the tastes of playwrights, actors, or spectators. Regarding acoustics, I can only note in passing its impact on the playtexts and staging. In comparing the verse of Thomas Kyd and James Shirley, say, we have to take into account not only two different temperaments at two different points in the development of English poetry but also two different kinds of acoustics—those of the large, outdoor amphitheaters and of the small, indoor hall playhouses. Thus, when Shirley in "A *Prologue at the* Globe *to his Comedy call'd* The doubtfull Heire, *which should have been presented at the* Black-Friers" has actors at the open-air Globe complain that they are forced "to break our lungs" in contrast to the easily heard speech at Blackfriars, we do not need to explain the difference between the ranting of Kyd and the slick proficiency of Shirley solely by recourse to perceived shifts in social and literary fashion from Elizabethan to Caroline times.[11] The form of their respective playhouses contributed a more direct influence on the kind of language appropriate to each. What is more, the acoustics available indoors affected at least one important element of staging. Richard Hosley has noted that the only significant difference between indoor and outdoor staging methods derived from the early use of a permanent music room at the indoor playhouses, inspired by the livelier acoustics there. These music rooms were visible to the audience and, hence, became available for discoveries "above" well before the practice took hold at the amphitheaters. Indeed, Hosley finds that the outdoor playhouses did not adopt the practice until the King's men began regular performances at Blackfriars.[12]

Similarly, it is surprising that only recently have scholars thought to compare the two kinds of theaters with respect to lighting, which, of all the elements of theatrical production, may well be the crucible wherein supposed differences or similarities can be tested. For while *King Lear* was performed by "his Maiesties seruants playing vsually at the Gloabe on the Bancke-side," it was also performed indoors "*before the Kings Maiestie at* White hall *vpon* S. Stephans *night in Christmas Hollidayes* [26 December 1606]," as the title page of the 1608 quarto testifies. At Whitehall, no natural sunlight could ameliorate the play's gloomy view of heaven; when Lear looked up to the sky there, both he and the audience saw something very different from what they had seen at the Globe. At Whitehall, chandeliers supporting dozens of candles hung overhead, which one could argue emphasized not Lear's helplessness in the face of unleashed natural forces but rather the artificial control that man could and did occasionally exercise over the powers of darkness. At Blackfriars, the King's men's indoor theater, natural window light and artificial candlelight mingled together to illuminate the stage, a combination from which one might develop still another iconographic interpretation of the scene.

Or to choose a more famous example, how did the bare light of Othello's candle in Desdemona's death scene behave in relation to the general illumination at the Globe, Blackfriars, and court? When Othello enters her bedroom *"with a light"* and compares it to Desdemona's life —

> Put out the light, and then put out the light:
> If I quench thee, thou flaming minister,
> I can againe, thy former light restore   (Q1 M)

—are we to see this lonely candle burning in a darkened hall, ironically signaling her true chastity in a nasty world? Or rather, are we to imagine it throwing out a feeble light on a brightly sunlit stage? Was the scene presented illusionistically at the indoor theaters with only Othello's flickering candle lighting the stage? In that case, the audience might have difficulty seeing Desdemona's horrified reaction to Othello's accusations whether or not he leaves the candle burning for the entire scene. Because Shakespeare specifically associates Desdemona with the light, we want to grasp its significance and know whether the emotional connotations of the scene changed as the King's men performed outdoors or indoors, during the day or night, that is, as the general illumination of the theater changed.

Such questions are worth asking for their own sake, of course. Along with sound, light is the means by which all performed plays are comprehended. Light participates in concert with language, sound effects, and music to produce meaning; the more we know about what Shakespeare's audience saw, the more we know about what it understood. Even Jonson's rejection of Jones's elaborate lighting effects pays genuine, though negative, homage to the power of light to affect the meaning of the drama, or at least the play-wright's perception of that meaning.

But perhaps more important for us, such questions should be raised because the answers to them can be found—and as these matters go, can be found rather easily. For a century, we have been agonizing over the internal structure of the first Globe playhouse, when the truth is we may never know what it looked like. Yet with the discoveries of the Rose foundation and part of the foundation for the second Globe, the quality and even the quantity of illumination on its stage can be estimated with a reasonable degree of accuracy. The elusive shapes of the various theater buildings enter into such calculations, to be sure, but estimates based on the most important variables regarding lighting—the size of the opening above the yard and the position of the heavens over the stage—can now be made with some assurance.[13] Indeed, with the completion of the International Shakespeare Globe Centre reconstruction of the first Globe, we can now experiment with staging practices in something very like their original physical setting. In like manner, the number of windows and candles employed indoors can be inferred and the kind and amount of light shed on the actors estimated. If we shift our historical inquiries away from the theater building, its stage, and physical properties, it is not because lighting is more important. Rather, it is because light possesses unique value for us as a kind of evidence that will last until the crack of gloom.

2

TUDOR AND EARLY STUART LIGHTING EQUIPMENT

Elizabethan, Jacobean, and Caroline plays refer to lights and lighting instruments that are familiar, if not commonplace, today. The lights most frequently mentioned in dialogue and stage directions—candles, tapers, torches, and lanterns—impose no large obstacles to an understanding of early English staging, because our conception of what these lights were like and how they were used is largely correct and productive. Yet, inevitable shifts in the meaning of some terms have taken place, and enough sixteenth- and seventeenth-century lighting nomenclature has become sufficiently unclear that a brief look at the technical principles of early lights should precede any examination of the uses to which they were put in the London playhouses.

The history of lighting is so poorly recorded that a good deal of conjecture must enter into even the most cursory review. Information can be gleaned here and there from casual references, pictures, and the very few early instruments that have survived; but for the most part, social and technological historians have failed to describe the lighting practices of each age and country. Why this is so has less to do with a failure to understand the importance of light in society than with the slow, nearly stagnant, development of lighting technology that makes writing any sort of connected history difficult. For a thousand years before the reign of Elizabeth I and for two hundred years after, lighting utensils remained relatively unchanged. Late Romans used lamps, candles, and torches similar to those of the Tudor and Stuart periods. In fact, lamps were not greatly altered from what the ancient

Greeks knew until 1784 when a method to control a uniform flow of air was introduced. Candles were not improved until self-snuffing wicks replaced twisted cotton strands in the late eighteenth century and refined waxes replaced tallow and beeswax in the early nineteenth. Modern experience teaches that technical arts progress steadily. But the history of lighting shows not only little or no progress for hundreds of years but also occasional reverses when improvements were lost in the shuffle of changing cultures, only to be rediscovered later or never at all.

Three main types of domestic lights were employed in early modern England: lamps, candles, and a miscellaneous category that includes rushlights, torches, links, and tapers. Of them, lamps provide an example of a well-developed means of illumination, popular in ancient Greece and Rome, that nevertheless fell into neglect during the Middle Ages and enjoyed only limited use in England in the sixteenth and seventeenth centuries.

Lamps

Lamps can be made—and were in ancient times—from any sort of concave stone or shell.[1] The hollow is filled with vegetable or animal oil, and a wick, almost always of vegetable material, is placed into the oil with one end protruding into the air. Like candles, whose only essential difference is that the fuel is always solid, lamps burn only when enough fuel can be drawn through its wick to replace the fuel that has been consumed. The wick itself also burns and must be replaced. But for both lamps and candles, the less the light is produced by the burning wick and the more it is produced by the burning fuel absorbed by the wick, the brighter and more efficient the instrument. Surviving Greek and Roman lamps resemble shallow clay teapots with one or more spouts used as supporting wick channels. Pottery lamps are ideal for Mediterranean climates where oils and some fats are naturally liquid and can easily flow to the bottom of the lamp where the end of the wick is usually positioned. The principal advantage of lamps is their convenience: only when the fuel is exhausted or the wick totally consumed do they require attention. The disadvantage is that early lamps produce much less light than candles. Increasing the thickness of the wicks creates more light but also produces significantly more smoke. The Italian scene technician Nicola Sabbattini used lamps extensively at the Teatro del Sol in Pesaro in the seventeenth century, for example, but generally only high above his scenes and away from the noses of his aristocratic audiences. Near the actors and above the spectators, he preferred candles. Although his description of stage lighting is the first record we have of lamp footlights, he nevertheless complains that they actually make the stage appear darker. "Lamps must have strong wicks if they are to give off a strong light," he explains, "[b]ut if the strong wicks are chosen, smoke will develop to such a density that a sort of haze will interfere with the view of the spectators, who will have difficulty in distinguishing the smaller details on the stage."[2]

In England, even simple household lamps with appropriately sized wicks were less than satisfactory, because fine liquid oil had to be imported and was prohibitively expensive. College and household account books rarely list purchases of oil, and when they do, salad oil is usually specified.[3] Solid and semisolid fuels like kitchen grease and suet were plentiful, though, and several attempts were made to modify lamps to such fuels. Thus, lamps came to be made of metal (usually iron) so that a portion of the flame's heat could be conducted down to melt the fat and cause it to flow to the bottom of the lamp. In the Middle Ages, what metal the English had went toward more important utensils; the candle and torch sufficed. But by the sixteenth century, metal became more abundant and metal lamps more common. Extant inventories of great houses almost never include lamps, but poor households in the north and in Scotland regularly owned iron "crusie" lamps filled with inferior tripe-oil. As early as the 1640s, settlers to America brought these open-saucer metal lamps with them, where they became known as Betty lamps.[4]

Lamps were associated with kitchens and the hearth where spattering grease and smoke was less troublesome than in other rooms. The process of melting the solid fat in the lamp was, after all, the slow frying of suet. The description in *The Comedy of Errors* (3.2) of Dromio of Syracuse's lover may be a not-unduly exaggerated picture of a typical setting for Elizabethan lamps: "Marry sir, she's the Kitchin wench, & al grease, and I know not what vse to put her too, but to make a Lampe of her, and run from her by her owne light. I warrent, her ragges and the Tallow in them, will burne a *Poland* Winter" (F 885–90). Careful rendering and clarifying of the suet could alleviate some of the most disagreeable side effects; but once householders had gone to this trouble, they apparently preferred to make candles anyway.

A few references to lamps seem to indicate outdoor use. John Stow's *Sur-*

vey of London tells how on the midsummer eve watch of Saints Peter and Paul in New Fish Street before 1538, "every mans doore . . . had also Lamps of glasse, with Oyle burning in them all the night."[5] Glass lamps with floating wicks had recently been introduced to England from Barcelona, but the inferior oils that the English had at their disposal made them unpopular for everyday use. In London, cheap, impure oil cost nearly four shillings a gallon and cleaner-burning oil a shilling or two more.[6] It is doubtful, therefore, whether habitual domestic use was made of such lamps, which at any rate appear to have been special floating-wick lamps, suitable only in warm temperatures or near the kitchen hearth. Apart from Stow, in fact, we hear of Londoners lighting lanterns and torches for such watches, not lamps. At court, where the cost of finer oils would have been less of a burden, lamps were nevertheless also used infrequently.

In sum, the Tudor and Stuart eras saw the reintroduction of the lamp after centuries of neglect. But because the period was one of relatively rapid change in regard to lamps, their place in typical lighting arrangements is difficult to assess. Shakespeare sometimes alludes to lamps in his dialogue, for instance, but not once do his stage directions call for lamps to be brought onstage. Even when his source specifically mentions a lamp (as North does in his description of a lamp's mysterious dimming on the appearance of Caesar's ghost to Brutus), Shakespeare changes the lamp to a taper. It may be that stray gusts of wind tended to blow out lamps more readily than tapers and candles; such was the case with the lamp reproductions I lit as an experiment at the "new" Globe. In fact, Shakespeare may have suffered from an aversion to lamps: of sixteen references to them in his plays, four center on comparisons with a lamp's being starved of oil. No doubt the need to replenish oil was sometimes a bother, but Shakespeare was the only dramatist to use such imagery.[7] At all events, only a handful of stage directions in all the plays of the period call for the use of lamps as stage properties, the most important one being the difficult-to-interpret stage direction at the beginning of scene 11 of Robert Greene's *Friar Bacon and Friar Bungay*: "*Enter Frier Bacon drawing the courtaines with a white sticke, a booke in his hand, and a lampe lighted by him, and the brasen head.*"[8] Perhaps Greene calls for a lamp here to convey an exotic, ritual flavor, or the lamp may be connected with the lightning that later flashes forth from the brazen head.

Candles

On the other hand, candles were the most popular lights of the day—both in private homes and at the theaters. Theatrical and household account books often record large purchases of candles, and several sixteenth- and seventeenth-century pictures show us what candles and candlesticks looked like and how they were used.

Candles were much as we know them today but much more awkward and dangerous to keep burning for any convenient length of time. Modern candles are made of plaited cotton wicks surrounded by molded cylinders of paraffin and other refined waxes. Tudor and Stuart candles were made of considerably inferior materials. Wicks were the pith of common soft rushes or were cotton or flax strands twisted together. Such wicks burned unevenly and did not bend over into the flame and consume themselves like modern plaited wicks, invented by Jean-Jacques Cambacérès in 1820. Early wicks had to be snuffed (that is, charred pieces of wick had to be cut off and removed) to reduce smoking and to prevent "guttering," the unfortunate result of a wick's falling down into the molten fuel, melting the top rim of the candle, and allowing liquefied fuel to run down the side of the candle. To prevent this waste of fuel, snuffing was regularly required, and a consideration of the artificial illumination of indoor theatrical venues must take into account the attendants who performed these important duties. For example, an eighteenth-century French advertisement for tallow candles boasted that they needed to be snuffed only eight to ten times an hour.[9] Moreover, dexterity was required to accomplish efficient snuffing, as it was all too easy to extinguish the flame in the process (hence, the usual modern connotation of "snuff"). A two- or three-hour performance in a hall theater lit by several dozen of these inferior tallow candles could therefore require hundreds of individual snuffing operations, but only rarely do playwrights make provision for this necessity in their texts.

The fuel used in most candles was as troublesome as the wicks. Due to its high melting point, beeswax was a relatively odorless, carefree illuminant, but because it was imported from the Continent, beeswax was expensive and reserved mainly for the church. On special occasions, the Stuart court used wax in the candles closest to the sovereign or in the elaborate torches carried by or for noble maskers; but typically, king and commoner alike suffered the

Fig. 1. Frontispiece to *Arden of Feversham* (London, 1633) showing the murder of Arden at the "game of tables" lit by candlelight. By permission of the British Library (643c2).

disagreeable effects of tallow. Only in the reign of Charles I were wax candles widely deployed for the illumination of plays.

The more common fuel in candles was tallow, which is merely purified or rendered meat fat, usually from sheep or oxen (Hal calls Falstaff "tallow" several times in *1 Henry IV*). One of the scavenging promoters in Middleton's *A Chaste Maid in Cheapside* explains the origin of tallow: "[W]e haue need to get Loynes of Mutton still, / To saue Suet to change for Candles."[10] But rendering was difficult to perform completely and could never disguise the fact that the burning tallow was essentially broiled suet. In *Cymbeline* (1.6), for instance, Iachimo gives us an idea of its smell when he likens Leonatus's conduct to "the smoakie light / That's fed with stinking Tallow" (F 721–22). Even as late as 1675, the fastidious Sir Fopling Flutter pinches a tallow candle in George Etherege's *The Man of Mode* (London, 1676) because he cannot "breath[e] in a Room where there's Grease frying" (63). Although few early English candlesticks survive, seventeenth-century examples in the Victoria and Albert Museum feature wide "grease pans" or "drip pans" circling the stems to catch dripping and splattering tallow.[11] Not until well after the Restoration was the fuel refined sufficiently to allow the gradual elimination of these drip pans from English candlesticks (see fig. 1).

Besides producing an obtrusive smell, candles smoked profusely. Always dwelling on the darker side of life, Malevole in *The Malcontent* advises, "Sticke candles gainst a virgine walles white backe, / If they not burne, yet at the least thei'le blacke"[12] William O'Dea, a keeper at the South Kensington Science Museum, had some tallow dip candles made up by the best means available and still found them "wretched and infuriating" devices:

> Snuffing was supposed to be necessary every half-hour with candles of the best London tallow. With those I tested the operation had to be done every twenty minutes and in some cases was necessary after five. An unsnuffed candle gave not only a fraction of the original light, but great gullies might appear in the pool of molten tallow beneath the flame. The molten tallow would pour down such a gully and in one candle left untended only 5 per cent of the tallow was actually burnt and the rest ran to waste. A candle of 8 to the pound was completely consumed in this way in less than half an hour; but even with constant snuffing it proved not unusual to lose more than half the tallow by "guttering."[13]

The regular snuffing of candles not only saves fuel, then, but also allows the flame to burn brighter. In the late eighteenth century, the French chemist Antoine-Laurent Lavoisier estimated that an unsnuffed candle lost four-fifths of its luminous strength, and according to early photometric tests conducted by Benjamin Thompson in 1792–93, an unsnuffed tallow candle could lose nearly two-thirds of its brilliance in eleven minutes.[14] In *Hamlet* (4.7), Claudius alludes to this decreased efficiency when he questions Laertes' love for his dead father: "There liues within the very flame of loue / A kind of weeke or snufe that will abate it" (Q2 L4^v).

The smoke and odor of tallow could presumably be ignored at the outdoor amphitheaters, but the low melting point of tallow candles may have caused other problems for the actors there because tallow could melt in the hot sun. In the manuscript play *The Launching of the Mary* (c. 1632), for example, a sailor complains that he is so hot "that all my fatt fades awaye like [stinkinge] Tallow agaynst the Sunne."[15] Even tallow chandlers who took the trouble to bleach their candles in the sun were obliged to undertake this process only in the early morning, lest their wares be ruined by the midday heat of the sun.[16] Drooping property candles may thus have occasionally inconvenienced players in the height of summer, although, as we shall see in chapter 5, direct sunshine rarely shone on the stages of the amphitheaters.

Ordinarily, such candles could not conveniently be mounted high in chandeliers or wall brackets, where they would be inaccessible to the attention they required. Instead, short and tall candlesticks were the rule, except in the halls of great houses where servants could attend to candles mounted in wall sconces and wooden or iron hoops suspended from the ceiling that could be lowered for snuffing. In the banqueting houses and halls that served as theatrical venues at court, large branched chandeliers, or branches, as they were called, provided the lion's share of the illumination. These branches, many of which were sumptuously garnished, could hold from four to fifteen individual candles each.[17] In the Middle Ages, candles had been held in place by impaling them on pricks or metal spikes, but with the rise of the guilds of wax chandlers and tallow chandlers in London in the fourteenth century, standardization in the size of candles gradually permitted the use of sockets.[18] During the sixteenth and seventeenth centuries, both methods of securing candles were used, larger candles generally by pricks, smaller candles in sockets. Caroline Revels Office accounts frequently mention "wallers" and an equal number of "prickers"; these were brackets supporting pricks on which large candles could be impaled, which were then hung on walls or pillars (the Caroline Revels Office once acquired "Pillered wallers and Hookes").[19] Even so, these lighting fixtures could still drip, smoke, and scorch; the Revels Office frequently provided plates or pans to catch drippings, pasteboards to protect low ceilings and nearby columns from burning, and pipes to shield the ropes from which the branches hung.[20]

Candles were sometimes made by householders themselves (by repeated dipping in molten tallow) or were purchased from the chandler by the pound. A few chandlers' bills for theatrical productions survive, and one way to estimate the number of candles that lit a performance is to divide the total cost of the candles by the price per pound and then multiply by the size of the candles as expressed by the number of candles in each pound. The price of candles increased severalfold during the era, however. In the early sixteenth century, a pound of tallow candles cost only a penny, but gradually rose to threepence at midcentury, four pence by 1600, and sixpence by the civil wars.[21] Wax candles were more dear: white (that is, bleached) wax candles were regularly four or five times as expensive, while yellow (unbleached) wax candles were two or three times as expensive as tallow candles, although for some reason yellow candles were not particularly common.

Tallow and wax candles were about the same size or a little larger than we use today. In homes, the average size was around six or eight in the pound. At court, candles were often larger, sometimes weighing a pound apiece or more. The legal "standard candle" in both the United States and Great Britain now weighs one-sixth of a pound but burns much more slowly and evenly than early tallow candles, owing to the use of refined waxes and plaited wicks. It is this candle that yields the now old-fashioned—but for our purposes, practical—unit of illuminating power, the footcandle, or the amount of light measured one foot away from such a candle.

Torches, Lanterns, and Other Utensils

In a third category, I group together lights essentially similar to the candle except that their wicks were much larger. Utensils such as rushlights, torches, links, flambeaux, and many tapers differed from candles in that they were not primarily made of fuel but were essentially all wick. The purpose of the little fuel in them was to help burn the wick, whereas in candles and lamps the wick served to burn the fuel. The most inexpensive lighting instruments in this category were rushlights. These were the thin piths of soft rushes, dipped briefly in kitchen grease. When supported by wire rush-holders, they served as utility lights and night-lights in humble bedrooms.

Torches and links worked similarly except that their wicks were usually several lengths of hemp rope, bound together around a wooden staff. The technical distinction between torches and links is not always clear, though. Torches were always three or four times more expensive than links, and their fuel probably included at least some wax in addition to the tallow and pitch common to links. To Americans, the word "torch" connotes a roughhewn club dipped in pitch appropriate for Ku Klux Klan parades. But torches were nearly obligatory lights in illuminating sumptuous masques, and a passage from *Westward Ho!* (1607) gives a truer picture of their status in early modern England. The authors tell how "the Cobler, in the night time walks with his Lanthorne, the Merchant, and the Lawyer with his Link, and the Courtier with his Torch."[22] Because a courtier uses a torch here, we must pre-

Fig. 2. Title page illustration of Thomas Kyd's *The Spanish Tragedy* (London, 1615) showing the discovery of Horatio's murder by smoky torchlight. By permission of the British Library (C117b36).

sume that it was no crude device, especially because the quotation implies habitual use. In consequence, our associations with some of these lights may stand in need of revision. In the storm scenes of *King Lear*, for example, the raw power of nature is accompanied not by knurled clubs burning primevally but by genteel torches whose staves were probably richly decorated. Thus, lights were associated with various occupations and levels of society, and the actors could use them as signals of character. Hymen's torch and the black torches of the Furies are obvious identifiers that even a modern audience may know, but we may not catch the pretension of Vittoria Corombona in *The White Devil* who has adorned her rooms "with seuerall kind of lights, / When shee did counterfet a Princes Court."[23]

Because of the smoke they generated, links and torches were typically employed out of doors (see fig. 2). Bardolph is such a "ball of wildfire" in 1 *Henry*

IV (3.3), for example, that he has saved Falstaff "a thousand Marks in Links, and Torches, walking with thee in the night betwixt tauerne and tauerne" (Q1 G2^v). But even as outdoor lights, they presented a danger when smoldering chunks of wick fell off the central staves. During midsummer watches when torchbearers festively marched through the streets of London, for example, householders regularly placed pots of water before their doors as a safety precaution.

As befits their sophisticated owners, torches were occasionally brought indoors into the great halls of the wealthy, where the smoke could rise and sufficient numbers of servants could attend to them. Perhaps a vestige of traditional mumming where torch-bearing mummers visited the houses of honored worthies at night, torches regularly accompanied indoor masques and other entertainments in the spacious halls of great houses and universities. Problems arose, however, when torches came near theatrical costumes in cramped quarters. In 1579, for example, when the Elizabethan Revels Office rented plumes for elaborate headpieces in a masque of knights, it was charged extra because four plumes "were dropte with torches" while three expensive heron feathers "were burnte with Torches."[24] No wonder that in the act 5 masque scene of *The Malcontent*, Bilioso berates a page for letting his torch drip where the ladies sit. Such dripping also obliged the Revels Office to spend large sums on gloves for the torchbearers. But in later Stuart masques, the torches that accompanied the masquers may not always have been lit; at least Jonson, Davenant, and others sometimes take pains specifically to call for *lighted* torches, implying that others may simply have been carried but not lighted. By the 1630s, masquers were sometimes accompanied by a species of the torch called the flambeaux, which was dearer even than the torch because, to reduce smoke and dripping, its thick wick was impregnated only by fine wax.

A strictly outdoor utensil that is less familiar to us now was the cresset (see fig. 3). These were iron fire-baskets usually carried or mounted on long poles in which woven frales or wreathes of rushes, pitch, rope, and tallow were burned. They had also been carried by the watches of London until the middle of the sixteenth century, but by the civil wars they were already forgotten. Their Elizabethan use was limited and apparently sometimes nostalgic. We know, for instance, that by the turn of the seventeenth century, they occasionally served as entrance lights mounted before the doors of inns, taverns,

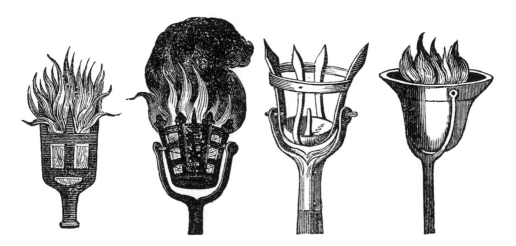

Fig. 3. Cressets from various early English prints and drawings published by Francis Douce in 1807. University of Illinois at Urbana-Champaign Library.

and stables where they illuminated the way of travelers and lent such establishments a traditional, even old-fashioned, ambience.[25] From early on, they were most often associated with outdoor wintertime activities where their heat would be as welcome as their light. We have only a few references to their use in professional theater contexts, but they are occasionally mentioned in connection with late amateur religious plays. In the N-Town *Betrayal* (c. 1500), Jesus is arrested by soldiers carrying *"cressettys, with feyr, and lanternys and torchis lyth"* (see John 18:1), and account books of the Capper's Company, Coventry, indicate that it owned six cressets for the pageants of *The Resurrection, The Harrowing of Hell,* and *The Meeting with the Maries* as late as the 1590s.[26] But some of these cressets may have had paratheatrical uses. The accounts of "the wache and play" of Wymondham, Norfolk, 1538, for example, contain payments for pitch, resin, and sixteen pounds of tallow for a cresset light, but a bonfire of this size may well have belonged to the watch, not the play.[27] Later, the term "cresset" seems to have been applied not only to the utensils themselves but also to the woven frales that, along with other combustible materials, were placed in the iron baskets. Such utensils required steady replenishment of fuel, as their large flames tended to consume themselves rapidly.

Lanterns were also for outdoor use. They were merely candles placed in wood or metal boxes with windows of oiled paper and parchment or, more frequently, horn; hence the usual spelling, "lanthorne." But again, we may miss the distinction between a normal lantern and a "dark lantern," such as Bosola carries in act 2, scene 3, of *The Duchess of Malfi*. Dark lanterns gave off no light at all until a small door was opened in the otherwise opaque shield. They were a favorite of thieves and highwaymen engaged in surreptitious nighttime adventures. Bosola's dark lantern thus fits his sinister actions well (he calls it his "falce-friend") and colors our response to Antonio at the end of the play when he, too, resorts to using a "darke Lanthorne" in his attempt to meet with the Cardinal.[28] Similarly, in *The Bloody Banquet*, Tymethes creeps into Roxano's bedroom "*hudwinckt*" and surprises her when he "*[o]pens a darke Lanthorne.*"[29]

Tapers were employed indoors, despite their also being made of rope. Tapers were usually single, thin ropes dipped in wax or tallow. They smoked and stank but had the advantage of requiring little snuffing. Hence, they were used as night-lights in bedrooms, where they could burn safely with little attention. Imogen has a taper in her bedroom in *Cymbeline*, and Lady Macbeth carries one from her bedroom while sleepwalking. Early emblem books often used lights of all kinds as images of life and death, but because of the taper's relative weakness as a light and its association with the bedroom, playwrights often use it to signal the frailty of human love and passion. Nowhere is this kind of symbol made more important to the meaning of a play than at the very end of *Bussy D'Ambois*, when Montsurry graphically shows his faithless wife the extinction of their love by putting out a taper:

> And as this Taper, though it vpwards looke,
> Downwards must needs consume, so let our loue . . .
> As when the flame is suffered to looke vp
> It keepes his luster: but, being thus turnd downe
> (His naturall course of vsefull light inuerted)
> His owne stuffe puts it out: so let our loue.[30]

This sense of frailty is sometimes shared by candles (Macbeth's "Out, out, breefe Candle," for instance [F 2344]); but on the whole, candles were more neutral in terms of their social connotations. Unfortunately, tapers were also placed in candlesticks and are easily confused with true candles: in *The White Devil*, for example, a *"hallowed candle"* is brought to Brachiano as he lies wounded in bed, but in the next stage direction, the candle is referred to as *"the Ho[ll]owed taper."*[31]

In fact, the major obstacle in attempting to reconstruct the artificial illumination of the early drama is that nearly every light could be and was confused with others. Torches and tapers were sometimes called candles, large candles were called torches, even tapers were called lanterns. Moreover, all of these instruments were frequently identified simply by the general term "light." Occasionally, a careful observer like George Cavendish distinguishes "lightes of waxe as bygge as torches,"[32] but more casual writers merely say "torches" and have done with it. In plays, for example, the requirements of the verse often take precedence over accurate description. On his way to Capulet's ball, Romeo demands, "A torch for me," but two lines later announces, "Ile be a candle-holder and looke on" (*Romeo and Juliet*, Q2 B4ᵛ). The everyday term was "torchbearer," not "candle-holder"; but as is typical of Shakespeare's early verse, a common word like "torchbearer" bows to elegant variation and the exigencies of the rhythm.

This muddle in terminology also applies to records written in Latin. While *lucerna* is normally translated as "lamp," one cannot always be sure that it does not refer to another kind of light. To choose but one example, *"lucernae"* were cited as employed for performances at Queens College, Cambridge, in 1545–46, but Alan Nelson has pointed out that they probably refer to candles, because they are also described as costing two pence per pound.[33] Whether from poetic license or indifference, early modern writers named lighting instruments imprecisely; or rather, there is enough sloppiness in the application of nomenclature that a given description must always be viewed skeptically.

There is no reason to believe that the professional actors used any other lights than the everyday, domestic utensils used in homes and businesses. Henslowe's *"Enventary tacken of all the properties for my* Lord Admeralles men, *the* 10 *of Marche* 1598" mentions only one light of any kind, a "beacon."[34] This may have been a cresset or some other large light, but Henslowe's grouping it with "ij stepells, & j chyme of belles" indicates he meant less a kind of light than a "signal station, watch tower," or "lighthouse," as the *OED* defines "beacon" in the sixteenth century. Perhaps this beacon was some kind of architectural set-piece rather than a special theatrical light, or a historically accurate replica of one.

At court, most of the lights that illuminated plays and masques were also versions of standard lighting utensils. The Revels Office spent large sums on chandeliers, candlesticks, and tallow and on occasion ordered elaborately gilded branches, perfumed wax candles, and specially fashioned torches (a torchbearer in Jonson's *Masque of Queens* carries a lighted torch "made of a dead-Mans arme," for example), but these were largely for the greater grandeur of the decoration and not for specifically theatrical lighting effects.

The only kinds of lights that served distinctly theatrical functions of illu-mination were apparatuses employed in early Stuart masques as a way of col-oring and concentrating light on the Italianate scenes. These instruments consisted of lights shining through colored paper or through glass vials filled with plain or colored fluid. The Italian designer Sebastiano Serlio recounted the use of paper and liquid-filled vials as coloring media for lamps in 1545, and his description of these techniques, in the second book of his *Regole gen-erali di architettura*, was published in English as early as 1611. If a particularly bright light is called for, Serlio adds, "then set a torch behind [a vial], and behind the torch a bright Bason."[35]

Serlio does not specifically mention it, but his vials filled with liquid will also focus light. In *The Mysteryes of Nature and Art* (London, 1634), John Bate describes *"How with one Candle to make as great a light, as otherwise of two or three of the same bignesse,"* and this feat of concentrating light in a par-ticular direction is accomplished, he says, by two glass globes—one to hold a candle, the other filled with distilled water to refract and focus the candle's light (157). A similar, but clearer, description is given in John White's *A Rich Cabinet with Variety of Invention* (London, 1651). Neither points to a the-atrical use of this invention, which later became known as "lacemakers' con-densers" because of the detailed work it permitted at night,[36] but Inigo Jones may well have employed similar instruments to represent shining jewels and other objects for his Stuart masques.

There is no evidence that professional actors employed colored or con-centrated light at their playhouses, and certainly at the outdoor amphithe-aters one imagines that attempts to do so might be unimpressive in daylight.

All the same, we may note that the contemporaneous *corrales* of Spain occasionally accommodated what appear to be lights similar to modern-day colored-paper lanterns on their daylit, but well-shaded, stages. In Lope de Vega's *La imperial de Otón* (1597), for instance, many lights "in colored papers" are revealed as the rear "tiring-house" curtain is drawn aside.[37]

Impulses toward theatrical spectacle on the one hand and concern for historical accuracy on the other will produce more elaborate lights and lighting techniques than were required in the home. We know that the actors paid attention to both these considerations on occasion. Spectacular lighting effects are not uncommon, and their use must have created sensations with the opening-up of hell in *The Tragical History of Doctor Faustus* or the burning of the town during Zenocrate's funeral in *2 Tamburlaine*. Moreover, if Henry Peachum's 1595 sketch of a scene from *Titus Andronicus* is any guide, Elizabethan actors paid at least cursory attention to historical accuracy in their costumes and hand properties.

Yet, however much the desire for spectacle or authenticity exerted itself in some areas of staging, the evidence for its implementation in lighting practice is thin. Spectacular lighting consisted largely of firecrackers set off. The scenes in *Doctor Faustus* and *2 Tamburlaine* are indeed memorable, but they belong to only a handful of scenes in the plays of the period, almost all of which can be staged with smoke, fireworks, and the rare rosin-flash. Of Shakespeare's thirty-seven plays, for example, not one calls for any lighting effect more complicated than a stroke of lightning—easily produced by setting off a squib. Nineteen of his plays require no lights at all; and only one or two plays, while they do not require more elaborate effects, might benefit from them. As for historically accurate or especially decorated property lights, we have only negative evidence. No record survives that even hints at any foreign, historical, or specially made lighting instrument for the professional playhouses. And as distinctively non-Elizabethan clothing and hand properties are specifically included in Henslowe's lists, we can only assume that the acting companies made do with readily available, contemporary lights.

3

EARLY LIGHTING SYSTEMS

WHEN John Brayne built the Red Lion playhouse in Whitechapel in 1567 and he and his brother-in-law James Burbage built the Theater in Shoreditch in 1576, they presumably based their designs on some idea or cluster of ideas about theater planning that they had learned by practical experience or through written sources. But what those ideas were and how much they affected stage production at the first London playhouses are questions that may never be settled. Among the stages that might have contributed to Elizabethan amphitheatrical design, the most frequently mentioned are the Roman theater as described by Vitruvius and his commentators; the medieval churchyard, tiltyard, pageant-wagon, and *platea* surrounded by scaffolds for seating; and the courtyard, inn-yard, animal-baiting house, booth stage, civic pageant, banqueting theater, and Tudor hall. All of these venues have similarities to the amphitheaters, and some were used by the acting companies as performance spaces before permanent houses were built. But whether they served as models for Brayne, Burbage, and other managers or builders is difficult to say. It is apparent that many of these possible influences were outdoor places of entertainment and that some surrounded the center of interest with spectators on more than one side. For a few, this is all the similarity that can be found. For others, more striking parallels are evident. Even so, similarities are not in themselves proof of direct or indirect influence. The daylit ring arrangement of the public playhouses and the near-circular shape of open-air theaters as old as those of the ancient Greeks may have in common only the obvious efficiency of seating a maximum number of people near the actors without the expense of building a roof.

The prominence given by an earlier generation of theater historians to church steps, pageant-wagons, inn-yards, and Shakespeare's Globe led many to believe that outdoor stage production was the characteristic mode of drama in England until the late seventeenth century. According to this scheme, the origin of the amphitheater lighting system was simple to discover: from the outdoor Corpus Christi plays to the street theaters of itinerant players derived a sunlit dramatic tradition nurtured wholly on English soil. Readers of introductions to the English theater were sometimes given the impression that once the players left the medieval churches and began to perform in the streets, they continued to perform outdoors and never returned inside until Shakespeare's company moved into the Jacobean "private" playhouse in Blackfriars. But research over the past twenty-five years has shown that this neat account of the derivation of public-theater lighting is misleading. Glynne Wickham and others have argued that throughout the late medieval and Tudor periods, the typical home of professional English actors was as likely to be indoors as outdoors; that the actors' construction of outdoor playhouses was a late-sixteenth-century innovation; and that far from prompting a new stagecraft reflected later in the private theaters, the entertainments at court derived from a long-standing tradition of indoor festivals, influenced only peripherally by Continental theatrical practice.[1] Wickham concludes that a professional actor's preferred environment was indoors and that only a financial desire for larger audiences and an impulse to escape restrictive City controls forced him outdoors.

If the use of permanent open-air arenas was an innovation, we may well wonder where the actors found the specific lighting arrangements they did if not in the familiar inn-yards and bear-baiting houses of London. Historians have long pointed to these venues as the immediate precursors of the amphitheaters, even though we know of few early plays that were definitely performed in either. In a preliminary summary of the findings of the Records of Early English Drama project, for instance, Alexandra Johnston points out how little evidence supporting performances at inns—either in rooms or in inn-yards—has been discovered.[2] And Oscar Brownstein and John Orrell have shown that early animal-baiting circles probably had few of the playhouse attributes that later animal arenas like the Hope displayed, although an Italian visitor to the Paris Garden in 1562 did note that the scaffolds surrounding that arena had "their awnings against the rain and the sun."[3] Seating arrangements for spectators at the inn-yards and bear-baiting arenas may well have adumbrated those at the amphitheaters, and builders may have borrowed ideas on construction from them. But neither inn-yards nor animal-baiting houses tell us much about the modification of light in the public playhouses. Completely unexplained is the derivation of the heavens or "shadowe" over the stage, as the Fortune contract puts it. No Tudor animal-baiting house is known to have had a roof over the pit, and the first we hear of a roof in an inn-yard is when the Boar's Head tavern underwent its second conversion into a permanent playhouse in 1599.[4] Just as likely an inspiration for amphitheatrical lighting arrangements can be found in churchyards, which Alexandra Johnston shows served as frequent theatrical venues in the provinces, not only for parish amateurs but also for professional actors.[5] In at least one instance, such churchyards were even equipped with canopies under which professional actors played: in 1339 the bishop of Exeter objected to "a balcony or canopy erected and constructed upon posts fixed in the ground . . . within the boundary of the churchyard of our aforementioned church of Exeter" under which "rogues, actors, whores, and other vile persons" performed "stage-plays."[6]

Since Richard Hosley, Richard Southern, and others have drawn attention to the prominent use of indoor halls by early acting troupes, an alternate model for the outdoor heavens is the ceiling of the Tudor hall.[7] This ceiling provided conveniences that the actors might not want to forego as they moved outdoors. They enjoyed its protection from the elements and hung from its rafters the hoisting apparatus needed for ascents and descents of actors. But when the professional troupes were forced outside the City walls by plague restrictions and Puritan intransigence, they could find few indoor halls available to them. Instead, shrewd speculators built large, multipurpose arenas that the actors shared with bear-baiters, fencers, rope dancers, and the like. Under these circumstances, early acting companies apparently made shift with what was available to them, because they could not at first insist that the speculators construct large roofs over the arenas solely for the benefit of occasional theatrical spectacle and a little protection from the weather.

Although no pre-Elizabethan outdoor stage leaves clear evidence of such a structure as the amphitheater heavens, several previous kinds of drama had facilities that anticipated the functions, if not the form, of the roof-canopy. The following review of early lighting systems, while not ignoring questions of derivation, seeks principally to describe antecedent lighting practice with which Elizabethan actors might have been familiar.

Classical and Early Neoclassical Precedents

Increasing attention has recently been paid to classical and neoclassical sources of inspiration to Elizabethan theater builders: John Orrell's *The Human Stage* (1988) adds an impressive array of evidence to support this thesis that was initially put forward by Francis A. Yates and Richard C. Kohler.[8] And it is true that the overall articulation of light at the English public playhouses approximated that at the amphitheaters of classical antiquity. Like Elizabethan plays, early Greek and Roman performances were given by daylight. At the Theater of Dionysos in Athens, performances from the fifth century B.C. on were apparently held from morning to afternoon under the sun. Early Roman plays also began in the morning but did not last quite so long.[9] So too, the ruins of Hellenistic, Graeco-Roman, Republican, and Imperial Roman theaters are almost all situated, like many English amphitheaters, so that the *skēnē* or *scaena frons* is to the south, southeast, or southwest.[10] This orientation meant that the sun shone from high behind the scene building during morning or midday performances. And finally, we know that as early as the fourth-century-B.C. *phlyakes* stages of southern Italy, roofs were sometimes erected over the stage.[11] The first wooden stages in Rome were probably without roofs, but once permanent stone theaters were built in the first century B.C., a narrow roof jutting forward from the *scaena frons* was a common facility in theaters throughout Magna Graeca.[12] The Romans were also in the habit of stretching large cloth awnings (*vela* or *velaria*) over their theaters to protect spectators from the sun. In the first century B.C., Lucretius described how light shining through these awnings could even tinge theaters in colored light:

> red, yellow, and brown
> awnings when, stretched across great theatres,
> flung wide over poles and beams, they ripple and flap.
> For they dye the whole thing under them: people, pit,
> stage, and scenery . . .
> and make it flow with bands of their own colors.
> And the more the walls of the theatre are enclosed

around, the more all that's inside is gay
and flooded with beauty when it has caught the light.[13]

Pliny and Martial tell us a purple awning was stretched above Pompey's theater in Rome in A.D. 66, and Cassius Dio describes a *velum* on which Nero
was depicted as a sun god riding a chariot among the stars.[14]

These Roman modifications of general lighting could not have directly influenced English actors. Although some early-sixteenth-century Italian
artists, among them Raphael, had measured and studied classical ruins, this
kind of firsthand knowledge was unavailable to early English builders. The
similarities between Roman and English outdoor theaters regarding time of
performance, theater orientation, and shelter for the stage may as easily be
ascribed to practical stage wisdom as to direct imitation. Still, T. F. Ordish
and Glynne Wickham have brought attention to the long-standing tradition
of open-air circular game-places in England going back to the ruins of the
Roman occupation and continuing through the Middle Ages with the Cornish *plen-an-gwary* rounds, which the Roman game-places may have influenced. Both scholars argue that these broad, shallow bowls dug into the
ground are precursors of the Tudor animal-baiting and theatrical arenas of
London and that these rounds may even be considered links between Roman
theater configurations and the Elizabethan playhouse's practice of surrounding the stage with spectators.[15]

Yet, even if these game-places did affect the shape of London amphitheaters, evidence of facilities for the modification of light in either the Roman
or Cornish arenas is meager. The English sun is seldom as hot as the Italian sun, nor does it shine down so steeply; it is doubtful, therefore, that
Roman soldiers bothered with large canvas *vela* simply to watch animal
fights. On the other hand, an iron counterweight found on the site of the
Roman theater at Verulamium (near St. Albans, Hertfordshire) may suggest
that its stage (enlarged around A.D. 200) featured a superstructure of some
kind to accommodate descents or an *auleum*.[16] And stage directions in the
Cornish *Ordinalia* (c. 1450) mention that stages, houses, and tents for the various characters were placed around the circumference of the round, again
possibly implying overhead coverings for some of the scaffolds.[17] But neither
the theater at St. Albans nor the Cornish rounds seems to have been accessible to Tudor theater-planners. Even though it is relatively close to London,
the Verulamium theater was not excavated until 1847. The Cornish rounds

at St. Just-in-Penwith and Perranzabuloe were not studied until the eighteenth century, although in 1602 Richard Carew wrote of an "earthen Amphitheater, in some open field" in Cornwall where "miracles" were performed, which he may have seen when he was high sheriff of Cornwall in 1586.[18] The tone of his description makes clear, however, that he assumed the average Londoner had never seen such a thing.

Although we must reject a direct Roman influence in the derivation of the London arena playhouses, it is true that the Elizabethans selectively followed what they believed to be classical precedent, especially written precedent. As a result, the Elizabethan heavens may be adumbrated less by what the Romans actually did than by what Renaissance interpreters, right or wrong, thought they had done.

The great conduit of ancient theatrical knowledge to the Renaissance was the first-century Roman engineer Vitruvius. In his famous book, *De Architectura*, Vitruvius does not mention the *vela*, but he describes the Roman theater as a "curved enclosure," open to the weather, with a roof above a colonnade "built at the top of the rows of seats . . . level with the top of the 'scaena.'" He advises that theaters should be laid out so as to avoid a "southern exposure," which, he says, creates an unhealthy climate by allowing the sun to shine from behind the *scaena frons* onto the curved rows of seats (5.3.2).[19] From what we know now, his account roughly coincides with actual practice during the Empire, except that the orientation of almost all known Roman theaters is exactly opposite to what he suggested. Unhappily, the drawings that formed an essential part of his explanations did not survive, and his descriptions are sometimes vague without them. What the *scaena* and its roof looked like, for example, he leaves completely to the imagination. It is not surprising, then, that when interest in him revived, a distorted notion of Roman lighting resulted.

By the Middle Ages, the Roman theater had already become confused with the popular mimic theaters. Tracing the word *scaena* back to the Greek *skēnē* ("hut" or "tent," akin to the Greek *skia*, "shadow"), early definitions of the *scaena* and its roof described a booth or house around which spectators assembled. As early as A.D. 620, the Spanish lexicographer Isidore of Seville defined *scaena* as a place within a theater *"in modum domus"* — in the form of a house. In Papias the Lombard's *Vocabulista* (1053), *scaena* is called an *umbraculum*, "shaded place," in which poets recited their plays. The in-

Fig. 4. Frontispiece to *Le Térence des Ducs*, fifteenth century. Terence is seen below while his play is recited and performed above in a circular theater with covered *scena*. Cliché Bibliothèque nationale de France.

fluential late-twelfth-century dictionary of Hugutius of Pisa defined *scaena* again as an *umbraculum* or "shaded place in the theatre covered with curtains" and likened it to the booths of merchants.[20]

Illustrations from early editions of Terence demonstrate this confusion. The frontispiece to the French Terence codex, *Le Térence des Ducs* (c. 1400), shows a round, open-air *theatrum* with a covered scaffold in the center, labeled *scena* (see fig. 4). In front of the *scena* are musicians and masked *joculatores*. One actor is making an entrance from a side curtain of the *scena*. Inside the scaffold, covered by an awning, the Roman grammarian and *recitator* Calliopius is seen declaiming from a book of Terence. What is significant about the miniature is not only that it portrays an early combination of a covered scaffold with an arena-style theater—a development that some assume occurred in England only with the introduction of booth stages into bear-baiting houses nearly two hundred years later—but also that this combination is represented not as an innovation but as a reconstruction of the Roman theater. The artist believed that the Romans placed a covered "tiring-house" within a ring of spectators that was in turn surrounded by a wall with exits and entrances. The actors are not protected from the sun, but the man reciting the text is, and the drawing represents one of the earliest modern uses of such protection in conjunction with a circular arena.

In his study of medieval English staging, Richard Southern has pointed out the strong resemblance between this quasi-Roman theater and several early circular theaters in England, including the *tenti* of the Cornish rounds.[21] For example, the diagram that accompanies the manuscript of the English morality play *The Castle of Perseverance* (c. 1425) resembles the French Terence theater, except that besides the central scaffold, five additional scaffolds are distributed around the perimeter of the *platea* (see fig. 5). Working from hints in the dialogue, Southern concludes that these scaffolds were covered with cloth awnings, presumably like those stretched over similar scaffolds in the well-known Fouquet miniature *The Martyrdom of Saint Apollonia* (c. 1460).[22] In the Fouquet miniature (see fig. 6), the elaborate immolation scene takes place in the open-air platea, but the actors and properties in some of the surrounding scaffolds make it clear that action also occurs under their protective awnings. In *The Castle of Perseverance*, most of the dialogue is spoken from the various scaffolds with only the climactic assault on the castle occupying the central area. As with the *Térence des Ducs*

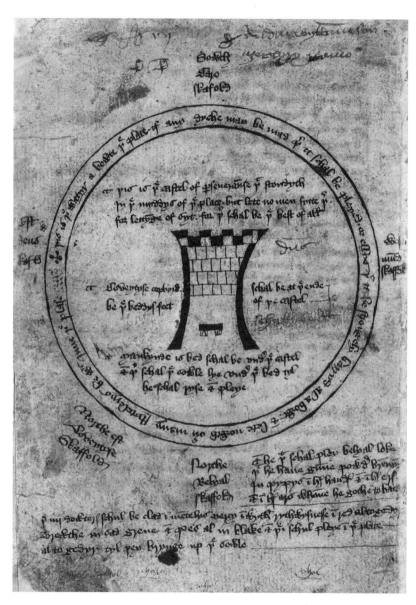

Fig. 5. Plan accompanying the manuscript of *The Castle of Perseverance*, fifteenth century. At each compass point is a "scaffold" for one of the major characters. By permission of the Folger Shakespeare Library.

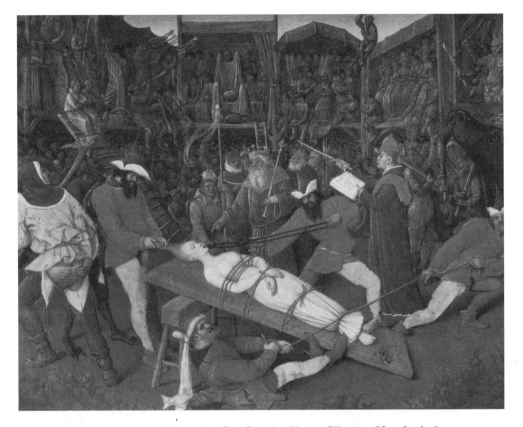

Fig. 6. *Le Martyre de Sainte Apolline* from *Les Heures d'Etienne Chevalier* by Jean Fouquet, c. 1460. Musée Condé, Chantilly. Photo: Lauros-Giraudon.

theater, these two religious plays document the early use of roof-canopies in connection with curved theatrical spaces long before the professional London acting companies set up their booth stages at one end of a Tudor inn-yard or bear-baiting arena.

A later Terence illustration exemplifies the growing sophistication of the Renaissance conception of the Roman stage cover. Johannes Trechsel's exterior view of an academic theater on top of a brothel in the Lyon *Terence* (1493) shows a polygonal *theatrum*, open to the weather, surmounted by a colonnade with a large canopy (see fig. 7). The building follows Vitruvius in

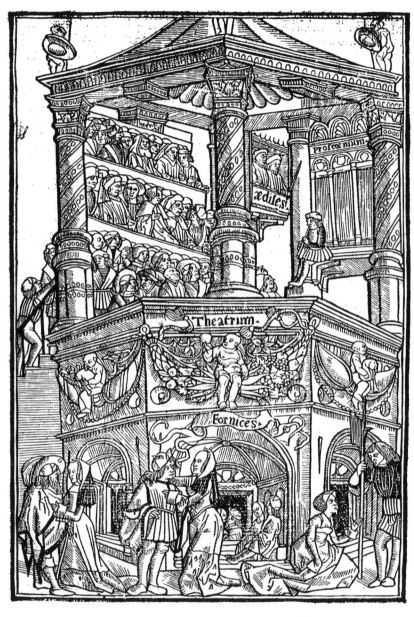

Fig. 7. Print of the frontispiece to Johannes Trechsel's edition of *Terence*
(Lyon, 1493). University of Illinois Theatrical Print Collection.

outline, save for the *velum* that Trechsel could have learned about from Ovid, Propertius, Pliny, Lucretius, or Martial or from the most influential fifteenth-century disciple of Vitruvius, Leon Battista Alberti. In the first printed commentary on Vitruvius, *De Re Aedificatoria* (Florence, 1485), Alberti described such a superstructure: "And over all this, as a Cieling to the Theatre, both to keep off the Weather, and to retain the Voice, they spread a Sail all strewed over with Stars, which they could remove at Pleasure, and which shaded the middle Area [the stage], the Seats, and all the Spectators."[23]

What is of interest is the degree to which the lighting arrangements of Trechsel's neoclassical *theatrum* parallel those in the later London amphitheaters. Trechsel shows an open-air, polygonal theater with sunlight emanating from behind the stage (from right to left in the picture). Pillars support a rectangular canopy whose underside displays a gadroon cloud motif that, if Trechsel followed Cassius Dio or Alberti, was decorated with celestial objects. Although the style of the theater does not recall that of Johannes de Witt's version of the Swan, the disposition of its parts controls light in a similar manner.

It is impossible to tell whether Tudor playhouse-builders had access to the source materials Trechsel had. Direct connection cannot be verified, but as Orrell demonstrates, there is circumstantial evidence to support a real, if unsystematic, adherence to Vitruvian theatrical principles in Tudor England. By 1577, William Harrison's *Description of England* could entertain a favorable comparison of English builders with "Old Vitruvius (Leo Baptista) and Serlo,"[24] showing that Vitruvius was known in England primarily through the edition of Alberti, who gives such a detailed account of the stage cover. The passage may even imply that an intelligent builder would have been aware of Vitruvian building methods. Francis Yates found evidence that several English libraries contained Latin and modern-language editions of Vitruvius, Alberti, and other later commentators by the 1570s.[25] Ben Jonson, for example, paraphrased Alberti's work extensively and owned several editions of Vitruvius.[26] Moreover, for the title page of his 1616 folio, Jonson had the English engraver draw a reconstruction of a Roman *theatrum*, based on what he had learned. The engraving is small and difficult to make out, but the *theatrum* has a surprisingly large hut above the stage, much more elaborate than any classical author could have led Jonson to believe. Although none was more plangent on the subject of classicism than Jonson, he may also have tended to identify the Roman *scaena* with the English tiring-house and heavens. And although the point of the remark has sometimes been ignored, some credence must be given to de Witt's conclusion around 1596 that the Swan's "form resembles that of a Roman work."[27] To be sure, the Swan drawing does not depict what we think of as a Roman theater, but there seems no reason to doubt de Witt that early theatergoers would have thought so. Certainly, the painting of its wooden columns in an "excellent imitation of marble" implies an attempt at the classical style.

A passage from Thomas Heywood's *An Apology for Actors*, written around 1608, may serve to summarize what an active man of the English theater knew about ancient theatrical lighting and the Roman stage roof. He explains that the "first publicke Theater was by *Dionysius* built in *Athens* . . . in the manner of a semi-circle." From it, he says, "the *Romanes* had their first patterne, which at the first not being roof't, but lying open to all weathers, *Quintis Catulus* was the first that caused the out-side to bee couered with linnen cloth." Later, after Pompey had built the first stone theater in Rome, Julius Caesar raised another, equally sumptuous theater that, according to Heywood, had a magnificent heavens, full of machines and spectacular devices:

> [T]he couerings of the stage, which wee call the heauens (where vpon any occasion their Gods descended) were Geometrically supported by a Giant-like Atlas, whome the Poëts for his Astrology, feigne to beare heauen on his shoulders, in which an artificiall Sunne and Moone of extraordinary aspect and brightnesse had their diurnall, and nocturnall motions; so had the starres their true and cœlestiall course.[28]

Heywood not only knew that the Romans built roofs over their stages but also suggests, by his reference to the Roman "couerings of the stage, which wee call the heauens," that he thought the Roman and English roofs were identical, or at least fulfilled identical functions such as astronomical displays. Like the Roman heavens, several Elizabethan and Jacobean amphitheaters had painted zodiacs over the stage, and there is evidence that celestial displays involving rockets mounted on pinwheels above the stage were popular, particularly at Heywood's favorite theater, the Red Bull. Henslowe's list of properties includes a "clothe of the Sone & Mone" that may have been hung from the heavens at the Rose.[29] And, of course, both the Roman and

English stages were equipped with facilities for the descent of gods. One theater historian claims that the builders of the English amphitheaters conscientiously followed Vitruvian theater geometry, especially in planning the Fortune, whose proportions exhibit an "exact mathematical correspondence" with the Vitruvian scheme.[30] This is possible, although why the Fortune was rectangular when Vitruvius and his commentators called for a semi-round theater is not convincingly explained.

An argument against a Vitruvian contribution to the public playhouse roof-canopy is that Vitruvian influence is much more evident in indoor rather than outdoor playhouses. By the seventeenth century, nearly every major court in Europe lavishly mounted indoor entertainments reflecting Roman pictorial and mechanical ideas. L. B. Campbell and Allardyce Nicoll recognized the contradiction that while Vitruvius described an outdoor theater, his ideas were largely adapted to indoor venues. They believed that early humanists had misinterpreted Vitruvius and thought he was talking about an enclosed rectangular theater. As proof, Campbell and Nicoll pointed to the theater plans in the first illustrated version of Vitruvius, the Jocundus edition (Venice, 1511), which are framed by heavy rectangles, implying, they believed, indoor rectangular theaters.[31]

But T. E. Lawrenson has shown that early editors of Vitruvius were aware that the theater he described was not only round but also open to the weather and that the rectangles in the Jocundus edition were merely the borders of the woodcuts. Describing the French Renaissance theater, Lawrenson concluded that

> the movement indoors is, as elsewhere, not the outcome of a transmitted mistake, but the breaking up of a collective popular art form, and a seeking not merely after show, for the pageants already had that, but after *trompe-l'œil*, in an enclosed space, and even in a darkened room, before an élite audience that, being élite, occupied less space and could be so accommodated.[32]

In England, Inigo Jones gave final shape to the Stuart masque from his personal knowledge of indoor Italian scenic conventions, for which he was called *Vitruvius Britannicus*. But the impetus for the masque was, at least in part, the much older English tradition of indoor disguisings and mummings that had comprised court entertainments since the Middle Ages. Thus, professional theater, both popular and elite, had found a home indoors long before the renewal of interest in ancient learning. Of this, I shall have more to say in connection with the lighting of the Jacobean hall playhouse. For the present, we may conclude that English professional players, accustomed to acting indoors, sought protection over the stage when in the 1560s and 1570s they were forced outdoors. To this end, they may have persuaded the owners of these open-air venues to imitate what they thought the Roman roof over the stage looked like. The roof-canopies built in the 1580s and 1590s undoubtedly reflected the owners' acceptance of the increased popularity of drama over other forms of entertainment, as well as a concession to the actors' desire to duplicate facilities they had enjoyed indoors and to cultivate an aura of antique legitimacy by building and decorating heavens that they believed followed classical precedent.

Medieval Theaters

Inextricably mingled with adulterated classical lighting techniques, indeed probably also influenced by them and certainly confused with them, were the contributions of native civic and religious theaters to facilities over the stage. Beginning in the Middle Ages and continuing into the Elizabethan reign, festivals such as tournaments and street pageants and religious shows such as the mysteries, miracles, and moralities provided an accessible source of outdoor theatrical custom on which to draw.

George Kernodle has brought attention to the similarity between the pre-Restoration stage and the *tableaux vivants*, or street pageants as they were called in England.[33] In London, these pageants were performed on two- and three-story platforms scattered along the routes that nobles rode on their way to special ceremonial occasions. The stages were not normally built in the streets but on preexisting structures — city gates, water conduits, and market crosses that lay adjacent to the major thoroughfares of London. Favorite scenic motifs were caves, gardens, ships, and the like, allegorically representing a political theme. But regardless of the motif, the upper level of the stage was frequently depicted as a "heaven." From it, gods, saints, and angels gave advice on the preservation of the commonweal blended with appropriate flattery to the honored worthy.

Apart from performance in the open air, these pageants resemble the later amphitheaters in that they often placed a heaven directly above the main acting area. No doubt because of space limitations in narrow streets, such pageants extended their playing areas vertically. In the religious staging exemplified by *The Castle of Perseverance* and *The Martyrdom of Saint Apollonia*, multiple stages had been arranged horizontally. On one side of a row or circle of scaffolds, a heaven (sometimes slightly raised) had balanced a hell or hell-mouth on the other. But in the street pageants, heaven found a place directly over the stage, which in turn represented the world. These pageant heavens give precedent, then, for the position that the heavens were later to take in the amphitheaters. Unfortunately, they do not leave behind good descriptions of what they looked like or clear proof that they were used for protection from the sun or weather. For the London reception of Richard II in 1392, several performers descended by means of cloud machines to pageant stages, but we do not hear whether the roofs they descended from shaded the stage or not.[34] Similarly, the York housebook for 1486 ordered that at the first city gate "a place in maner of a heven" be constructed and that "under the heven shalbe a world desolaite."[35] But a description of a pageant for the Emperor Charles V in June 1522 suggests that a celestial roof protected at least one acting area. This open-air pageant at the Little Conduit in Cheapside was surmounted by a heavenly scene "in a type in the top."[36] A type is a small dome or cupola; it presumably covered the heavenly scene, but it may or may not have shaded the actors below.

A similar effect is called for in a 1533 pageant performed in the Leadenhall marketplace for the London reception of Anne Boleyn. Raphael Holinshed described a pageant "with a type and a heauenlie roofe, and under the type was a roote of gold set on a little mounteine." Later, "out of the type came downe a falcon all white & sat upon the roote and incontinent came downe an angell with great melodie."[37] Although some of these early heavens may have amounted to little more than angelic perches, the increasing popularity of descents and ascents from and to heaven implies a type or some other structure above the stage to house or hide the required apparatus. Apparently, this is the significance of a device built for the coronation of Edward VI in 1547. For it, there was a "double Scaffold one above the other," and underneath the upper scaffold was "an Element or Heaven, with the Sunn, Starrs, and Clowdes very naturally . . . out of which there descended a Phenix downe to the neither Scaffold."[38] As this heaven was under an upper scaffold, we may presume that the higher scaffold provided facilities for the hoisting equipment and, perhaps, some sort of covering for the performers. Whether these roofs and types affected the light on the main stage is open to question.

Although the English Corpus Christi pageant-wagons were not vertically arranged like the street pageants, surviving records for them also hint at roofs and covers. Our conceptions of medieval staging have changed so rapidly in recent years, however, that one hesitates even to summarize the evidence. The notion that all the great Corpus Christi cycle plays were performed on pageant-wagons, one play to each wagon, at various "stations" throughout a city has been called into question. Alan Nelson has argued that cycle plays at York, Lincoln, and Chester may have been performed indoors in town halls and guildhalls and that several related religious plays, especially those at Norwich and Coventry, were indoors as well.[39] Only at Beverley and at Coventry (where there were likely only two or three outdoor stations) are we positive that the cycles were performed in processional fashion out of doors. Nelson goes so far as to suggest that some pageant-wagons were part of a separate Corpus Christi tradition, a parade of pageants held in the morning before the cycle plays were performed. On these pageant-wagons, he concludes, not true plays but tableaux and short declamations were given. Nelson's argument for nonprocessional staging of the York play has met with skepticism,[40] but he nevertheless reminds us that we may underestimate the variety of environments—including luminary—in which the mystery dramas were acted.

However the pageant-wagons were deployed, they nevertheless provide evidence of roofs and raised heavens. Despite Archdeacon Rogers's claim, recorded in 1609, that pageant-wagons at Chester were "all open on the tope that all beholders mighte heare & see," there are assorted references to roofs covering wagons in other cathedral towns.[41] A 1565 inventory of equipment owned by the Norwich Company of the Grocers includes a "Pageant, that is to saye, a howse of waynskott paynted and buylded on a carte with fowre whelys," above which was "A square topp to sett over the sayde howse."[42] Whether or not such a top extended over the acting area, this pageant-wagon plainly was not completely open to the weather. Guild account books at Coventry record that in 1480, sixpence was "paid to a carpenter for the pagent rowf," and there are several payments regarding a "wynd," or windlass.[43] A roof supporting a windlass suggests that the whole structure was above the stage. Wickham and F. M. Salter believe that substantial roofs were mandatory to hide machinery for ascents, although medieval stage technicians did not always disguise how such effects were produced.[44] What the ascents certainly imply is that some structure was above the stage to support the necessary equipment.

Some of the extant accounts of Corpus Christi festivities mention torches and tapers, leading several scholars to conclude that dramatic performances continued into the night under artificial illumination. But these lighting utensils appear to refer to liturgical and pageant processions and watches and not to the cycle plays themselves. The processions began so early in the morning (shortly after 4:30 A.M. at York and 5 A.M. at Wakefield)[45] that torches may have been necessary to organize them. Several of the processions were called "lights," implying very early or very late starting times. There are a few records of artificial lights for indoor religious plays but none for the mystery plays themselves. In fact, a notice of the outdoor cycle at Coventry having to stop prematurely one day in 1457 on account of darkness suggests that no nighttime performances by torchlight were given there.[46] Some artificial lights were used for stage properties, of course, but in considering their use for general illumination, it should be remembered that the cycles were performed in a season when the days were the longest of the year. Cressets and torches are also occasionally associated with civic pageants, but their function was primarily ornamental or, again, connected with nondramatic festivities.

Neoclassical Ceilings and Machines

If early outdoor stages established a tradition of a superstructure above the stage and a garbled knowledge of Roman precedent reinforced the practice, then we have still to account for the size of the amphitheater roof-canopies that, by the mid-1590s, often covered half or more of the stage. Because such substantial covers are rare in previous outdoor theatrical venues, we are left to assume that the actors were attempting to approximate the accommodations afforded by the ceilings of indoor venues such as temporary banqueting houses and Tudor halls.

These ceilings offered protection from the elements, of course, but they also provided facilities for such important theatrical functions as ascents and descents. Far from representing an innovation, the installation of the heavens at the outdoor theaters meant that techniques previously employed indoors could continue. For example, it is significant that among the Tudor dramas in our possession, the earliest hints of suspension-gear are associated not with outdoor but with indoor stages. Queen Elizabeth saw a play, probably at Greenwich, written and performed by gentlemen of the Inner Temple as early as the winter of 1566 or 1568 in which a "Cupide cometh downe from heauen."[47] Although the play was later printed, the manuscript from which this stage direction is drawn undoubtedly refers to the initial performance indoors. A cupid could descend by walking down stairs or climbing down a ladder, to be sure, but ten years later the Elizabethan Revels Office furnished a performance of *The Three Sisters of Mantua* with "A rope A pulley A basket to serve in the Earle of warwickes men plaie."[48]

In contrast, the earliest use of suspension-gear at the outdoor theaters seems to have been no earlier than 1588 or so, more than twenty years after the Red Lion had been built. This first documented use of flying apparatus at a professional playhouse is in Robert Greene's *Alphonsus, King of Aragon*, which opens with the stage direction, "*After you haue sounded thrise, let* Venus *be let downe from the top of the Stage.*" And at the end of the play we get the complementary, "*Exit* Venus. *Or if you can conueniently, let a chaire come downe from the top of the stage, and draw her vp.*"[49] We are uncertain of the auspices of the original production; the play may even have been first performed indoors. The play is associated with the repertory of the Queen's men, however, who around 1588 were performing at the Theater, Curtain, and Bel Savage. Even so, the uncertainty expressed in "*if you can conueniently*" indicates that Greene was unsure whether the necessary apparatus would be available.

And this uncertainty may reflect the evidence we have about when the heavens became a permanent part of the amphitheaters. For it was just in the late 1580s and early 1590s that the actors regularly began to furnish the outdoor theaters with superstructures above the stage. Henslowe, for instance, installed a heavens at the Rose only in 1592 and provided a "throne In the heuenes" in June 1595.[50] Perhaps this was the flying chair Greene was hoping for, because his play was definitely offered at the Rose sometime around 1594. Evidently, the revival missed by a few months the convenience of this equipment. At any rate, if the use of ascents and descents tells us anything about what was above the stage, then we must conjecture that the integration of the indoor ceiling into the *mise en scène* was the anterior development and that the heavens and roofs of the amphitheaters followed only several decades later and owed their existence, in part, to the inspiration of the earlier form indoors. "Boys were flown in *The Widow's Tears* [c. 1605] and *Cupid's Revenge* [1608] at Blackfriars, but at the Globe Hymen in *As You Like It* and Diana in *Pericles* both entered on foot," Andrew Gurr points out, concluding that "the plays written after 1608 used flights."[51] In fact, ascents and descents were never so frequently practiced at the amphitheaters as they were indoors, a demonstration that throughout the period, suspension-gear was more characteristic of the Tudor hall and private playhouse where it was more easily accommodated under their sturdy roofs and ceilings.

Not only does the active use of the indoor ceiling in the production of drama predate the installation of the heavens, but, as John Orrell has carefully documented, the ceilings of several early indoor theaters bear a strong resemblance to what was later built outdoors.[52] For instance, the habit of painting astronomical motifs on the underside of the heavens, probably on some kind of cloth stretched across the corners of the roof-canopy, is antedated by many years. One of the very earliest modern theaters in Rome, for example, commissioned in 1513, was a temporary structure of wood painted like marble. Built in the classical style with no roof, it nevertheless featured a "ceiling" of blue and white cloth.[53] Henslowe's "clothe of the Sone & Mone" was not inventoried until 1598, but by 1520, when Henry VIII built a theater at Calais for the entertainment of Charles V, an elaborately painted and studded blue cloth with "starres, sonne, and mone" was stretched over a circular theater underneath a more substantial, waterproof roof.[54] The cloth was supported by a giant wooden column providing "for the formation of a handsome and well-proportioned covering, like a pavilion." Although completely enclosed, this wooden theater was remarkably similar to the Elizabethan public theaters: a circular shape was approximated by a sixteen-sided polygon, and spectators were arranged in three tiers of galleries surrounding the stage on three sides. The dimensions of the galleries are even within a few feet of those in the Fortune contract. Unluckily, a great wind blew the star-studded roof off, and the revels had to be moved to another building. Perhaps frustrated by this stroke of fate, Henry ordered the great Hans Holbein to design another temporary disguising theater and banquet house in the tiltyard at Greenwich in 1527. For the disguising theater, another double roof was constructed, the outer layer of thick canvas and the inner of buckram extravagantly gilded with celestial representations. A fascinated observer, Edward Hall, described how "the rofe of this chambre was conninglie made by the kynges Astronimer, . . . and in the zodiak were the twelue signes, curiously made, and aboue this were made the seuen planettes."[55] English aristocrats were familiar with a heavens above the stage long before the first permanent amphitheaters were built.

Charles V emerges as something of an authority on the heavens as he witnessed another indoor entertainment with a heavens nearly identical to later ones at the public theaters. In August 1549, Charles and his son Prince Philip (shortly to become Philip II of Spain and Prince Consort to Mary I of England) were feted at Binche in present-day Belgium. At midnight they entered a hall in which an "enchanted chamber" had been prepared. This chamber featured a *vaissellier*, a baldachin-like canopy supported by large columns much the same as in the Swan drawing (see figs. 8 and 9). The canopy was, in fact, a revolving astronomical display of great ingenuity that produced artificial thunder and lightning, perfumed rain, and sugar sleet.[56] But the evening's climax came when three tables sumptuously decked with feasts magically descended from the heavens. The drawing of the event is a composite, showing all three banquets in different positions, but a Spanish observer who accompanied Philip makes clear that the tables descended one at a time, stopped at the pedestals (*antipecho*) supporting the columns, and then "instantly" disappeared back into the heavens. The trick was accomplished, he says, by rope pulleys near the top of the columns, hid so subtly that no one could see them. As the tables were hoisted up and down, the thunder and lightning from above distracted the audience's attention, and the tables were made mysteriously to appear and disappear. The use of smoke and flashing light to distract an audience's attention is an old magician's trick, but the use of thunder and lightning from above in unison with descents is especially characteristic of the English theater. Indeed, so frequently do thunder and lightning accompany descents that they are almost obligatory. Familiar examples are in *Cymbeline* ("*Iupiter descends in Thunder and Lightning, sitting vppon an Eagle*" [F 3126–27]) and in Heywood's *The Silver Age* ("*Thunder, lightnings*, Iupiter *descends in his maiesty, his Thunderbolt burning*").[57]

Thus, the indoor banqueting theaters provide a model for extending the heavens beyond the floor of the hut into a large canopy covering a good part

Fig. 8. The *vaissellier* with practical heavens in an "enchanted hall" for a fête at Binche, 1549. Bibliothèque Royale Albert Ier, Brussels.

Fig. 9. The Swan playhouse, c. 1596. Sketch of Johannes de Witt as copied
by Aernout van Buchel. Bibliotheek der Rijksuniversiteit te Utrecht.

of the stage and suitable for depictions of the firmament. In the [U]nfortu-nate Traveller (London, 1594), Thomas Nash employs then-current play-house nomenclature to describe a banqueting house "built like a Theater with-out, within there was a heauen comprehended both under one roofe." This heaven, writes Nash, "was a cleere ouerhanging vault of christall, wherein the Sunne and Moone and each visible Starre had his true simili-tude, shine, scituation, and motion" (14ᵛ).

Jacobean and Caroline hall playhouses continued the use of such false ceilings. At the second Blackfriars and the Cockpit-in-Court, winches hung from the main roof, while a ceiling, analogous to the underside of the heav-ens, apparently hid the apparatus. At the Cockpit-in-Court, part of the false ceiling could be drawn aside for ascents and descents; and later amphithe-aters probably also had facilities to draw a cloth aside or to open a hatch in the heavens to permit the audience to see blazing stars, lightning flashes, and other special effects. A theater set up by John Spencer and his English actors in Germany in 1613 had a four-cornered opening in the roof above the stage through which beautiful "Actiones" could be seen.[58] In Cymbeline, after de-scending to thunder and lightning and predicting a happy outcome, Jupiter "[a]scends," and Leonatus describes a similar opening in the heavens: "The Marble Pauement clozes, he is enter'd / His radiant Roofe" (F 3157–58). The descent and ascent in Cymbeline may have been added for later perform-ances at St. James and may not have been part of the original production at the Globe in 1611. Based on the paucity of references to descents in play-texts associated with it, Bernard Beckerman doubts the existence of any hoist-ing apparatus at the first Globe, although John Astington points out the difficulty in basing such assessments exclusively on textual evidence.[59] Yet, even if the suspension effect was an interpolation, it remains an indication of the popularity of such effects indoors and of the inspiration the indoor ceil-ing could provide to the outdoor heavens. The first Globe may have been re-medial in its use of special effects from the heavens: Shakespeare's plays reveal a poverty of such spectacle, and we must remember that the first Globe was, essentially, the Theater rebuilt. Other playhouses—specifically the Rose, Red Bull, and the second Globe—could certainly accommodate hoisting apparatus, and nearly all the amphitheaters reveled in fireworks and light displays from above.

In contrast, the indoor playhouses relied much less on fireworks (for safety reasons) but used their ceilings to support suspension-gear and celestial pictures earlier and apparently more actively than the outdoor theaters. Perhaps some amphitheater heavens were too flimsy to support such paraphernalia. The Red Lion's thirty-foot turret seems to have been a fairly substantial edifice all by itself and may well have served such a purpose, but the recently discovered legal documents pertaining to it fail to mention any sort of cover over the stage. Without assuming a steady evolutionary development of the heavens, we may nonetheless note that with the building of the second Globe and its massive superstructure, an amphitheater heavens appropriated several functions identified with indoor production. Nor should we forget that the first private theater—the playhouse at St. Paul's—was undoubtedly in active use several years before the Theater was built. Lacking any information to the contrary, we may consider the indoor theater the anterior form and the indoor ceiling the seminal model for the amphitheater heavens, even if neo-Vitruvian and early native traditions contributed a parallel impetus or sanctioned a development already initiated by the actors' desire to duplicate circumstances indoors. Performing in town halls and inns in the afternoon or at night, early actors must have often played in low light. When they planned new outdoor venues, they sought not to make the stages as bright as possible but rather installed covers and positioned the stages where they would be shielded from direct sunlight.

Early Artificial Lighting

That the light indoors was not always brilliant is evidenced in the more easily traced history of indoor theatrical lighting. In fact, evidence that early actors were at home indoors and that their move outdoors in the 1560s and 1570s was a novelty is provided by the unbroken string of indoor entertainments under artificial light and window light from the Middle Ages to the Interregnum. The better documented of these indoor performances are medieval mummings and disguisings, early Tudor masques, and university plays. Such entertainments leave records of ample illumination in the halls of wealthy nobles, at court, and at the great universities. But the more direct precursors of professional Elizabethan lighting practice for adult players are the humbler interludes performed by itinerant acting troupes that established the more modest general illumination used later in the professional private playhouses.

The lavish spectacles and revels performed for, and sometimes by, the nobility are better documented, of course, because they involved the doings
of important persons. Court instructions regarding "disguyssing" show that
as early as 1494, Henry VII ordered his lord chamberlain to provide "lights in
the hall afture the quantitie of the hall and youre discrecion rowme enough
for them."[60] By all accounts, such discretion afforded more than adequate
light. Henry VIII's 1520 circular theater, whose double ceiling I have described, was brilliantly illuminated, for example. A Venetian witness wrote
that the inside was to be lit "by cornucopias, serving as candlesticks, fixed
around the outside of the banqueting area, and by great chandeliers, 'tri-
omphans a merveille,' hanging from the ceiling, alternating with silk-clad
wickerwork figures bearing torches in their hands."[61] The 1527 banqueting
house and theater were perhaps even brighter. In the banqueting house (approximately one hundred by thirty feet), the walls supported at least forty-four
candlesticks in addition to many windows.[62] Forty more pricket candlesticks
lit a great arch, and fourteen candlesticks of silver plate decorated a table or
surrounded the king. From eighteen wainscot beams hung an unspecified
number of chandeliers with a total of 230 wooden candle sockets, all expen-
sively garnished. In addition, there was a special pageant of lights with twenty
figures holding candlesticks.

After dinner in this glory, the guests retired to a disguising theater, also
known as the long house. The name implies a larger space than for the banqueting hall, but slightly fewer lights were employed, indicating either a
smaller area to be lit or that the theater was not meant to be as bright as the
dining hall. The Revels Office acquired eighty silvered basins for the theater
to be fixed on sixteen pillars in order to support and catch the drippings of
"greate braunches of white wax." Twelve ornately turned candlesticks supplemented these basins. A payment for 106 pounds of cotton candles is also
recorded, but since the accounts we have are works accounts, these candles
were apparently ones by which the artisans prepared the hall and were not
used for performances. Assuming that the candles for the chandeliers
weighed something on the order of five to ten in the pound and that the
larger candles on the sides weighed up to a pound apiece, one night's
lighting in the banqueting hall must have cost more than ten shillings and
lighting for the disguising theater only slightly less.

Early University Theaters

Records of court entertainments yield some of the few early accounts of indoor theatrical illumination in England that are specific enough to allow us to count the number of lights. But the court had resources of which most early Tudor acting companies never dreamed, and we should prefer accurate descriptions of their less sumptuous arrangements. Documents collected in the Records of Early English Drama project fill in some gaps, but few records of provincial performances give details about the provision of theatrical lighting. The best evidence comes from account books of various colleges at Cambridge and Oxford, and the fullest descriptions are of college performances for Queen Elizabeth, one of whose many thrifty habits was the annual summer progress, during which she would tour the kingdom and be entertained largely at her hosts' expense. In the 1560s, for instance, two summer progresses to the universities—one to Cambridge in 1564 and one to Oxford in 1566—leave detailed accounts of lighting.

At Cambridge, the queen saw a play at 9 o'clock at night in the chapel of King's College lit only by torchlight. The University Registrary wrote that the entrance of the college's officials was accompanied by "a multitude of ye garde with them havyng everye man in his hand a torche staffe for ye Lightes of ye playe for no other Lightes was occupied."[63] His specification that no other kinds of lights were used might indicate that a subdued effect was desired, but we cannot be sure of this because we do not know how many torches were involved. The Registrary makes clear that the guards holding torches stood to either side of the stage, so perhaps all he meant was that the rest of the chapel was not lit or that no ordinary candles were used.

Not to be outdone, Oxford invited the queen two years later. Her stay was carefully chronicled, and it is apparent that Oxford did not want to suffer by comparison with the arrangements at Cambridge. An enthusiastic John Bereblock told of splendid lighting in the Common Hall of Christ Church for a performance of the first part of *Palaemon and Arcyte* at night:

> Lucernae, lichni, candelaeque ardentes clarissimam ibi lucem fecerunt. Tot luminaribus, ramulis ac orbibus divisis, totque passim funalibus inaequali splendore, incertam praebentibus lucem, splendebat locus, ut et instar diei micare, et spectaculorum claritatem adjuvare candore summo visa sint.[64]

Accurate translation is difficult owing to the muddle in lighting terminology not only in English but also in Latin. In an often-cited rendition, W. Y. Durand translated it this way:

> Cressets, lamps, and burning candles made a brilliant light there. With so many lights arranged in branches and circles, and with so many torches, here and there, giving forth a flickering gleam of varying power, the place was resplendent; so that the lights seemed to shine like the day and to aid the splendor of the plays by their very great brightness.[65]

Although much of the nomenclature was interchangeable, Durand's translation of *lucernae* as "cressets" is unfortunate; no early Latin-English dictionary gives such a definition. Typical translations of *lucerna* are "lanterne" in Thomas Elyot's *Dictionary* (London, 1538) and "[a] candle, a lamp, a light" in Thomas Thomas's *Dictionarium* (London, 1588). Durand's "lamps" for *lichni* is also misleading. Thomas Cooper's *Thesavrvs Lingvae Romanae & Britannicae* (London, 1565) identifies *lichni* with the wicks of any lighting instrument, and the *OED* hints that the English word "link" is metathetic for the Latin *lichinus*, "wick" or "match," out of which links were made.

I raise these points because several scholars have cited Durand's translation to prove that cressets and lamps were common lighting utensils for early indoor plays, even though corroboration does not proceed from contemporary dictionaries.[66] In the first new translation since Durand's, Wickham corrected these inaccuracies but made others himself. He translates *luminaribus* as "so many lamps,"[67] whereas early dictionaries all give more general definitions; Cooper's translation of *luminare* is "[t]hat which geueth light." For *funalibus*, Wickham has "so many candles." This is not wrong, but as the word's etymology derives from *funis*, "rope," Cooper's translation of *funale* as "[a] torch: a corde" is clearer and probably more accurate, especially for us who are unfamiliar with how these lights were manufactured. In fact, Cooper's famous dictionary boasts a special authority in deciphering Bereblock's Latin, because the dictionary was published only one year before the queen's progress and because both Bereblock and Cooper were Oxford fellows at the time, presumably sharing the same languages.

Bereblock is given to hyperbole, and we should have preferred fewer superlatives in his description and more specific numbers and locations of the lights. In this regard, Cambridge serves us better than Oxford. College account books at Cambridge list many payments for lighting equipment. As most of this equipment was intended for nonroyal entertainment, the accounts give us a look at more modest production methods. Based on a thorough review of these records, Alan Nelson shows that most of the plays at Cambridge were presented at night and that anywhere from a dozen to three or four dozen candlesticks were generally bought.[68] But large purchases of candles are also frequent, lumping together expenditures for unspecified numbers of plays and performances in a single entry. One of the rare instances when particular performances are listed is found in the Trinity College steward's book recording expenditures for plays performed at Christmastide 1550:[69]

for Candell at Mr Cocrofte plaie	x[d]
for Candelles for Mr Cocrofte play	xiij[d]
for Candelles for stilles play	x[d]

The inclusion of two separate entries for Mr. Cocrofte's play, as well as the use in all three entries of the singular "play," seems to indicate that each payment covers lighting expenses for only one performance. Because of inflation, the pound of candles that had cost only a penny in 1527 now cost threepence. Trinity College provided not much more than three pounds of candles for each performance, therefore, and the total number of candles was only two dozen or so, depending on their size. We do not know where plays were performed at Trinity College until after the Restoration when a special Comedy House was constructed, but the room in which plays were presented could not have been large, because neither the chapel nor the great hall was erected by 1550—the college having been founded only in 1546. The account books of the founding year mention an expensive "great Rownd Candelsticke for the stage In the hall," which I take to refer to the preexisting Michael House Hall, now surviving only in fragmentary foundations.[70] The foundations suggest a hall of not more than fifty by thirty feet.[71] We may visualize, then, a small stage above which a large, circular chandelier was suspended with perhaps two dozen candles. I presume the chandelier was suspended because fourteen years later a new "knot of Corde to hange vp ye great candlesticke" was purchased, although by this time I suspect the location for playing had been moved and the great chandelier was being rehung.[72]

That the number of candles did not increase appreciably over the years is suggested by a payment of four pence at Jesus College, Cambridge, "for 2 pounde of candles att Robinsons showe," during the Christmas season of 1595–96.[73] The largest and most likely site at Jesus College was its hall, approximately fifty-seven by twenty-five feet, which is still standing.[74] Considering the weight of the candles purchased, only a dozen or two candles were used. Thus, early and later evidence implies that theatrical lighting at the universities was not always particularly bright, at least by our standards. Perhaps the nocturnal search for the needle in the early Cambridge play *Gammer Gurton's Needle*, first performed around 1550 but revived several times before it was published in 1575, was made plausible by dim light. On the other hand, there is no evidence that the colleges stinted in allocating what resources they had. In at least one instance, in fact, a college saw fit to provide more resources than it owned: in 1561, King's College, Cambridge, was obliged to beg candles from other colleges for its play. A sour note in the Trinity accounts complains that Trinity students "hadd no candles bicause of the playe[s] that wa[re]s at the Kynges Colledg as vpon this night," giving evidence that King's, at least, provided more light for these plays than it would have for a regular nighttime supper or meeting.[75]

University plays were generally performed without the benefit of window light. Most plays were acted in the wintertime and at night (9 o'clock is the most common starting time at Cambridge), but some daytime performances are recorded for which the window shutters were occasionally closed. At Queen's College, Cambridge, a performance of *Laelia* was given in 1595 "after dinner, the Day being turned into Nyght."[76] On 12 March 1623, King James visited Trinity College where he "dined before eleven, then went to the Hall, which being darkened, the play began presently."[77] King Charles went to St. John's, Oxford, in August 1636 and saw two plays, one in the afternoon and one at night. Archbishop Laud tells how after lunch, "I caused the windows of the Hall to be shut, the candles lighted, and all things made ready for the Play."[78] Perhaps the windows were closed only to prevent drafts from blowing the candles out; or it may be that officials desired to emulate the nighttime entertainments at court for their royal guests. If the universities habitually closed the windows to outside light, it would have been contrary to the custom adopted for all but occasional "nocturnals" at the professional private theaters in London. On the other hand, it is likely that many afternoon university performances did indeed find the windows open.

Church Plays

Because the preponderance of plays acted at churches were performed indoors rather than in the churchyard, it is not surprising that churches also sponsored artificially lit plays.[79] At Sutterton in Lincolnshire, churchwardens' accounts for the annual play on the Feast of the Assumption refer to lights in the church. The earliest record dates from 1520–21, when sixpence was "payd for makynges of yᵉ plaaris [players] candelles." In 1522–23, only four pence was paid for lighting, but in 1525, thirteen pence was "payd for ij li wax to owr ladys lyght."[80] Two pounds of wax will yield only about twelve or eighteen candles.

In London, plays were also occasionally performed at night in churches. For instance, a play was performed on the church holiday in Silver Street, 29 July 1557, "at eight of the clock at night" that "continued until xij at mydnyght, and then they mad an end with a good song."[81] In 1564, the City of Norwich sponsored a play by school boys and "payed for Torches to Show lighte in the Chappell when they played . . . iiiˢ."[82] Three shillings is a large sum, but lights that were called "torches" varied so widely in price that it is difficult to estimate their number. Because these torches were used to light a large room (one hundred by thirty-three feet) that was no longer used for ecclesiastical purposes, perhaps some two dozen inexpensive torches were used.[83] After the accession of Elizabeth and the Church's attendant reversion to Protestantism, churches ceased theatrical activities.

Early Professional Troupes

As for the early professional actors themselves, we have only scraps of information regarding their lighting procedures. Early morals were performed out of doors: *The Castle of Perseverance* and *The Pride of Life* (c. 1350–1450) are explicit in this regard. But studies by T. W. Craik and Richard Southern show that references to halls, doors, and nighttime performances begin to appear in interlude texts in the late fifteenth and early sixteenth centuries, indicating indoor venues, most likely Tudor halls.[84] Several early Tudor interludes include the fireplaces common to such halls in the action of the drama, and in winter, at least, these fires may have provided much of the illumination present.[85] Torches and candles could easily have supplemented this firelight, but it would have been expensive for the players or sponsors to buy enough candles to make the ambient illumination of halls much brighter than that produced by a fire. Instead, there is evidence that hand-held lighting utensils were used to "highlight" particular actors and actions. In John Heywood's *The Play of the Weather* (c. 1527), for instance, the Vice steps out from the audience in answer to a call for volunteers and asks a torchbearing bystander to give him more light:

> Brother holde vp your torch a lytell hyer
> Now I beseche you my Lorde loke on me furste
> I truste your lordshyp shall not fynde me the wurste.[86]

In a situation where the cost of candles came directly out of the actors' or innkeepers' pockets, such a utilitarian system of lighting is easy to imagine. What is more, this "spotlighting," as Southern calls it, demonstrates that the playwright was aware of the ability of concentrated light to draw attention to specific actions as well as the realism possible when lights intended for general illumination are woven into the texture of the drama.

In the provinces, early troupes preferred to perform in town halls; and under Elizabeth, city officials generally offered them these facilities, occasionally even constructing stages for them and defraying the cost of artificial illumination. In the chamberlain's accounts of Gloucester for 1561–62, we learn threepence was "payed to Mr Ingram for a pounde of candelles at the . . . playe."[87] The purchase of only one pound of tallow means that only four to eight average-sized candles lit the room. Perhaps the actors supplied additional lights, although one doubts the actors spent any more money than was necessary. At Bristol, the 1577–78 treasurer's account mentions a payment to Leicester's men "at the end of their play in the Yeld Hall before Mr Mayor and the Aldermen and for lynks to giue light in the euenyng."[88] As links are associated with outdoor use, these at Bristol were probably for festivities following the play.

Later on, provincial officials were less pleased to suffer the visits of touring acting companies. Typical disenchantment is expressed by the York City Corporation, which in 1592 forbade actors the use of the town hall because the windows, benches, and doors of its Common Hall were broken by spectators attending plays.[89] Sybil Rosenfeld concludes the players resorted to inns and private houses, but records of such performances are few and far between.[90] Some performances must have been outdoors in private gardens and inn-yards, but surviving provincial accounts tend to mention such venues only when there was trouble; in June 1583, for example, we hear of an afternoon performance in the yard at the Red Lion inn in Norwich only because of a scuffle there.[91]

From the frequent provincial prohibitions against nighttime entertainments, however, it is clear that actors commonly attempted to perform in the evening when the largest number of people were free to attend plays. The Burgmote books for 15 April 1596 complain of plays stretching into night and ordered that performances "not exceede the hower of nyne of the clock in the nighte."[92] Similarly, Pembroke's men were allowed to perform in the Norwich town hall in 1598 only until nine.[93] But at Chester in 1615, where the city fathers had been disturbed by a "Scandall" occasioned by plays, performances were forbidden to extend beyond six o'clock.[94] We cannot be sure that night performances were the rule, but these frequent restrictions prove they were not out of the ordinary, at least before the cities undertook sterner measures to discourage them.

We can infer from evidence late in the period that early provincial lighting was not brilliant. Once the urban private playhouses had established their regular afternoon performances, one might expect touring companies to emulate the lighting procedures of their London counterparts. But as late as 1636, methods reminiscent of earlier lighting practice persisted in the provinces. The London private playhouses regularly performed in the afternoon, for instance, but in 1636 the mayor of Canterbury was complaining to Archbishop Laud that "night plays continued until midnight, to the great disorder of the city."[95] So, too, the York Corporation minute books record apparently vain attempts to stop nighttime performances in halls, taverns, and private homes.[96] More tellingly, the candlelight that by that time typified the London hall theaters was sometimes considered an extravagance in the provinces. This can be adduced from a letter written on behalf of Prince Charles's men, also in 1636. The company had recently gained an unsavory reputation, and in seeking permission to perform in Norwich, they attempted to impress the city with the refinement of their productions. The actors requested that only the best people be allowed to attend and by way of lobbying for their cause had a sympathetic citizen write to one of the city fathers regarding the lavishness of their plays. "I pray tell your sons that the Red Bull company of players are now in town," the citizen writes, "and have acted one play with good applause and are well clad and act by candlelight."[97] Since acting by candlelight is represented as a mark of sophistication, we may assume that less prosperous companies often acted by fewer utensils or none at all. If candles vouched for refinement as late as 1636, then we may surmise that they were as rare or rarer when professional acting troupes were in infancy some eighty years earlier.

In London, interludes were performed inside inns and private houses before and after animal-baiting and public arenas were built. As early as 1569, the City of London authorities worried that plays at "Innes and other places of this Citie" were spreading the plague by causing the spectators to be "close pestered together in small romes, specially in this tyme of sommer."[98] On 11 January 1580, the Lord Mayor was displeased to learn that nighttime plays were being given within the City gates. He attributed recent civil disorder to plays acted "by night in diu[er]se suspecte places" from 7 or 8 until 11 or 12 o'clock.[99] Plays lasting until twelve midnight in "suspect places" imply indoor, artificially lit venues and not the open-air inn-yards, marketplaces, and animal-baiting arenas so often mentioned as the forebears of the first amphitheaters.

A fellow of Trinity College, Cambridge, is helpfully more specific regarding the locations of such performances. In 1583, Gervase Babington (later bishop of Worcester) bewailed "prophane & wanton stage playes or interludes" and reasoned that "[i]f they be dangerous on the day time, more daungerous on the night certainely: if on a stage, & in open courtes, much more in chambers and priuate houses." Nighttime inn performances were the more to be avoided, he said, because "there are manie roumes beside that, where the play is, & peradue[n]ture the strangenes of the place & lacke of light to guide them, causeth errour in their way, more than good Christians should in their houses suffer."[100] Although Babington attributes lack of light to the inns, we should not construe his parallelism to mean that plays in open-air theaters and inn-yards were always performed by daylight and that plays in tavern and inn chambers and at private houses were only at night. But he leaves little doubt that indoor night plays were frequent enough to arouse concern. By 1608, in fact, a suburban innkeeper was tried by the Middlesex justices "for sufferinge playes to bee played in his house in the night season."[101] Babington's naive claim that darkness at the inns caused the faithful to lose their way invites skepticism. Thomas Nash probably gives a truer picture of nighttime inn life when he tells of a young country gallant gone to "reuell it" in London who will "haue two playes in one night" and "inuite all the Poets [that is, actors] and Musitions to his chamber the next morning."[102]

References to nighttime indoor entertainments give us a notion of the prevalence of artificial theatrical illumination. But artificial light also accompanied indoor entertainments in the afternoon. In fact, we possess a picture of an afternoon masque in a private house that makes prominent use of torchlight. The picture is a detail from a portrait of Sir Henry Unton, diplomatist and soldier, that shows his wedding feast and an accompanying masque around 1580 or so (see fig. 10). Sir Henry, his bride, and guests are at table, while exotically costumed masquers climb the stairs and enter the dining room. Ten nude children bearing long, slender torches accompany the masquers, but the principal illumination comes from two large windows in the background and perhaps others in the fourth wall that has been cut away. Painted shortly after Unton's death in 1596, according to his widow's memory, the detail makes no attempt to indicate that much light derives from the ten torches. They are drawn without halos and cast no shadows. Instead, the room is brightly and evenly illuminated by natural window light — the torches merely adding highlights to the otherwise conventionally lit space. At court, masques were usually at night with artificial light replacing all natural light. But plays at the professional hall theaters were in the afternoon, and they may have looked something like this masque.

Why some indoor plays were performed in the evening and others in the afternoon is not always clear. City prohibitions and regulations were important, but other factors came into play. The nobility and gentry were largely free during the day to pass the time as they saw fit. Afternoon entertainments like Sir Henry's may thus have been more refined, as a whole, than many evening entertainments catering to tradesmen in need of diversion after a hard day's work. The evening may also have been the only time available to moonlighting actors busy during the day at the public playhouses. Except for entertainments at court, then, which in this and several other ways were unique, professional performances lit totally by artificial means must not be thought of as necessarily more well bred and expensive than performances

Fig. 10. Detail from a portrait of Sir Henry Unton, c. 1596.
By courtesy of the National Portrait Gallery, London.

that mixed both natural and artificial light. Nighttime plays requiring artificial light were always suspect, after all, and rarely officially sanctioned. Sir Henry was a rich, important person, a friend to Essex and even Henry IV of France. His use of natural light was hardly to scrimp on the chandler's bill but rather the result of now unknowable scheduling considerations. In the provinces where troupes were not occupied during the day at permanent theaters, plays for the nobility could be given indifferently by day or night. The fourth earl of Cumberland, for instance, a wealthy and powerful peer, hosted a dozen plays at his home in Londesborough from 1611 to 1612, of which about half were before supper and half after supper.[103]

Around 1604, we get a theatrical portrait of what is considered extravagant lighting for a professional play in the hall of a private home. Thomas Middleton's *A Mad World, My Masters* (London, 1608) satirizes the wealthy Sir Bounteous Progress who prides himself on the hospitality of his house. In the last act, his spendthrift nephew disguises himself as a player and absconds with several costly trinkets, "borrowed" as properties for the play that he and his cohorts perform for his uncle's guests. As usual, Middleton infuses the scene with realistic detail, and we learn a good deal about conditions at what Sir Bounteous believes is an indoor professional performance.

At the opening of the scene, Sir Bounteous and his servants are seen preparing for a large supper: tables are set up and guests are ushered into the "Hall" where "theres a good fire" (G4^v). As the bogus players arrive, Sir Bounteous welcomes them with "[s]ome Shirry for my Lords players there. Sirra, why this will be a True feast, a right Miter supper, a play and all, more lights—I cald for light" (H1). As a good host, Sir Bounteous's first concern, after offering drink, is the provision of lighting. Final preparations are made; the guests assemble for the play. But true to his humor, Sir Bounteous continues to fret over the lighting arrangements. He orders, "More lights, more stools, sit, sit, the play begins" (H2). Inductions to later hall theater plays sometimes include the lighting of candles just before the plays proper begin. If this play-within-a-play is any guide, the practice was not unique to the private theaters. But as the satire is based on Sir Bounteous's indiscriminate hospitality, Middleton's audience at the St. Paul's children's theater may have detected a certain excess to the provisions made. It was always a social obligation to provide adequate lighting—old Capulet requests more torches at his ball, as do such worthies as Lasso and Bilioso for private masques in *The*

Gentleman Usher and *The Malcontent*. But Sir Bounteous's twice calling for lights in addition to the fire and lights already present for the supper must accordingly be considered an indulgence.

Sir Bounteous's comparison of his feast with "a right Miter supper, a play and all" also confirms that artificially lit plays accompanied evening meals at taverns. The Miter was an old tavern in Fleet Street, later frequented by Dr. Johnson, that apparently was famous for its evening plays. Neither Chambers nor Bentley discusses the Miter, but it seems to have been an important indoor theatrical venue. Punning allusion to its use as a theater is found in *Your Five Gallants* when the title characters consider where they should sup while planning their intrigue. One gallant suggests the Mermaid, but they settle on the Miter—"For the truth is this plot must take effect At Miter."[104] This logic is based on a syllepsis, "plot" meaning both "intrigue" and "the action of a drama," with an associated satirical thrust at the type of dramatic fare popular at such taverns. Twenty tears later, the prodigious gossip John Chamberlain admired the duke of Buckingham's generosity to forty of his gentlemen when he spent one hundred pounds "to make them a supper and a play the next night [24 April 1618] at the Miter in Fleet-street."[105] At something over two pounds spent on each gentleman, the provisions for this nighttime play were munificent indeed. Forty-two years later still, Mr. Pepys overheard a performance taking place in what seems to have been a special hall for entertainments when he went "to the Mitre in Fleet-street, where we heard (in a room over the music-room) very plainly through the ceiling."[106]

Sir Bounteous's wealth and Buckingham's patronage give presumptive evidence that the lighting at Sir Bounteous's house and the Miter tended toward the sumptuous. The lively Buckingham took an avid interest in court theatricals and had the makings of a showman in him. Three months before his Miter play, Buckingham had the presence of mind to fill in a "lag" in Jonson's *Pleasure Reconciled to Virtue* by jumping out of his seat near the king and cutting a score of "lofty and very minute capers" under the "two rows of lights" that lit the first Jacobean banqueting house in Whitehall.[107] The efforts to please his own men rather than the king may not have been quite so taxing, but I should not wonder if a man this taken with theatrical affairs would have provided brilliant arrangements at the Miter as well. Like Sir Henry Unton's masque, these plays were for the enjoyment of the fortunate gentry and nobility. Run-of-the-mill citizens probably saw indoor plays lit simply by available window light or by the more homespun varieties of artificial light.

On hearing that a play is toward, the ingratiating Sir Bounteous Progress thinks immediately of lighting. But from the thousands of notices of early indoor entertainments that make no mention of it, I gather lighting was customarily not the major worry or expense of either the actors or their hosts. Our ignorance of the humbler forms of drama both indoors and outdoors means that the evidence we do have regarding the quality of lighting is not statistically representative of the whole but weighted disproportionately on the side of sophistication and splendor. The clearest picture we have of theatrical lighting is from court, but there is no reason to believe that private theater lighting happened to develop from the practices we know the most about. In any case, general illumination at court, as opposed to its special masque effects, differed from popular lighting less in kind than in sheer quantity. Many of the acting companies who moved into the Jacobean hall playhouses had already performed at court, but when they returned to their theaters, they had neither the money nor the leisure that the court lavished on its once-a-year entertainments. Rather, they relied on the window light and minimal candlelight of their Tudor forebears.

4

AFTERNOON PERFORMANCES
AT THE OUTDOOR PLAYHOUSES

SUNLIGHT FLOODING a platform stage is a familiar picture to anyone who has glanced at the many conjectural reconstructions of Elizabethan and Jacobean public playhouses. We see actors standing at the front of the stage bathed in bright light, even if darkness engulfs the tiring-house facade and galleries around them. There is a roof of sorts above the stage; but all too conveniently, it casts a shadow only over those parts of the theater for which we have no good description. The controversial discovery space, music room, lords' rooms, and "above," for example, remain in darkness, while the fore-part of the stage is covered with direct sunlight. It looks as though the actors were spotlighted by natural sunshine.

Although we know that the public playhouses usually mounted their plays in the afternoon, it is by no means certain that their stages looked like this picture. Behind our image of starkly lit actors moving in front of dimly seen architectural details lurks, in fact, a suspiciously modern theatrical conception, one only a little different from that of many productions in our modern theater, where Hamlet at Stratford, Siegfried at Bayreuth, and Didi and Gogo in Paris regularly stand in bright light before a pervasive gloom.[1] It is possible that we have returned to a mode of staging once popular in early modern London. But it is just as likely that we are confusing very different, older techniques with our own. Inevitably, each age interprets the sparse information about Shakespeare's stage based in part on its own aesthetics and theater practice. The great eighteenth-century theater historian Edmond Malone possessed much of the information concerning early English staging that we do, for instance, but could not imagine the Globe stage without two hanging chandeliers for lights.[2] He believed this even while knowing the Globe was an open-air playhouse, because the theater with which he was familiar—the theater of Cibber and Garrick—had them. Similarly, the naturally spotlighted actor may be the creation of our own bias, and a thorough look at the lighting of the public amphitheaters is in order before we proceed to the more complicated artificial lighting in the private hall playhouses.

Although there are many records of afternoon public theater performances throughout the Elizabethan, Jacobean, and Caroline periods, only a few vague contemporary references survive that describe the actual light inside the theaters. There is no reason to doubt that the actors performed by daylight, but we do well to recall that the first clear assertion of this comes as late as 1699 in a pamphlet, *Historia Histrionica*. "The *Globe, Fortune* and *Bull*, were large Houses," it states, "and lay partly open to the Weather, and there they alwaies Acted by Daylight."[3] The *Historia* purports to represent the memories of an "Honest Old Cavalier" looking back on the theaters he frequented as a youth. As such it is not the kind of evidence on which one likes to rely, because it was published over fifty years after all the theaters mentioned had been closed by Parliament. Still, it is the only description of light at the public theaters that may claim even a minimal weight of first-hand authority behind it.

Performance Times Before 1594

In order to evaluate the *Historia Histrionica*'s information and determine the availability of daylight, it is first necessary to learn at what times of the day the outdoor playhouses in London gave performances. We are fortunate to have several contemporary references from diaries, letters, and such, telling when people went to the playhouses, although the evidence is fragmentary and often in disagreement. And yet even this evidence must be used with caution. From a syncretic desire to discover the starting time of plays at a "typical" London public playhouse, early investigators averaged the many different times we find recorded into a mean starting time of two o'clock.[4] Taking such an average ignores not only the diversity of the ten or so public theaters built before the Restoration but also the changes in theatergoing habits that took place throughout the period, especially during the reign of Elizabeth. The times of performance were not as standardized as they are in our modern theater, and because one source says that the Globe began at two o'clock, we must not conclude that all public playhouses began at two o'clock or that the Globe always began at two o'clock throughout its history or during different seasons of the year.

The changes that took place in regard to Elizabethan theatergoing were caused principally by changes in churchgoing. Apart from a general antagonism between Protestants and the acting companies, leading finally to the 1642 closing of the theaters, public afternoon performances specifically conflicted with the observance of evening prayer. As various accommodations on both sides were offered, the time of performance shifted so as not to interfere with this important religious service. In its original Catholic form, vespers had formed part of the rigid set of seven canonical hours of prayer for each day.[5] The first English prayer book of 1549 eliminated all the canonical hours except matins and vespers, reorganized these, and renamed them morning and evening prayer. The pious were still called on to attend these services daily just after sunrise and just before sunset, but the sharp break with tradition had altered the public's view of its religious duty. Churchgoing, especially weekday churchgoing, suffered as a result. A century before, foreign visitors had wondered at the devotion of the English parishioners attending common prayer twice a day. But toward the end of the sixteenth century, the English began to neglect divine services except on Sundays and holy days, and might have neglected services on these days as well had it not been for strong fines imposed for nonattendance. In 1592, for example, the name of Shakespeare's father appeared in a list of Sunday church delinquents at Stratford. By the latter half of the sixteenth century, large numbers of Londoners never went to church on weekdays at all.

The problem for the acting companies was that for centuries, Sundays and holy days had been the occasion for merrymaking in general and theatrical entertainment in particular. Plays, fairs, and sporting events were reserved for Sundays and the large number of saints' and feast days in the old Catholic calendar. The Corpus Christi plays and St. Bartholomew fairs are familiar evidence. But under the increasingly puritan rule of the City authorities, these revelries were frowned on because they recalled the old Catholic way. One of the prime tenets of anti-Catholicism was the strict observance of the entire Sabbath as a day of rest and prayer. Nicholas Bownde's *The doctrine of the sabbath plainly layde forth* (London, 1595), to cite an extreme example, promulgated rules so stringent that even animals were enjoined not to work or frolic on Sundays. This puritan emphasis on devout Sunday worship therefore produced a scheduling conflict with the playhouses, because both the churches and the acting companies by tradition had asked the people of London to gather on Sunday and holy-day afternoons. Ultimately, the conflict was resolved when the actors, anticipating larger economic rewards, bowed to civic pressure and relinquished once-a-week Sunday performances for the greater number of weekday performances. But before that, the actors were obliged to juggle the times of performance at inns and early amphitheaters so as not to interfere with the celebration of evening prayer.

Before the Reformation, vespers or evensong was said at sunset shortly before going to bed. According to the *Regularis Concordia*, the medieval collection of rules for monastic ceremony, monks in England said vespers at about 4:15 P.M. in the winter and at 6 P.M. in the summer.[6] But a monk's day was long, and vespers for the laity was sung earlier in the afternoon, well before supper. In 1375, the bishop of London allowed the parish of St. Michael Cornhil to hold vespers on weekdays at 2 P.M. and on holy days "according to the lawdable custome of the Citee."[7] Under the Tudors, custom rather than regulation also seems to have determined the time of evening prayer; at least few specific times are indicated in church service records of the period. In 1553, the City prohibited plays before 3 P.M. on Sundays and holy days so as not to interfere with evening prayer, indicating the services began around 2 P.M. or so.[8] Around 1600, a memorandum by William Percy indicates that evening prayer at St. Paul's was completed by 4 P.M., suggesting a 2 or 3 P.M. starting time.[9] Unfortunately for us, no specific time was required by the ecclesiastical authorities. The bishop of London's visitation articles of 1571 stipulated only that services of common prayer be said "at convenient hours."[10] Even though the name given to the service was *evening* prayer, most contemporary descriptions place it in the afternoon. Two modern scholars state that evening prayer began at 2 P.M., which is reasonable enough, although the time varied from parish to parish.[11] Even within a parish, the time of evening prayer could change from season to season, hence the lack of particular starting times in church documents. Two o'clock is certainly the earliest these services began.

To avoid a Sunday afternoon conflict, the City ordered players to wait until after evening prayer was done to begin performances. In December 1571, the

London Court of Aldermen granted a license to Leicester's men to play "at convenient howers & tymes, so that it be not in tyme of devyne service."[12] The next year, the aldermen reiterated the prohibition, ordering house-keepers of inns "not to suffer the same playes to be in the tyme of devyne service . . . in there howses, yardes, or back sydes."[13] Although only one more-or-less permanent outdoor playhouse (the Red Lion) had been in operation before these orders, they show that prohibitions against playing during evening prayer applied equally to outdoor and indoor stages.

If the actors performing in such venues obeyed these orders, plays could not have begun much earlier than 3:30 or 4 P.M. The prayer service was traditionally one hour and perhaps lasted even longer with the inclusion of the newly popular sermons, many of which were quite long. If the services began at 2 P.M. and lasted until 3 or 3:30, then there would be a convenient thirty minutes for the playgoers to walk to the inn, pay admission, and take a seat before the play began. Thus, many performances in the early 1570s must have begun more towards 4 P.M. than 2 P.M. On the other hand, the necessity of repeating the prohibition suggests that it was not always enforced.

The difficulty with a 4 P.M. starting time in regard to lighting is the early sunset in London, particularly in the winter. In mid-December, London's sunset is about 3:45 P.M. In November and January, it is just after 4 P.M. (see table below).[14] Players who began after evening prayer—as Leicester's men were ordered to do in December 1571—would find themselves performing in darkness soon after their play began.

Of course, some of these late performances must have been given indoors. Andrew Gurr has shown that, in the provinces at least, actors generally played indoors in both summer and winter, because Elizabeth's 1559 edict generally allowed players to perform in a city's largest hall.[15] But in Tudor London, large civic halls had long been unavailable, and actors relied on inns from very early on. Based on their familiarity with provincial guild-halls, the companies probably preferred indoor venues at these London inns, although the City's prohibitions against both indoor and outdoor venues in all seasons show that the companies did not always get their way.

A reason why companies like the Admiral's men could perform outdoors throughout the winters in the 1590s without concern for darkness was a series of changes in performance times. These changes were the practical solutions to controversies that occurred regularly between the actors and the

Sunset Times in London, 1598 (Old-Style Dates)

	1st	7th	14th	22nd	28th
January	3:57	4:06	4:14	4:27	4:37
February	4:46	4:51	5:10	5:26	5:38
March	5:40	5:52	6:06	6:20	6:24
April	6:24	6:54	7:06	7:21	7:31
May	7:37	7:45	7:55	8:04	8:09
June	8:11	8:14	8:15	8:13	8:09
July	8:06	8:01	7:53	7:40	7:30
August	7:13	7:13	7:00	6:44	6:33
September	6:26	6:14	5:58	5:44	5:33
October	5:26	5:14	5:00	4:45	4:34
November	4:27	4:17	4:07	3:57	3:51
December	3:48	3:46	3:45	3:48	3:52

City. The political and religious background to attempts at governmental in-
tervention has been discussed by Richard Dutton; here we can only trace specific prohibitions that affected the times of performances.[16]

In December 1574, an Act of Common Council enforced the permanent
prohibition against playing during evening prayer and ended the first of these
controversies by precipitating the flight of the acting troupes to suburbs not
under City control.[17] If lack of surviving records is an indication, trouble died
down with the building of the Theater and Curtain playhouses in the mid-
1570s, taking a large part of the audience away from the London inns and out
of immediate official concern. But a flurry of complaints arose again in the
late 1570s and early 1580s when the City, spurred on by puritan preachers,
sought to ban performances on Sundays and holy days entirely.

Taking the side of the actors, the Queen's Privy Council suggested a
compromise and ordered the lord mayor to permit plays in the City on all
weekdays, including holy days, after evening prayer but not to permit performances on Sundays. In April 1582, they ordered the lord mayor "to reuoke
your late inhibition against their playeng on the said hollydaies after euening prayer onely forbearing the Sabothe daie whollie according to our

former order."[18] The order makes clear that by this time, the actors were willing to give up Sundays for the more numerous and lucrative weekday performances.

What the Privy Council does not make clear is whether the requirement to play after evening prayer applied only to holy days or to all weekdays, on most of which people never went to church anyway. Restoration testimony suggests that the actors did delay performances even on regular weekdays. In his *Short Discourse of the English Stage* (London, 1664), Richard Flecknoe said Elizabethan plays were performed "on Week-dayes after Vespers," but he may have been referring to performances by boy actors connected with religious choir schools.[19] The 1581 minutes of the Privy Council record only their desire that actors should play "upon the weeke dayes only, being holy dayes or other dayes, so as they doe forbeare wholye to playe on the Sabothe Daye, either in the forenone or afternone."[20] That the acting companies did wait until after evening prayer is admitted to by the lord mayor in his answering letter to the Privy Council. But he found the actors' compliance unsatisfactory in other ways. For while the players had indeed delayed their actual starting times, they had enterprisingly opened their doors several hours before, luring parishioners from their religious duty. Indulgently, the lord mayor wrote of the Privy Council's inexperience in such matters and vowed that allowing plays on holy days after evening prayer "can very hardly be done." He explained to the Privy Council:

> [F]for thoughe they beginne not their playes till after euening prayer, yet all the time of the afternone before they take in hearers and fill the place with such as be therby absent from seruing God at Chirch, and attending to serue Gods enemie in an Inne; If for remedie herof I shold also restraine the letting in of the people till after seruice in the chirche it wold driue the action of their plaies into very inconuenient time of night.[21]

Thus, if the starting times at the City inns were to be postponed by only so much time as was required for spectators to assemble after evening prayer, then the end of the play could fall into night. What is more, this deferment "into very inconuenient time of night" was contemplated in April when sunset was after 7:30 P.M.

The playhouses outside City jurisdiction were nominally free to ignore these prohibitions, occasionally offering plays early in the afternoon. Such is the tenor of a letter the lord mayor wrote to Walsingham, the queen's secretary, in May 1583, complaining of "p[ro]phane spectacles at the Theatre and Curtaine and other like places . . . wch be otherwise p[er]ilous for contagion biside the withdrawing from Gods s^rvice."[22] But there is also evidence that these playhouses sometimes performed later in the day after evening prayer, as did the players at the inns within City control. In the continuation of Holinshed's *Chronicles*, for instance, we learn that actors at the Theater, and probably at the Curtain as well, were performing at "about six of the clocke" on 6 April 1580 when an earthquake shook London.[23] To be performing at 6 P.M., these northern theaters probably began their plays after evening prayer. An even worse disaster occurred on 13 January 1583 at the Bear Garden in Paris Gardens when several scaffolds full of spectators collapsed at "about foure of the clocke in the after noone," just the time of the early winter sunset.[24] And on 9 June 1584, a fight broke out "very nere the Theatre or Curten at the tyme of the Playes," and the City recorder found the street full of police watches at "night."[25] The fight might have begun before midsummer nightfall, but the recorder's letter lends support to a later starting time than early afternoon. At any rate, the incident brought tension between the City and the actors to a head yet again, and the Privy Council suppressed all playing in London, forcing the acting companies to flee the City and travel or use the suburban playhouses for the remainder of summer.[26]

In the autumn or winter of the 1584–85 season, the newly formed Queen's men petitioned the Privy Council to let them return to the City.[27] We do not know what action the Privy Council took, but an answer to the petition from the Corporation of London has survived that speaks to lighting conditions in the public theaters. In their petition, the actors had complained that bad winter weather made performances outside London difficult. The City replied that if winter darkness was a problem for them, the solution was not to bring the plays into the City but to continue to perform in the distant liberties and shorten the plays: "If in winter the dark do cary inco[n]uenience: and the short time of day after euening prayer do leaue them no leysure: . . . the true remedie is to leaue of that vnnecessarie expense of time whereunto God himself geueth so many impediments."[28] The City's answer indicates not only that winter performances at the northern amphitheaters encountered problems with darkness but also that, despite being technically free of City control, the suburban playhouses after 1583 or so nonetheless sometimes began after evening prayer. The City appended a list of "remedies" to their reply: "That no playeing be on holydaies but after euening prayer. . . . That no playeing be in the dark, nor continue any such time but as any of the auditorie may returne to their dwellings in London, before sonne set, or at least before it be dark."[29] The City's phrase "playeing . . . in the dark" could mean either playing in bad light outdoors or under artificial lights indoors—at a hall in an inn, for example. But the City's careful phrasing in the last remedy suggests that an effort was made to include both suburban public playhouses and City inns with or without open-air inn-yards. The document is susceptible of the interpretation that natural daylight may not have served quite to the end of some winter open-air play presentations, although the City's emphasis on spectators walking home in the dark also suggests that the Queen's men continued to play right up to the onset of darkness, after which they left departing spectators to fend for themselves in the dark.

As it had done once before, the controversy between the players and the civic government died down for about ten years, only to flare up again at the beginning of the 1590s when at 8 P.M. on Sunday, 11 June 1592, a mob of feltmakers' apprentices, who were attempting to free a fellow apprentice from the Marshalsea, assembled themselves "by occasion, & pretence of their meeting at a play."[30] With the sun setting about 8:10 P.M. in the middle of June, 8 P.M. is rather late to give the pretense of meeting at a playhouse, presumably the Rose, approximately a quarter of a mile away from the Marshalsea. We should be able to confirm that there was a performance at the Rose on that day, but unfortunately the pertinent entry in Henslowe's diary is ambiguous. Figure 11 shows it along with the preceding and succeeding entries.

The entry for *A Knack to Know a Knave* is unusual because instead of giving a date, Henslowe supplies only an interlined note reading "day." Preceding the word is a mark that editors transcribe as a "1," but which is simply the characteristic backward-"C" bracket-mark that Henslowe regularly made at the beginning of each rule separating the year and the amount of money collected. In this case, Henslowe was a bit sloppy: the bracket mark is a little above the rule, and as he finished the mark, he failed to lift his pen quickly, resulting in a flourish mark more like a "V" than anything else. Between this mark and the word "day" is a faint smudge. Greg describes it as "a faint trace of a figure which has apparently been erased."[31] In their edition of the diary, Foakes and Rickert transcribe the smudge as a "o" and the bracket

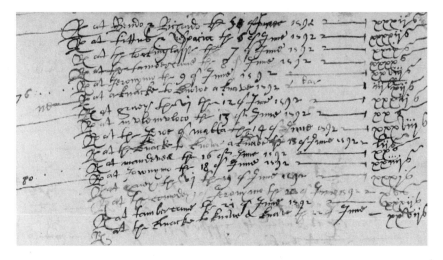

Fig. 11. Detail of folio 8 of Henslowe's diary (the entry for *A Knack to Know a Knave* is the sixth line down). Dulwich College Library, London.

and smudge together as "10," making the note refer to the tenth of the month, a Saturday.[32] But as I make it out, the smudge might signify just about anything or—for that matter—nothing; it is very faint indeed, and elsewhere in the diary Henslowe tends to strike out mistakes rather than erase them. Because the play is marked as new, perhaps Henslowe meant "1 day," meaning the first day of performance. Editors transcribe the note "10" rather than "11" because later on, the Admiral's men regularly skipped Sunday performances in accordance with City wishes, but the habit of not performing on Sundays was only solidly established at the Rose two years later in the summer of 1594 by the Admiral's men. In the summer of 1592, the Rose was occupied by Lord Strange's men who seem to have performed on several Sundays, as they apparently did a week later, offering *Jeronimo* on Sunday, 18 June 1592.[33]

Hence, the apprentices' riot might well have involved the Rose. And there is further evidence to support this suggestion. Two weeks later, all playing was forbidden in and about London by the Privy Council, which dreaded such civil disorders.[34] When the noble sponsors of the acting companies asked for relief from the prohibition on behalf of their troupes, Lord Strange's request was granted only if his company not perform at the Rose but at the more distant theater in Newington.[35] The Privy Council had a specific de-

sire that the Rose remain empty, which tends to link it to the original dis-
turbance. Thus, Strange's men may have performed at the Rose at 8 P.M., just
the time of summer sunset.

This last controversy between the City and the players resolved itself when
the acting companies requested and evidently received permission to perform earlier in the afternoon at the same time as evening prayer. As we have
seen, prior to the 1590s the government had been most concerned with keeping the time of divine service free of more alluring activities. Although there
had long been nighttime curfew laws in London, officials believed that playing after evening prayer posed less harm to moral health than did allowing
Londoners to miss church altogether.[36] Thus, the City had mollified its objection to late performances; at least there are fewer night prohibitions in
their regulatory documents of the 1580s and early 1590s than in the 1570s. But
after the Southwark riot and other instances of unrest, both City and Crown
became more concerned about avoiding civil disorder at night than protecting the Church in the afternoon. At both Guildhall and Whitehall, concern
for religious observance succumbed to fear of social protest.

It was in this climate that Henry Carey, Lord Hunsdon, the queen's lord
chamberlain, wrote to the lord mayor on 8 October 1594 requesting early
wintertime performances at the Cross Keys inn. Lord Hunsdon wrote not
in his official capacity but as the patron of the Lord Chamberlain's men who
must have moved from their summer home at the Theater to the Cross Keys
earlier that autumn. Thanking God for the abatement of the plague, Hunsdon promised that "where my nowe companie of Players . . . haue vnder-
taken to me that where heretofore they began not their Plaies till towards
fower a clock, they will now begin at two, & haue don betwene fowe[r] and
fiue."[37] In all likelihood, the lord mayor would previously have rejected an
offer to begin plays at 2 instead of 4 P.M., because the earlier time conflicted
with evening prayer. But by 1594, social conditions had changed, and Hunsdon could represent the early starting time as an advantage to the City fathers. Still, he admits that before October, his company was in the habit of
beginning at 4 and finishing at 5 or 6 P.M. at the Cross Keys.

We should like to know whether such performances were indoors or out.
Early autumn performances at inns lasting until 6 P.M. tend to suggest indoor
venues. Glynne Wickham has argued that the habit of assuming plays at inns
were normally outside in the inn-yards is unsupported by the evidence.[38]
Still, David Galloway points out a clear reference to an inn-yard scuffle in

Norwich "in the after noone . . . at a play in the yard at the red lyon" in June 1583.[39] And in London in 1557, a "Lewde playe" was about to be "plaied this daye" at the Boar's Head inn, presumably in the yard that was later converted into a fairly elaborate playhouse.[40] Regarding the Cross Keys inn, moreover, we have Richard Flecknoe's statement in his brief history of English drama that the Cross Keys was an inn-yard theater. He described how "Companies . . . set up Theatres, first in the City, (as in the Inn-yards of the Cross-keyes, and Bull in Grace and Bishops-Gate Street at this day is to be seen . . .)."[41] Flecknoe's account was published in 1664; it may or may not be reliable. We have no records of the Cross Keys being used as a theater after Hunsdon's request in 1594, and it is not clear whether Flecknoe meant that the theaters in the inn-yards were still to be seen or merely that the inns themselves were still standing in the early 1660s. Yet, Flecknoe's report is early in the Restoration, and we know that he was alive and old enough to travel alone to the Continent before the Interregnum.[42] Thus, when he says the Cross Keys accommodated a theater in its yard, we cannot ignore his evidence merely because we also have records of late afternoon wintertime performances there.

Although Wickham may well be correct that actors typically performed on indoor stages in winter and on outdoor stages in summer, we must not consider his observation a hard-and-fast rule, because there is contradictory evidence, many plays being given indoors in the summer and outdoors in the winter, although, in the latter case, to smaller audiences.[43] John Webster complained that the premiere of *The White Devil* at the Red Bull *"was acted, in so dull a time of Winter, presented in so open and blacke a Theater, that it wanted . . . a full and understanding Auditory."* Similarly, a player in Jonson's *Poetaster* (1602), who is identified with the Globe, complains of low receipts in winter.[44] In short, an actor's virtue was flexibility—the ability to perform under a variety of conditions in nearly any sort of playhouse. In all the letters that passed hands among the troupes, their patrons, the City Corporation, and the Privy Council, the aesthetic question of theatrical illumination never arises. The closest we come to such a concern is when the City sympathized with playgoers walking home in the dark from the Theater and Curtain in 1584. Actors may have preferred indoor winter quarters in the City, but we have no documentary evidence for believing that they did so because of bad outdoor lighting in the amphitheaters. The winter migration of a few companies to the private hall playhouses took advantage of artificial light, no doubt, but their primary motive was a desire to perform as close to the center of population as possible.

We lack sufficient information to trace accurately the movements back and forth of the early acting companies, but a similar form of entertainment, fencing, leaves records suggesting that weather and lighting were less important motives for migration than plague restrictions and precautions. The "Register of the Masters of Defense" shows that the fencers preferred to hold their prize matches in all seasons at the City inns but that the regular resurgence of the plague, almost always in summer, obliged them to flee to the suburban amphitheaters where they could ignore the City's prohibitions against public assembly.[45] Presumably, one can fence less safely in the bad light of winter than one can act in it, but light does not seem to have been a worry for the fencers or for the actors. Indeed, the variety of evidence about whether performances at inns were indoors in a hall or outdoors in a yard suggests that the actors were not very particular about their lighting arrangements. When Lord Hunsdon requested earlier playing times for the Cross Keys inn, the change seems to have been prompted by political concerns and not by technical lighting requirements. And Webster's and Jonson's real complaint is that the winter weather inhibited large audiences from gathering at the outlying playhouses, especially an *"understanding Auditory,"* as the patrons would have to stand in the yard unprotected from the weather. Webster does not lament that the *"open and blacke"* Red Bull made it difficult to see but that it prevented or discouraged patrons from making him a popular playwright.

Performance Times after 1594

The 2 P.M. starting time suggested by the patron of the most famous acting company of its time has been so widely accepted as a norm that it is surprising to discover on what little evidence it is based. Not only are we unsure if Hunsdon's starting time refers to an outdoor playhouse, but also we do not have the City's reply to the request. Nor do we have subsequent letters with time indications from the City and the actors. In fact, once their arguing finally died down in the late 1590s, we have only a handful of allusions to performance times. And among this handful, there is little agreement as to a standard time for the public playhouses. Indeed, only one indication of a regular starting time survives: in April 1614, an actor in Lady Elizabeth's troupe at the Hope agreed to a contract requiring him "to begyn the play at the hower of three of the clock in the afternoone."[46] Otherwise, we must rely on the usually vague allusions in extant letters, diaries, and the like as to when spectators arrived at the theater. E. K. Chambers states flatly that "before the end of the sixteenth century the time for beginning had been fixed at 2 o'clock," but for proof he cites only Lord Hunsdon's suggestion and a statement by the Swiss visitor Thomas Platter that on 21 September 1599 he rode over the Thames "ettwan umb zwey uhren" to see a production of *Julius Caesar*, presumably at the newly opened Globe.[47] Even so, the reference may imply a commencement later than 2 P.M. If Platter crossed the river "about" 2 P.M., then we may suppose it took him at least several minutes to reach the playhouse and find a seat.[48] And because we know that spectators often expected to wait in their seats before the play began, the performance Platter saw may not have begun until close to 3 P.M.[49]

Well before Chambers, Malone's study of Shakespeare had announced just as emphatically that "[p]lays in the time of our author, began at one o'clock in the afternoone."[50] Malone offered only one piece of evidence, an epigram by Sir John Davies published around 1590, which is hardly precise. The epigram describes a town gallant who "goes to Gilles, where he doth eate til one, / Then sees a play till sixe, and suppes at seauen."[51] Later, J. Payne Collier objected to Malone's estimate and declared, "In fact the performance of plays began at three o'clock."[52] For his argument, Collier collected three citations from the eighty-year period covered in his study. The first is from a children's theater satire, *Histriomastix, or The Player Whipt*, in which a "player" advertises his company's performance will begin "At three a clocke."[53] The second is the contract, mentioned earlier, between the actor Robert Dawes and Henslowe and Jacob Meade requiring him to begin acting at 3 P.M. And the third is a passage from an entertaining book called *Amanda, or The Reformed Whore*, that summarizes Amanda's afternoon schedule in neat heroic couplets:

> At two a clocke, thou goest to dinner tho
> With thy Land-lady, and her mayd below.
> At three unto the Play-house backe agen,
> To be acquainted with some other men.[54]

Apart from the small number of such time references, very few of even these provide satisfactory evidence regarding the amphitheaters. Hunsdon's request reveals pertinent information about an inn, but we do not know if the request was adopted or if plays there were performed in an open-air yard. Davies's epigram about the gallant who eats lunch until one, sees a play until six, and begins supper at seven is of unsure date and could refer to any sort of theater. But it hardly refers to a 1 P.M. starting time, as Malone suggests. If it took one hour for the gallant to go from the playhouse to supper, then we may suppose it took him an hour to get to the playhouse from lunch. Thus, 2 P.M. is the earliest likely starting time, and even that would mean spending four hours watching the play and leave no time before it to secure a good seat. In fact, the play's not finishing until 6 P.M. implies a still later commencement. The three o'clock reference in *Histriomastix* is precise, but Collier was pushing his evidence rather hard. The play is a satire of a rag-tag provincial acting company that hopes to perform in the local town hall. It refers neither to professional London actors nor to an outdoor theater. The date of Platter's two o'clock description is better fixed, but the two or three different places at which he says plays were acted are difficult to choose from the list of possible sites—the Curtain, Rose, Swan, first Globe, Newington Butts, and the indoor second Blackfriars and St. Paul's theaters, all standing in 1599, the date of his visit to London.

The 1614 actor's contract giving a three o'clock starting time is more definite as it clearly refers to a regular starting time at a specific playhouse, the Hope. Unfortunately, the contract is now lost and cannot be authenticated. But Collier's other bit of proof—the citation from *Amanda*—is too vague to be of use, because it also fails to indicate at what theater or even at what kind of theater Amanda conducted business before her long-delayed reformation. At any rate, Amanda's arrival at the playhouse to find clients at three o'clock does not necessarily imply that she was particularly eager to see the beginning of the play.

To these references should be added a half-dozen others that confirm no one standard starting time but demonstrate instead considerable flexibility in regard to when plays were performed. In Thomas Dekker's pamphlet *The Guls Horne-booke* (London, 1609), a man who would be a gallant is advised to go to lunch at 11:30 A.M. and see a play across the river directly afterwards.[55]

Depending on the length of dinner, Dekker suggests a 1 or 2 P.M. starting time. But a letter from John Chamberlain in August 1624 implies a later time for the Globe. That summer, Thomas Middleton's *A Game at Chess* was drawing large crowds of Londoners, fighting their way in to see it before the Privy Council suppressed it. Chamberlain admitted that he would have liked to see the play, too, "but that I could not sit so long, for we must have ben there before one o'clocke at farthest to find any roome."[56] How long Chamberlain would have had to sit is again left vague. Accounts of other plays describe a one-hour wait as expected, and the second Blackfriars theater presented a one-hour concert before each play. Since Chamberlain implies that a one o'clock arrival would mean an unusually long waiting period, we may estimate the performance began sometime after 2 P.M.

Looking at the whole period, we can say with confidence only that the public playhouses usually began performances anywhere from 2 P.M. to 4 P.M. Chronologically speaking, the times recorded before 1594 refer most often to around 4 P.M., at the turn of the century perhaps more towards 2 P.M., and closer to 3 P.M. some fifteen years later. Gurr believes there is enough evidence to say that different playhouses may have established different starting times: the Globe at 2 P.M., the Hope an hour later.[57] This is entirely possible, but there are several references to spectators deciding to leave one theater in order to catch a play at a rival theater, which would be made difficult, but by no means impossible, by disparate starting times.[58] On the other hand, variations in starting times may have been a function of the season, with wintertime performances beginning earlier than summertime performances.

There is one entry in Henslowe's diary that specifies a nighttime performance by the Admiral's men: "lent vnto the company when they fyrst played dido at nyght the some of thirtishillynges wch wasse the 8 of Jenewary 159[8]."[59] The early-twentieth-century scholar T. S. Graves used this entry to prove that "night performances in the public theatres were rather frequent in the days of Shakspere."[60] To be sure, there is evidence for performances stretching into twilight, but Graves went further and insisted that full nighttime performances lighted by torches and cressets were common in the pre-Restoration amphitheaters. To reinforce his argument, Graves jumbled together references to private, court, and even Restoration productions. The Henslowe entry is his prime bit of evidence, because the only playhouse Henslowe owned or had business associations with at the time was the Rose.

But the form of the entry (lending money to the company simply for a performance rather than for the usual scripts, costumes, or properties) is unusual and probably signifies nothing more than extra expenses incurred for a private performance indoors, such as the transportation costs that Henslowe paid a year later when the Admiral's men "played in fleatstreat pryvat."[61] A private venue is also supported by the entry's reference to a Sunday performance, when, by this date, the Rose normally went unused. At any rate, one nighttime performance does not suggest a regular pattern.

Records of nighttime professional performances in the provinces are more frequent, but they usually do not specify performance sites. In April 1615, for example, the city of Hythe in Kent allowed actors to perform "in the daye tyme or Eveninge (the same playes beinge fully ended before eight of the Clock at nyght in ye winter & in the Sumer before nyne of the Clock at night)" but announced a twenty shilling fine to the "ownor of any house within this Towne [who] shall suffer any players to play in their houses or backsides" in contravention of these and other conditions.[62] Winter performances ending at 8 P.M. undoubtedly took place "in their houses," but summer performances ending by 9 P.M. could reasonably take place in the "backsides" of inns or in large rooms. In the article "Public Night Performances in Shakespeare's Time," Marvin Rosenberg draws attention to a passage in Thomas Heywood's *An Apology for Actors* (London, 1612, G2) to support Graves's theory of London nighttime public theater playing.[63] In defending the acting profession, Heywood takes pains to recite every conceivable benefit that might derive from plays. To demonstrate an unexpected military advantage, Heywood tells a fantastic story of a group of Spanish marauders who landed one night on the shores of Cornwall and were about to pillage an English town when they were scared off by the sound of drums, trumpets, and military alarms arising from a local play. Rosenberg believes that the ease with which the invaders heard the stage battle meant the performance was out-of-doors. This might be the case, but just such noise disturbed the neighbors of the indoor second Blackfriars and the indoor Rosseter's Blackfriars theaters.[64] Moreover, of the references to night plays in provincial records that indicate specific venues, most put the performances in town halls, guildhalls, or, increasingly after 1614–18, in rooms in inns.[65] At any rate, Heywood's story is probably apocryphal and does not concern the London theaters.

Although Henslowe's contract and the street cry in *Histriomastix* both give a specific 3 P.M. time for the beginning of plays, it may be true that patrons did not expect plays to begin as regularly or as promptly as we do. Handbills advertised coming plays, but although no authentic playbills have survived, it is doubtful that particular times were specified. An advertisement for bear baiting in Henslowe's papers gives no indication of the time spectators should assemble, nor does the playbill for a bogus play, *England's Joy*. Indeed, English playbills did not indicate performance times until the middle of the eighteenth century, although a German bill for English actors in 1628 does advise the audience to gather at 2 P.M.[66] This lack of concrete notice suggests that some plays began at only approximate times or simply when the actors were ready. Modern theaters are darkened for the sake of dramatic illusion, and latecomers are not permitted to destroy it by wandering down the aisles looking for their seats. A well-advertised starting time is mandatory for a theater like ours that has little kinship with the kind of theater where spectators could come and go with little regard for a strict schedule or social pressure. Consequently, there may have been less need to designate a certain hour as an official starting time.

Yet even if the majority of plays began around two o'clock, it is difficult to understand how daylight could have served quite to the end of many plays performed in the winter. Although the "two hours' traffic" of the stage from the prologue to *Romeo and Juliet* is often quoted normatively, it is likely that most full entertainments at the public playhouses lasted closer to three hours. As in the case of starting times, there is much conjecture but little hard evidence regarding the length of performance. In the most influential study of playing times, Alfred Hart argued for a standard two-hour "allotment." Hart summarized his evidence: "Prior to 1614 [the terminus for his article] at least a dozen allusions were made by ten very important dramatists and actors connected with the principal companies and theatres to the prevalent custom of allotting two hours to the representation of a play. Only one dramatist speaks of a three-hour playing time."[67] But David Klein argues for longer playing times, listing a half-dozen other allusions to three-hour performance times.[68] Unfortunately, neither Hart nor Klein distinguishes between public and private playhouse auspices. Moreover, they both accept a two o'clock starting time as obligatory. Thus, Klein bolsters his argument for a three-hour allotment by citing allusions to five o'clock finishing times.

Still, Klein's point that several, perhaps many, plays continued longer than the conventional two hours is well taken. What is more, the actors often presented a jig after the completion of their plays. Chambers makes the intriguing suggestion that shorter plays may have been reserved for the winter.[69] But this kind of scheduling may have been difficult to arrange, considering the nature of the repertory system. At least, a check of the performance schedules in Henslowe's diary reveals no seasonal emphasis on plays known to be either short or long. Presumably jigs could be shortened more easily than plays; perhaps they provided the actors some flexibility in accommodating uncontrollable natural light. After a careful review of the evidence, Andrew Gurr concludes that performances lasted "somewhere between two and three hours in all."[70]

The assumption that a complete entertainment at the theater lasted between two and three hours means that some representations finished in twilight. Even if plays began promptly at 2 P.M., a three-hour duration would push the end of the play past sunset for four months a year, from the second week in October until the third week in February. When plays began at three o'clock, the end of a three-hour play would continue past sunset for half the year, from the middle of September until the middle of March. At the Hope on 31 October 1614, for example, Lady Elizabeth's men performed *Bartholomew Fair*, which, as Jonson tells us in his induction, lasted "two houres and an halfe, and somewhat more."[71] As the actor's contract signed the previous spring gives it as official company policy to begin at 3 P.M., the play would have stretched more than one hour past sunset, unless, of course, the company reverted to an earlier staring time for the autumn and winter. Such was the procedure at the *corrales* in Madrid, where plays started at two o'clock in winter and as late as four in summer.[72] It is improbable, though, that this delay was caused by any artistic inclination of the Spaniards to perform plays through the year under similar levels of brightness. More important was the practical desire to avoid the blazing midafternoon sun in Madrid, where even today the city closes down from one to four o'clock in summer. A custom like this is unnecessary in London.

If early darkness caused difficulties and no indoor venue was available, English actors probably simply shortened the play, as we know they sometimes did from the complaints of irate authors. For example, the title page of *The Duchess of Malfi* tells us that the text was printed "with diverse *things*

. . . that the length of the Play would not beare in the Presentment." Because early sunsets would be one of the principal reasons for cutting a play, we may guess that there was a limit to how much past sunset a performance could last.

Weather

No matter what time of day plays began or ended, the quality of light was also affected by a largely uncontrollable factor—the weather. Regardless of the time or the season, the possibility that the sun directly lit actors on an open-air stage could not have been great. London is not famous for its sunshine, and what evidence we have indicates that the weather in Shakespeare's time was rather worse than it is now. In typical summer weather today, only two of every five daytime hours is sunny in London, according to measurements recorded at Kew over the past fifty years.[73] In spring and autumn, the sun shines on average only one-third to one-fourth of the time from sunrise to sunset.

But climatologists refer to the period from 1550 to 1680 as the first phase of the "Little Ice Age," a period of relatively cooler, more unstable weather than we have enjoyed since about 1850.[74] It is difficult to generalize from the sparse anecdotal evidence, but apparently early-seventeenth-century winters were frequently more severe than we are used to (the Thames freezing over on a number of occasions), while summers tended to uncomfortable extremes—wet and cool, for the most part, but occasionally hot and dry. All in all, London's mists and rains must have reduced the amount of light at least as often as we should expect them to do today. Although climatologists ascribe the severity of London's fogs to the effects of the industrial revolution in the nineteenth century, diarists as early as the Restoration lodge familiar complaints of smoky mists and thick fog covering the City. And it does not seem to be true that performances were regularly canceled on rainy days, as C. Walter Hodges has asserted.[75] A 1623 almanac predicted rain showers at the Red Bull and Curtain amphitheaters, where "they shall sit dryer in the Galleries, then those who are vnderstanding men in the yard."[76] Dekker advises a gallant at the Bankside theaters that "if . . . indisposition of the weather binde you to sit it [the play] out," mewing at the actors and criticizing their music are in order.[77] At the Rose, the Admiral's men must have often played in bad weather; ticket receipts in Henslowe's diary record uninterrupted strings of performances by the company six days a week over many seasons. And we know that, while "unseasonable" summer weather reduced income at the Globe, it did not cause performances to be canceled.[78] In short, the dismal picture Webster drew of the premiere of *The White Devil* at the Red Bull may not be the mere exaggeration of a disgruntled playwright.

5

ILLUMINATION OF THE OUTDOOR PLAYHOUSES

B ESIDES THE NATURAL EFFECTS of sun and clouds, the playhouses themselves affected the quality of the daylight that illuminated them. The configurations of the amphitheaters built in Shakespeare's London may never be determined to our complete satisfaction, of course, but from the Swan drawing, extant playhouse contracts, perspective maps of the Bankside, and the partially excavated foundations of the Rose and second Globe, we know enough about the shape, size, and orientation of several outdoor theaters to make intelligent surmises about the amount and kind of light that illuminated their stages. The variables are the position and size of the stage and the "heavens" above the stage, the altitude of the sun above the horizon, and the proportions of the playhouse. Diagrams *a* through *f* (see fig. 12), based on Richard Hosley's reconstruction of the Swan, demonstrate the principles.[1]

Let us assume that sunlight comes from the southwest, as it does on average in the midafternoon from spring to autumn. In diagrams *a* and *b*, the stage is placed at the northeast side of the theater, opposite the sun. Diagram *a* shows the articulation of light in the Swan at 2 P.M. on the summer solstice. It will be seen that at the height of summer, the altitude of the sun at 2 P.M. (about fifty-four degrees) is high enough to light nearly the entire stage. Diagram *b*, however, presents a more typical performance situation — 3 P.M. on the autumn or spring equinox. Here the altitude of the sun is about twenty-seven degrees, and only a small area high on the tiring-house wall is lit directly by the sun. In winter, the sun is so low in the sky even at 2 P.M. (only

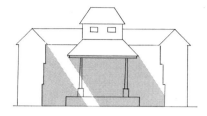

a. NE stage: 2 P.M. in summer

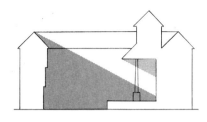

b. NE stage: 3 P.M. in spring or autumn

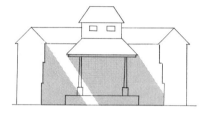

c. NW stage: 2 P.M. in summer

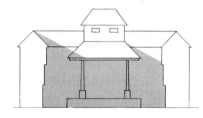

d. NW stage: 3 P.M. in spring or autumn

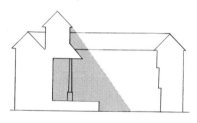

e. SW stage: 2 P.M. in summer

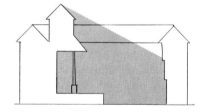

f. SW stage: 3 P.M. in spring or autumn

Fig. 12. Conjectural diagrams of the Swan

eleven degrees above the horizon on the winter solstice, for instance) that the stage can never be lit by direct sunshine.

Diagrams *c* and *d* are cross sections of Hosley's reconstruction with the stage and heavens at the northwest side of the arena (or the mirror image of its complement, the southeast). In *c*, the early afternoon summer sun can light about half the forepart of the stage, while the walls of the playhouse and the heavens shade most of the rest. Only a thin band of light is allowed to cross the stage from front to back. Diagram *d* demonstrates that on an autumn or spring day at 3 P.M., no direct sunlight could strike the stage at all.

Diagrams *e* and *f* represent the corresponding situations when the stage is at the southwest, the same compass point from which the sun is shining. It will be seen that even at the height of summer at 2 P.M., no frank sunshine could reach the stage.

Orientation

To obtain the best light, a modern lighting designer would undoubtedly put the stage at the northeast side of the yard, as in *a* and *b*. Judging by the shadows in pictures of their reconstructions, several early theater historians put the stage there, too, as did the planners of many American outdoor Shakespearean festivals. But the practice in Shakespeare's time was less predictable; in many of the amphitheaters, in fact, the orientation appears to have been the exact opposite to what we might expect.

A summary of the most important evidence for the orientation of amphitheater stages and the structures above them follows.

Red Lion. The recently discovered legal description of the construction of the Red Lion indicates that its stage was erected in a "Courte or yarde lying on the south syde" of a garden belonging to a farmhouse.[2] About the court were galleries, and within the court the carpenter built a stage forty feet north and south and thirty feet east and west. Because other amphitheater stages were wider than they were deep (Richard Hosley estimates an average ratio of eight to five), we may conjecture that the stage of the Red Lion faced either east or west.[3]

Theater. Abram Booth's *View of the City of London from the North toward the South* (c. 1599) shows a large gabled hut indefinitely centered above the yard. The hut appears to be wider along the east-west or northeast-southwest dimension, while the west (or southwest) side is fairly heavily crosshatched. These details might indicate a northwest location for the stage, but the picture is so crudely drawn that conjecture based on it can be given little weight.

Curtain. Booth's *View of the City of London* may also show the hut of the Curtain playhouse. Because the galleries are hidden by another building, no evidence regarding the orientation of the stage is discernible.

Rose. The foundations uncovered in 1989 reveal the stage was positioned just a few degrees west of due north both before and after the remodeling of 1592.[4] This position roughly confirms the apparent orientation in John Norden's *Civitas Londini* panorama (1600), generally regarded as one of the most accurate maps of Elizabethan London (see fig. 13). Norden shows a simple gable roof with a fenestrated gable-end on the northwest side of the yard facing southeast. Because we know that the stage was in fact to the north, Norden implies that the ridge of the roof was perpendicular to the front of the stage with the gable-end facing the yard.

Swan. Norden's panorama shows no superstructure above the yard of the Swan, while J. C. Visscher's notional engraving (c. 1616) shows a hut at the west facing east. The de Witt sketch (c. 1596) seems to show light coming from behind the tiring-house and hut.

Fig. 13. The Rose (*left*) and the first Globe (*right*). Detail of a panoramic view of the Bankside, London, from John Norden's *Civitas Londini*, 1600. Royal Library, Stockholm.

Boar's Head. Although documents connected with the Boar's Head place the stage and tiring-house on the "[w]est syde of the greate yard," Herbert Berry has shown that, because Whitechapel High Street actually ran diagonally from southwest to northeast, the true orientation of the stage was to the southwest.[5]

First Globe. Norden's 1600 panorama also includes the first Globe, but the evidence is difficult to interpret. As he does for the Rose, Norden shows a superstructure with a gable roof, whose gable-end is clearly facing southeast. Orrell sees Norden's representation of the superstructure at the first Globe as essentially similar to his depiction of the Rose—that is, a gable roof with its ridge running radially and with the gable-end parallel to the front of the stage.[6]

If this is the case, the stages in Norden's Rose and first Globe would share the same orientation, and the Globe stage and roof would be at the north or northwest side of the yard. But we would not expect this orientation based on the evidence we have regarding the second Globe. Because the first and second Globes were built on the same foundation,[7] and because Wenceslaus Hollar's sketch (c. 1643) puts the heavens of the second Globe at the southwest (see fig. 14), we would predict a similar placement for the first Globe. To account for this anomaly, Orrell suggests that Norden's original sketch of the first Globe, drawn from the perspective of the tower of St. Saviour's Church (now Southwark Cathedral) to the east, was copied unchanged into his panorama that ostensibly shows the Bankside from a southern viewpoint; hence, Orrell argues, true west in Norden's preliminary sketch appears as north in the engraving. One can easily imagine this happening, but as we now know that the Rose stage was in fact to the north, we must then wonder why this apparent rotation occurred only for the Globe and not for the Rose, which was presumably also sketched from the same vantage point but whose superstructure is drawn close to its true orientation. One way around this problem would be *not* to assume that the first and second Globes shared the same orientation. If the foundations were laid out symmetrically, it is possible, but perhaps not likely, that when the Globe was rebuilt in 1613, its planners shifted the area allotted to the tiring-house from the northwest quadrant to the southwest.

A more plausible solution may be inferred from Norden's panorama if the gable-end he saw did not face the yard. If we imagine that the ridge of the

Fig. 14. The second Globe. Detail from Wenceslaus Hollar's *West part o[f] Southwarke toward Westminster*, c. 1643. Yale Center for British Art, Paul Mellon Collection.

hut in Norden's depiction of the first Globe lay parallel to the front of the stage, then the stage and its superstructure would find themselves at the southwest, confirming Hollar. In this orientation, the gable-end would not lie parallel to the front of the stage but would be perpendicular to it. The hut would then resemble that shown by de Witt at the Swan, except that instead of the Swan's hip roof, the hut of the first Globe would be topped by a simple gable roof. Norden's view of the Globe is sometimes difficult to make out, but I wonder if the crosshatching to the left of the hut's roof might be an indication, not of thatching on the gallery roof, but of some sort of saddle connecting the gallery roof with the roof of the hut, as suggested in my very conjectural redrawing of Norden's Globe (see fig. 15). In this case, the superstructure above the first Globe stage would not be integrated into the framework of the galleries, as Orrell suggests, but would be a freestanding turret, as argued by Hosley.[8] Although certainty is unattainable, the most likely placement of the stage at the first Globe is at the southwest.

Fig. 15. Conjectural redrawing of Norden's *Civitas Londini* Globe

First and second Fortunes. No pictorial evidence is available for either play-house. Hosley argues that the stage of the first Fortune was to the north, based on inferences he draws from Agnes Henslowe's 1616 assignment of her spouse's lease to Edward Alleyn's moiety of the Fortune property.[9] This assignment mentions a street on the "south side . . . of the house from one doore of the said house to an other."[10] Although C. Walter Hodges placed these two doors on the stage side of the playhouse to allow the audience to enter along gangways into the yard, Hosley places them opposite the stage, believing that entering spectators would clog up these side alleys near the stage. On the basis of symmetry, he places both doors to the south, but because Thomas Platter implies that only one door was needed by spectators, one of the doors along this street may have been positioned opposite the stage while another might communicate with other parts of the house from the side of the playhouse. The lease implies that Alleyn himself used these doors, and their "large & ample" size may imply uses other than audience admission.[11] Hence, the orientation of the first (and second) Fortune remains unknown.

Second Globe. Hollar's sketch shows a mammoth hut to the southwest facing northeast.

Red Bull. No evidence is available.

Hope. Hollar shows the gallery-roof peak at the southwest facing northeast.

Regarding the orientation of the amphitheaters for which we can draw conclusions, then, the evidence indicates one stage to the north, one to the east or west, one probably in the west, one probably in the southwest, and three in the southwest. Although variation is apparent, we cannot fail to notice the preponderance of stages situated in the west or southwest. Thus, the lighting at many public playhouses seems to have been as depicted in diagrams *e* and *f*. In these cases, we must conclude that direct sunlight rarely illuminated the actors.

The implications of southwest stages may be disturbing to modern theatergoers. Direct sunlight would not only miss the stage but also sometimes shine fully in the faces of those sitting or standing opposite to it in what we should consider the choicest locations in the house. Thus, Alan Young believes that "practical men of the theatre" would not normally have placed the stage on the southwest side where the actors would be shaded from the southwest afternoon sun.[12] Young concludes that some extraordinary explanation must account for this "odd" orientation of the Elizabethan stage. But there is no evidence that Elizabethans considered this arrangement odd, nor do the explanations Young offers seem very plausible. His first explanation is that, in orienting their theaters, businessmen like Burbage, Henslowe, and Langley felt a desire to emulate medieval church iconography where the chancel (God) was situated to the east and the nave (man) to the west. But it hardly seems useful to equate the galleries opposite the stage with the presence of God, nor does it make much sense to equate the stage ("the little world of man") with the nave: if anything were analogous to the nave, it would have been the galleries and yard where the audience gathered to watch the play.

Young's second explanation suggests that Elizabethans placed their stages at the southwest side of the playhouse in accordance with complex Vitruvian triangulations. But this is one point Vitruvius is not complex about. He clearly states that a southern exposure is to be *avoided* because the sun shining all day from behind the stage house on to the auditorium seats creates a hot, unhealthy environment in the *cavea*.[13] But London is so far to the north that direct sunlight could rarely have shone in the theaters where, in any case, one imagines a little warmth might have been welcomed. In Rome the problem was the opposite. And because the prevailing wind in London is from the southwest (Rosalind compares stormy Silvius in *As You Like It* to "foggy South, puffing with winde and raine" [F 1823]), it is not surprising that stages were put in positions where the actors, properties, and costumes would be most protected from the elements.

Although a southwest orientation might be unacceptable to us, Shakespeare's audience apparently thought otherwise. For one thing, the lack of perspective scenery meant that the stage could be properly seen from many viewpoints, not just opposite the stage. We know that the king faced north at medieval English tournaments so as to avoid squinting into the sun, and a similar custom prevails at bullfighting arenas where seats in the *sombra* are a good deal more expensive than those in the sun.[14] If there were any choice seats at the amphitheaters, they were consequently probably near the stage, shaded from the sun. Thomas Dekker's *The Guls Horne-booke* implies as much when it places the lords' rooms in "the Stages Suburbs."[15] And Dekker confirms that these exclusive rooms were in shadows when he complains that they were "contemptibly thrust into the reare, and much new Satten is there dambd by being smothered to death in darknesse." During recent summer visits to the full-scale reconstruction of the first Globe in Southwark, which has its stage positioned to the southwest, I was interested to see that spectators, as they entered the theater, initially stood or sat directly opposite the stage where habit had long taught them they could best see the performance. They gravitated to these areas even on hot summer afternoons with bright sunlight shining down on them. But as the performance began, and the spectators turned their attention to the actors, they sometimes found themselves uncomfortable in these areas. This discomfort was most notable when frank sunshine entered the playhouse from behind the stage. With direct sunlight shining down on them, many spectators found themselves either too hot or obliged to squint directly into the sun. But even on cool, overcast days, many spectators in the back of the yard gradually migrated to the sides of the auditorium because, as they looked up at the stage, they still found themselves squinting into a sky considerably brighter than the shaded stage.

The most important exception to the prevailing southwestern orientation of the amphitheater stages was the Rose. By way of accounting for this deviation from the apparent norm, Orrell plausibly suggests that the placement of the Rose stage to the north may have been determined by a necessity to have its main entrance face Maid Lane to the south.[16] Whatever the explanation, daylight would generally shine down on the interior of the Rose from the stage-right side, occasionally lighting the stage with direct sunlight in the early afternoon in midsummer. But because the Rose in its first phase was so small in diameter (approximately seventy-two feet), less light could have entered its interior that at other theaters, whose apparent average diameter was close to one hundred feet. Assuming the galleries about the Rose's circumference were the same height as those stipulated in the Fortune contract, this smaller diameter would also mean that the galleries would block out a higher proportion of the available daylight. Figure 16, based on C. Walter Hodges's reconstruction of the Rose in its first configuration, shows that at 3 P.M. on the summer solstice, only about one-half of the stage could be lit by direct sunshine.[17] On the equinoxes, when the sun is much lower in the sky, only a few sections of the two upper galleries on the actors' left could be lit by direct sunshine; no frank sunshine could have lit the stage at all.

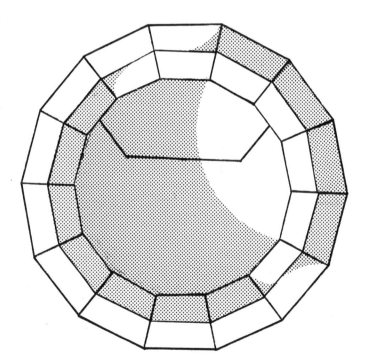

Fig. 16. Conjectural insolation of the Rose, first phase, at 3 P.M. on the summer solstice

Stage Covers

Hodges's reconstruction of the Rose in its first phase (1587 to 1592) includes no superstructure over the stage. The archaeologists found no evidence for pillars, which would be required to support anything but the smallest of roofs jutting out from the tiring-house. Henslowe's diary makes clear that extensive remodeling took place at the Rose in 1592, however, and the archaeologists duly found the foundations of a second stage (some seven feet north of the original stage), within the perimeter of which two substantial bases were discovered, presumably to support the pillars of a stage cover, much as depicted in the de Witt rendition of the Swan.

Thus, the original Rose seems to have been built without a stage cover, and evidence from other early amphitheaters may indicate that some of the first purpose-built outdoor playhouses did without the familiar heavens over the stage. The legal proceedings regarding the Red Lion say nothing of a roof over its stage, although a thirty-foot-high turret was erected "uppon" the stage, which may have served to shade certain areas, even if its principal purpose was to house hoisting paraphernalia or provide an "above." Although Booth shows a large hut or turret above the Theater, his *View of the City of London* comes nearly twenty-four years after the Theater had been built and may not represent its original configuration. Based on the relative absence of stage directions calling for descents in plays written before the 1590s, Wickham suggests that a heavens may have been added sometime after the building of the playhouse but before 1599.[18] On similar grounds, Herbert Berry concludes that early versions of the Boar's Head may also have lacked stage covers. In the summer of 1598, the stage was located in the southwestern portion of the central yard but not, apparently, directly against the tiring-house, making a large roof difficult to support. Because none of the surviving plays associated with the Boar's Head calls for descents, Berry infers that the stage constructed in this first major renovation may well have lacked a roof.[19]

But other amphitheaters built or remodeled in the 1590s give clear evidence of stage covers. Although the Rose was only five years old in 1592, Henslowe undertook to add a very large roof indeed. We know that this roof extended over and beyond the stage because a depression line, formed by rainwater dripping off the roof, is in evidence in the yard some four feet three inches in front of the stage.[20] A later remodeling at the Boar's Head in 1599 also included the addition of a stage cover, because we know that, when the stage there was moved southwest to adjoin the tiring-house, a "cou*e*runge ou*e*r the stage," apparently a substantial roof, was added.[21]

When new theaters were built—the Swan (c. 1595), the first Globe (1599), and the first Fortune (1600)—they were designed with substantial stage covers from the start. De Witt's sketch of the Swan shows a heavens extending well out from the hut and covering half the stage. The Fortune contract is vague as to size, prescribing only a "shadowe or cover over the saide Stadge," telling us in the name "shadowe" something, perhaps, of its purpose and effect.[22] At any rate, the contract testifies that the Fortune was planned with a cover in mind and that it was not an afterthought as at the Rose and Boar's Head. We may also assume that the Swan's cover was planned as an original part of the playhouse, because de Witt drew it only a year or so after the playhouse opened.

We have no direct evidence about the roof-canopy at the first Globe. Perhaps the Globe had a less substantial cover than other playhouses built about this time. The first Globe was constructed hurriedly, and it may have lacked something in the way of opulence, at least in comparison to the second Globe. Shakespeare's plays from 1599 to 1608 display a poverty of hoisting effects, and Alois Nagler has pointed out that because the Fortune contract instructs the builder, Peter Streete, to copy the Globe (which Streete had built the year before) in details not stipulated in the contract, the provision for a large stage cover at the Fortune could indicate that the first Globe did not provide a suitable model.[23]

On the other hand, Hamlet may have pointed to a beautifully decorated first-Globe heavens when he directs Rosencrantz and Guildenstern's attention to "this most excellent Canopie the ayre; looke you, this braue orehanging firmament, this maiesticall roofe fretted with golden fire" (Q2 F2). Although we have no information regarding the size of the heavens at the first Globe, we do know that three years before the Lord Chamberlain's men moved there, James Burbage had attempted, unsuccessfully, to lodge the troupe indoors at Blackfriars. It may be that subsequent plans for the heavens at the two Globes reflected his inclination to perform in as shaded a space as possible.

We are ignorant of the form of the stage cover at the next amphitheater to be set up, the Red Bull (c. 1606), although the many ascents on large, floating properties in Heywood's Red Bull plays point toward a substantial heavens there. But we are well informed about the next two public playhouses to be built—the Hope (1613–14) and the second Globe (1614). The Hope contract calls for a "[h]eavens all over the saide stage," but one which was not supported by posts arising from the stage because the stage itself was removable to accommodate animal baiting.[24] Confusingly, though, the contract elsewhere speaks of "turned cullumes vppon and over the stage"; these, perhaps, were associated with the tiring-house. If the heavens there actually did extend "all over" the stage, it must have been quite large, because the stage itself appears to have been at least as substantial as that at the Swan, the basic model for the Hope. One wonders how such a broad structure, together with its lead rain-gutters, was adequately supported without stage pillars.

The Hope was hastily planned just after fire destroyed the most prestigious amphitheater in London, the Globe. The Globe was rebuilt by the summer of 1614, and many patrons leave testimony to its increased splendor. Although its overall dimensions must have been nearly the same as the original Globe and Theater before that, Hollar's sketch shows a large heavens covering not only the stage but also half of the entire theater. In a detailed study of the second Globe, C. Walter Hodges reconstructs a great double-gabled timber roof spanning sixty-seven feet across the yard and reaching over thirty feet from front to back.[25] Hodges realized that such an arrangement would make the stage dim and suggests that the onion-domed turret situated in a valley between the two slanting roofs of the stage cover was a glazed cupola or lantern, illuminating the stage below.[26] This idea is attractive to us who are accustomed to brightly lighted actors, and we know from Restoration paintings and records that the two Cockpit theaters were also equipped with overhead lanterns. But at the Cockpit-in-Court, which was remodeled specifically for the King's men in the early 1630s, a blue buckram ceiling was placed above the actors, and the lantern was positioned not directly above the stage but above the auditorium.[27] In this position, its Globe counterpart was not Hodges's lantern but the opening above the yard.

Although it may seem reasonable to us that the King's men would have wanted more light onstage, the growth in the size of the canopy over the years demonstrates that bright light was only a subsidiary concern. Hodges's identification of the cupola's purpose may be correct, but it means that the floor of the heavens must be removed, making the support of suspension-gear difficult. Hodges puts the winch and windlass inside the tiring-house in order to permit light to reach the stage. In that case, one wonders what the purpose of the second Globe's heavens was, because, as Hosley points out, such a heavens could neither obstruct sunshine nor provide a means of supporting hoisting machinery.[28]

If extra light had been the primary concern, it would have been more practical first to increase the number and size of the windows in the walls of the galleries and the tiring-house. But as all the panoramic maps of the Bankside agree, only a few small windows were put in the walls of any playhouse. Hodges believes these windows were also to help light the stage, but Richard Southern has shown that most of them lighted the dark passageway behind the middle gallery.[29] Their small size, limited number, and (in Hollar's view) special placement halfway up the exterior walls corroborate Southern's description. If their purpose had been primarily to increase the brightness onstage, many more and much larger windows could more easily have been constructed than the elaborate cupola tower Hollar shows. The Fortune contract does call for "convenient windowes and lights [that is, window panes] glazed to the saide Tyreinge howse," which might mean that additional light was desired there.[30] But the reference is probably to exterior windows for the illumination of dressing rooms and property storage areas in the tiring-house behind the stage. This sort of utilitarian rather than aesthetic purpose is confirmed by Henslowe's leaving it to the builder to determine convenient positions and numbers.

The cupola in Hollar's view of the second Globe is small and pushed back toward the galleries and tiring-house, not directly over the center of the stage. What appear to be glazed windows are also quite small, and the whole tower is set in a deep valley between the two steeply gabled roofs, an inefficient place for light to enter. Stuart Baker has pointed out that one would normally expect such a lantern on the ridge of a gable roof, not in a valley.[31] He argues, moreover, that such a valley would require substantial support and that a turret arising from the stage, much like the one at the Red Lion, must have been placed directly underneath such a cupola. In this position, a turret would have severely reduced the amount of any light descending from such a lantern. Baker concludes that, if the cupola was a lantern, it probably lighted only the room where suspension-gear was housed.

One motive for erecting broad ceilings above otherwise open playing spaces may have been the desire to exploit the emblematic possibilities that such ceilings afforded. As noted in chapter 3, playing had occurred under the painted canvas ceilings of banqueting halls for more than a hundred years before the Cockpit-in-Court was remodeled. But ceilings are rarely constructed solely for the purpose of painting them. Since Hosley has cogently argued that the indoor Tudor-hall screen provided a source for the outdoor tiring-house facade, as likely an inspiration for the outdoor heavens was the ceiling of the Tudor hall. Such ceilings provided conveniences that the actors would not want to do without as they were forced outside City walls into the public arenas. They enjoyed its protection from the weather, and they could hang hoisting machinery on its rafters. The enlargement of the heavens in emulation of the indoor ceiling was probably prompted more by a desire to avoid rain than to avoid sunlight, but it is difficult to do one without the other, especially in playhouses with stages to the southwest. The inevitable result was to protect the stage from all the elements.

Articulation of Light

Although the gallery walls and stage cover occluded most of the direct rays of the sun, much indirect light entered the theaters through the opening above the yard. Unfortunately, precise levels of brightness cannot be calculated owing to the large number of unknown quantities—the size and shape of the opening and cover, the changing densities and reflecting capacities of the clouds overhead, the time of day, the season of the year, and the reflective capacity of the interiors of the playhouses. The decoration of the auditorium and stage is significant, because the amount of light reflected back by different surfaces varies widely—less than 10 percent for black velour hangings, 20 percent for finished walnut, 40 percent for unfinished oak, and 70 percent for white paint.[32] We know that Henslowe spent a good deal of money to paint the Rose, but we are not told the color.[33] There is a possibility that much of the auditorium of the first Fortune was unpainted. The contract directs the contractor to paint only the lords' rooms, two-penny rooms, and the stage; otherwise, the Fortune, which was to resemble the "fashion" of the Globe, seems to have been largely oak framing and lyme-and-hair walls.[34] Assuming that the interior decoration of the Swan resembled that of the Fortune, rough approximations of the amount of light onstage can be made by consulting tables of seasonal variation in daylight at London, estimating the fraction of this light that the playhouse permitted inside, and adjusting for the light absorbed or reflected away by the interior.[35]

Thus, in spring, an average illumination level at 3 P.M. near the front of Hosley's Swan stage works out to something on the order of 150 to 200 footcandles, this in contrast to about 8,000 footcandles produced by strong, direct sunshine; about 1,000 footcandles from a bright, overcast sky; and about 50 to 100 footcandles in commercial stores and factories. In summer, the average brightness at 3 P.M. would rise to around 250 to 350 footcandles. In autumn, the level recedes to 150 to 250, and in winter drops to under 100. As averages, though, these figures are misleading, because on any given day, the light could vary widely. On a dull, gray winter day, for instance, the level of illumination could be well under 50 footcandles. On the other hand, a clear, cold winter afternoon might illuminate the stage to 300 footcandles or more, nearly equal to the levels of the brightest days of summer.

By way of comparison, bright but not brilliant general purpose lighting on the modern stage is commonly rendered by 50 to 100 footcandles, or somewhat more in very large theaters. But 100 footcandles on the modern stage will appear brighter than 100 footcandles on the Swan stage because of the greater contrast between the bright stage and darkened auditorium in our typical proscenium and arena theaters. The modern practice of shielding the audience from the glare of the sources of light and of accustoming their eyes to semidarkness while waiting for the play to begin increases the disparity between house and stage. In the public playhouses, light was dispersed throughout the theater, and the emphasis that present-day lighting designers bring to the stage by means of light contrast was unavailable to early English actors. Modern lighting can vary widely during the course of a play, but it differs so little from performance to performance that computers now regularly control the levels of brightness. Early modern actors performed in very different circumstances. English weather can also change quickly, but such changes will rarely coincide with the atmosphere of the play. Except for chance variations, then, the light remained more or less constant throughout major periods of a performance, while it could change drastically from one performance to another. Audiences saw Hamlet bathed in warm light one day and shrouded in cold, dull light the next.

The variability of light intensity from day to day or even hour by hour and the relative uniformity of light within the theater at any given moment raise questions regarding the effect of the *mise en scène* on the original performers and their audience. Under such unpredictable circumstances, actors today might boast of adapting themselves to unplanned changes in the lighting, modifying this or that aspect of their performance to compensate for or to take advantage of specific weather and lighting conditions. But it is much more likely that the same impulse that rejected the need for elaborate scenic decoration caused both actors and audience to treat prevailing weather conditions as nonartistic factors in the enjoyment of drama—similar, perhaps, to the way we view theater acoustics today. Certainly the pervasive verbal descriptions of scenes and moods represent a more compelling contribution to the audience's aesthetic perception of the performance than did the weather overhead. And yet, Renaissance Londoners could hardly have remained completely unaffected by *A Chaste Maid in Cheapside* performed in the gloom of winter or a *King Lear* in the glory of summer.

Theatrical propriety is largely conventional, of course, and we have learned over many years to expect to see our tragedians in the dark and our comedians in the light. But the convention, in other forms, is at least as old as the Tudor era. At the beginning of *A Warning for Fair Women*, for example, History debates with Comedy and Tragedy over their relative merits and unmistakably identifies Comedy with the light and Tragedy with the dark. Alluding to the black stage hangings, History remarks:

> Looke Comedie, I markt it not till now,
> The stage is hung with blacke: and I perceiue
> The Auditors preparde for Tragedie.

Acknowledging the convention, Comedy grumbles:

> These ornaments beseeme not thee and me,
> Then Tragedie, kil them to day with sorrow,
> Wee'l make them laugh with myrthfull ieasts to morrow.[36]

Inasmuch as the actors and the audience accepted the convention, it is difficult to understand how the reception of a play could not have been influenced by lighting conditions that were anticonventional.

The New Globe

With the construction of the full-scale replica of the Globe in London at the International Shakespeare Globe Centre, our estimates of lighting levels in Hosley's Swan can be tested and the overall effect of the illumination assessed. Thus, on a typical sunny day in early August, the level of light at the front of the new Globe stage measures over 400 footcandles at 1 P.M. and recedes to approximately 300 footcandles at 4 P.M., 200 footcandles at 5 P.M., and under 100 at 6 P.M. (GMT). In absolute terms, such figures represent more than adequate levels of illumination. But the ease by which one can view a particular object is dependent, in part, on the relative brightness of that object when compared to the level of light to which one's eyes have grown accustomed, what psychophysiologists call the brightness adaptation level.[37] In consequence, spectators standing opposite the stage in direct sunlight are forced to squint at an otherwise well-lit stage that therefore appears less bright than it would if light shining from behind the tiring-house wall could somehow be eliminated.

Figure 17 shows the new Globe photographed at 2 P.M. under such conditions. The frank sunshine of a hazy-sunny sky floods the galleries directly opposite the stage and a good portion of the yard.[38] Spectators sitting or standing in this direct sunshine find themselves peering into a stage-space that is, in measurable brightness, more than a hundred times dimmer than

Fig. 17. The new Globe, 2 P.M. (GMT) in August

the light to which their eyes are adjusted, and in terms of perceived bright-ness, more than ten times dimmer. Spectators sitting in the shade of the upper galleries or to the right or left of the stage can view the stage much more comfortably, but even they must compare the level of illumination they perceive onstage with the levels they perceive in other parts of the playhouse. Because our eyes adjust themselves not to the lowest level of brightness we see but to the average of the brightest areas in and around the center of our field of vision, it follows that if spectators in the shade are nevertheless in a position where they can see substantial sections of bright sky through the opening above the yard, they, too, perceive the stage as less than brilliantly lit, at least in contrast to their overall impression of the theater's illumination. This contrast in brightness, then, makes the darker areas in our field of vision appear slightly darker than they actually are. Concomitantly, visual acuity also decreases in areas perceived as dark—that is, we not only see such areas as less bright but we also see details in them less clearly. Thus, even early in the afternoon with bright daylight streaming down from the sky, the southwest stage of the new Globe *appears*, at least to many in the audience, as only moderately well illuminated.

The contrast between the illumination onstage and that in the auditorium is most pronounced, of course, under direct sunshine, but a considerable dis-crepancy between dark and bright areas of the new Globe remains even on overcast days. Under a cloudy sky, the absolute levels of brightness are re-duced proportionally in every part of the playhouse, but clear differences in brightness persist. On an overcast day at 3:30 P.M. in August, for example, light at the front of the new Globe stage measures between 350 and 400 foot-candles, the brightest areas in the yard opposite the stage measure over 1,000 footcandles, and gazing directly up into the sky overhead registers something on the order of 3,000 footcandles (see fig. 18). The ratio between the light on-stage and the light opposite the stage thus falls from one to ten on a sunny day to one to three on an overcast day. This change is substantial, but as per-ceived brightness is a function of the cube root of measurable brightness, the contrast between the lighting onstage and that in the yard on an overcast day would be perceived as only one-half the contrast present on a sunny day. In short, the audience would continue to experience much of the effect of brightness contrasts produced by frank sunshine.

Fig. 18. The new Globe, 3:30 P.M. in August

   This effect of perceiving the stage as slightly dimmer than it is in actuality is particularly true for audience members standing in the yard or sitting in the lower galleries, because they are obliged to look up to see the faces of the actors and, hence, find it more difficult not to gaze also into the bright sky above the playhouse. Although we tend to think that the groundlings occupied a nearly ideal vantage point from which to view the stage action (apart from the inconvenience of having to stand), the severe angle at which they were obliged to look up at the actors inevitably caused them to adjust their vision to a higher level of light than those spectators in the highest galleries or galleries close to the stage. The new Globe confirms that the more comfortable and efficient positions for spectators to see the actors were to the rear of those galleries relatively close to the stage, as shown in figure 19. Here spectators can easily adjust their eyes to the light onstage without the danger of glancing up at the bright sky overhead, because the floors of the galleries above the spectators act as awnings. Even more effective vantage points are

Fig. 19. The new Globe, 4 P.M. in August

at the rear of the stage itself or in the windows of the tiring-house, where the audience sits in virtually in the same light as the actors. It is not surprising, therefore, that the lords' rooms were found in such locations. In addition to good acoustics, proximity to the actors, and an opportunity for sumptuary display, seats near or even on the stage provided those who could afford them the most advantageous lighting environments in which to view the play.

But if spectators avoided looking up into the light, the opposite was true of the actors. Because the principal source of light (the opening above the yard) illuminated them from a steep angle, actors were obliged to hold their heads high to be well lit. This is obviously the case if the actors wanted to be seen (and heard) by spectators in the upper galleries around the auditorium, but it even holds true if the actors wanted to make an impression on the groundlings, because if the actors let their heads droop, shadows would obscure their faces. Whereas modern lighting designers regularly light actors with instruments mounted in positions forty-five degrees above the stage,[39] the average angle of the principal illumination at the new Globe is roughly seventy degrees. With the playhouse walls intercepting light from lower angles, the actors are effectively lit from above.

The amount of light on various parts of the new Globe stage falls into a regular pattern of light concentration with minor, but clear, changes in the amount of light as one moves about the stage. In general, the stage is brightest at its front and grows darker toward the tiring-house wall. Whether the day is cloudy or sunny, the time early afternoon or near dusk, the center of the foot of the stage always remains the brightest location. The left and right front corners are consistently 90 percent as bright as downstage center, dead-center stage 60 percent as bright, the left and right rear corners 50 percent, and the rear-center against the tiring-house wall only 35 percent as bright as downstage center. These differences in absolute measures of light seem large, but at the levels we are considering (100 to 400 footcandles), the human eye perceives brightness logarithmically and, hence, construes such disparate levels of brightness as more equal to each other than they are in actuality. Put another way, the light on an object must be increased eightfold for the eye to perceive that it is twice as bright. Although the front of the stage is, on average, nearly three times as bright as the rear, the audience perceives actors at the front of the stage as only 1.4 times brighter. The eye can discern this difference, but numerous researches have established that illumination must be doubled to produce significant improvements in seeing.[40]

Although the eye makes poor judgments about the absolute quantity of light, it nevertheless can make fairly accurate distinctions between what it sees as "more" and "less" light. While the perceived difference between the light at the front and the back of the stage is subtle, it is nonetheless discernible, as it was to Johannes de Witt, who accurately indicated that the rear of the Swan stage was marginally darker than the front by the crosshatching there. Knowing that the audiences at the Swan and other amphitheaters surrounded the players, several theater historians have been puzzled as to why the actors in de Witt's view have arrayed themselves more or less in a straight line near the front of the stage, as though they were nineteenth-century actors huddled up near the footlights of a proscenium stage. Possible explanations include a desire to be near the largest number of spectators, acoustical considerations, and the like, but I would not be surprised if early modern English players were not as prone to "find the light" as contemporary actors are.

Even after sunset at the new Globe, visibility remains surprisingly adequate, because the eye gradually grows accustomed to the decreasing amount of light. Details of movement and facial expression become less clear but in some ways are compensated for by the pleasant, but no longer glaring, glow of the setting sun above and to the west of the heavens. On certain days, it is as though a golden halo surmounts the stage and heavens. At the same time, the loss of visual acuity tends to blur the action onstage and invites the spectator to pay closer attention to the language. Sitting in the new Globe now, one can imaginatively reconstruct Thomas Platter's response to the conclusion of *Julius Caesar* that he witnessed at the newly opened Globe on 21 September 1599. For when dusk crept over the playhouse around 5:30 P.M. that day, Platter heard a stirring apostrophe to the setting sun:

> O setting Sunne:
> As in thy red Rayes thou doest sinke to night;
> So in his red blood *Cassius* day is set.
> The Sunne of Rome is set. Our day is gone.   (F 2545–49)

Platter seems not to have understood the native tongue, but he may well have seen how this "lighting effect" participated in the scene as actively as any costume or stage property.

Light and Staging

I leave it to others to determine if dramatists wrote with an open-air lighting system in mind. We may note, however, that only certain modes of staging will benefit from such lighting conditions. The lack of strong contrasts in brightness meant that the audience's attention could not be directed to specific actors or properties by means of conveniently placed pools of light or by color differences. Theatrical emphasis was accomplished by what we take to be the more conventionalized techniques of Elizabethan dramaturgy—soliloquies, ceremonial entrances, poetic set speeches, and the like. The relative uniformity of the light necessitated, in part, the use of more explicit signals and pointers onstage than we care for in narrative drama. But consider an advantage of early English lighting systems. Although the "heightened realism" of the modern lighting designer can more subtly emphasize and deemphasize actors, that realism, once established, will not allow for the moment the poet wants the audience to concentrate wholly on his words. Rhetorical displays like Gertrude's on Ophelia's death or Eno-barbus's on Cleopatra's barge were neither highlighted by anti-illusionistic spotlights nor motivated by realistic lighting. They had to spotlight and jus-tify themselves in a luminary atmosphere more closely resembling modern lecture halls than modern theaters. By never employing our sort of illusion in their lighting, Elizabethan dramatists were free to direct the audience's at-tention to some telling stage business or to catch their imaginations by the language.

This sort of outdoor stage lighting must also be distinguished from the uni-form stage and auditorium illumination advocated by such modern theater artists as Antonin Artaud, Bertolt Brecht, and Jerzy Grotowski. They yearn for a return to the active rapport between spectators and actors that an au-dience, sitting submissively in the dark, can never establish.[41] Their experi-ments have had some success, but we must not confuse their aims with Shakespeare's. Light shining on the modern audience is a reaction against Victorian illusion and produces its effect in part by dislodging the spectators' realistic expectations. To Shakespeare's public, there was nothing jarring about being as much in the light as the actors and, hence, no dislocation of normal sensibilities and no shocking reminder of the artifices of the theater. The temptation is to view Shakespeare's lack of illusion as equivalent to the conscious anti-illusionism of much modern stagecraft. To us, the convention that permits nighttime scenes on a daylit stage may be a "perverse *tour de force*," as J. L. Styan puts it.[42] But it is doubtful that an audience unfamiliar with dimmers and rheostats would have been so deeply impressed by a con-vention that, after all, went back to the Corpus Christi plays and beyond. Our response to the convention, however accurate, tends to be too conscious.

Nevertheless, some plays appear to demand the convention in order to ex-plore the full repercussions of their action. Critics have long spotted the irony when the blind Gloucester jumps, he thinks, off the cliffs at Dover but in re-ality merely falls to the stage floor in glare of the day. Here the light onstage comments unmercifully on physiological darkness, but a similar irony often attaches to pretended nocturnal darkness. What to Cassio and Roderigo is dark confusion, for example, is clear to us who can see Iago furtively wound Cassio in their fight. At court, elaborate lighting effects in the masques em-blematized, if anything, the control, or putative control, of the king over every aspect of his realm. At the outdoor theaters, the actors may have been powerless to control their light but could still employ it to convey meaning.

There is, for example, a sense in which the natural illumination, because it was ungovernable, could occasionally complement one of the age's more persistent notions—that heaven could, but does not, respond to man's tragedy. When Faustus asks the ever-moving spheres to stand still, or when Bosola reminds the Duchess of Malfi that the stars shine still, we must recall that the sun was continuing to travel across the sky, refusing to respond to the pathetic fallacy. In *The Atheist's Tragedy*, such references to uncontrollable, natural light are explicit and go far toward defining the competing views about nature in the play. When D'Amville commits murder, the sky draws "the curtaines of the clouds betweene those lights and me about this bed of earth"; but when he begins to feel the horror of his sin, "that Bawd, the skie, there" exposes his crime and "meetes me i'the face with all her light corrupted eyes."[43] It is as though man's inability to regulate his world was occasionally reflected in the actors' inability to regulate their stage light.

In comedy, we are less concerned with the powers of nature and the workings of fate than with social relationships and practical experience. Sometimes a "one day" convention is adopted, frankly accepting the limits of lighting variation possible in the afternoon at an outdoor theater. But often, imaginary darkness is employed to confuse the characters onstage. While the lovers of *A Midsummer Night's Dream* meander through the woods, sunlight sorts out their complicated relationships for us. Dissembling onstage can be similarly revealed. In William Haughton's *Englishmen for My Money*, performed at the Rose in 1598, a sly fool pretends to offer assistance to two foreigners groping their way through the dark streets of London. Instead, he leads both of them straight into two poles (perhaps the columns supporting the heavens).[44] The simpleminded joke is founded on our clearly seeing them head for and then bump into these obstructions. Were the darkness convincingly realized, the scene is pointless. In *1 Henry IV*, it is supposedly dark during the Gad's Hill robbery scene (2.2), but the audience must also be able to see the action clearly because Hal and Poins have already made a point of the necessity of differentiating and recognizing those who are and are not clad in buckram.

To accommodate themselves to the unchangeable light, playwrights may have adopted a "daylight convention," such as Styan posits, in which the neutral light of the sun complemented the unlocalized, wide-ranging drama. To Styan, the uniformity of the sunlight freed the imagination of the spectator and offered "a challenge to the poet to conjure special illusions."[45] This challenge was sometimes answered by properties associated with night or by other special effects, Styan points out, but more often by a saturation of references calculated to evoke a sense of darkness. Certainly this is often the case, although Styan's attribution of the effect to daylight and outdoor production may be too narrow, inasmuch as the light indoors was nearly as uncontrollable and even more uniform than the light outdoors; and other sunlit drama—Greek tragedy, for instance—is often well localized and seldom wide-ranging. The interchangeability of hall and amphitheater repertories could hardly have allowed dependence on a convention that was inaccessible half the time.

Even so, the summoning up of pretended darkness remains a convention simply because it was so familiar and readily accepted. But we must take care to evaluate the convention on its own terms and not on our own. I am skeptical that any tour de force can rightly be thought a convention in the traditional sense. Whereas the term "convention" once meant those theatrical practices sanctioned by long use and agreement between actors and audiences, it now tends to mean those anti-illusionistic practices asserted, sometimes ruthlessly, by eager actors on a bewildered audience. For example, the Chorus's apologies for nonrealistic staging in *Henry V* are often cited to demonstrate Shakespeare's reliance on theatrical convention. Yet, a theater thoroughly imbued with what we now call the presentational style hardly needs to invite the spectators' indulgence when night must be evoked by a plea to

> entertaine coniecture of a time,
> When creeping Murmure and the poring Darke
> Fills the wide Vessell of the Vniuerse.   (F 1790–2)

Here and elsewhere, the Chorus assuages realistic, not conventionalistic, expectations of the audience. Whether or not realistic darkness was ever artificially achieved, it redounded to the audience's enjoyment to believe that they were witnessing a natural representation of life onstage.[46] The Chorus's apologia for pretended darkness in *Henry V* predated the beginning of Jones's illusions by a half-dozen years or so, but it hardly represents a patronizing invitation to childlike spectators to imagine themselves in a world where natural laws do not adhere. Sir Philip Sidney's *Defense of Poesy* (1595) and Jonson's prologue to *Every Man in his Humour* (1598) had already made scathing fun of such naivete.

But although daylight reinforced some theatrical tropes, we must not assume that playwrights and actors regularly relied on sunlight or open-air production for the proper presentation of their dramas. The more prosperous acting companies performed both indoors and outdoors, and most of the plays I have mentioned in connection with outdoor illumination—*Othello*, *Macbeth*, *A Midsummer Night's Dream*, and *The Duchess of Malfi*, among them—are also known to have been performed indoors at private playhouses or at court. One might suppose that indoor lighting produced quite a different effect, yet it must be realized that the mixture of window light and candlelight in the permanent hall playhouses was nearly as difficult to control as the light outdoors. Indeed, the evidence we have regarding the structures of the private playhouses suggests that they were well provided with windows admitting substantial amounts of natural light.

Although some contemporary theater practitioners have embraced a uniform illumination of their stages and auditoriums as a means of fostering audience participation, the interplay between actors and spectators in the early modern English theater is difficult to assess, because English drama had never used any other lighting system. Whatever one can conclude about current practice, the contribution of uniform lighting to such interaction is probably of secondary importance when compared to the personality of the public to begin with and the manner in which it is invited to participate. Were light chiefly responsible for the nature of theatrical communication, we could expect the same sort of interplay between fifth-century-B.C. actors and spectators as we find in the eighteenth century. For although the Italian scenographer Leone di Somi had advocated darkening the auditorium as early as the 1560s, houselights across Europe remained lit and theater light evenly distributed until the introduction of gas illumination in the mid-nineteenth century.[47] Indeed, some light brightened the larger auditoriums of London well into the nineteenth century. The indignation of old-timers at Covent Garden when it was proposed to darken the auditorium for Wagner's *Ring* in the 1890s gives us an idea how recent the practice is.

Artificial Light

The possibility that artificial light supplemented failing natural light has occurred to several researchers concerned about late performance times and
early winter sunsets. E. K. Chambers found it "doubtful whether, in the
depth of winter, daylight could have served quite to the end" of the plays.[48]
But the evidence for artificial light in the amphitheaters is slim, resting
largely on the definition of *falot* in Randle Cotgrave's French-English *Dictionarie* (London, 1611): "A Cresset light (such as they vse in Play-houses)
made of ropes wreathed, pitched, and put into small and ope[n] cages of
yron." Assuming Cotgrave is referring to English practice, the playhouses he
mentions in 1611 may be either amphitheaters or halls. The smoke of such
crude instruments might well eliminate their use indoors, although cressets
could still be employed there to illuminate entranceways for spectators. The
only stage direction calling for cressets that I can find comes from Jonson's
outdoor pageant *King's Entertainment in Passing to his Coronation* (London,
1604), where a lady holds "in her one hand a lampe, or cresset."[49] But here
Jonson was surely following literary rather than practical concerns: cressets
were heavy metal devices requiring constant replenishment of its messy fuel.
If the lady did hold a cresset in one hand (the other hand rang a bell), then
we may be sure it was a miniature one and probably not lit. At Trinity College, Cambridge, the senior bursar's accounts for 1547–48 reveal large payments for cresset materials (pitch and basket frales) in connection with
"[e]xpensae circa theatru[m] et ludos,"[50] but we know that university plays
were often associated with outdoor festivities, processions, and the like for
which cressets would have been more appropriate than for small indoor
halls, which served as the predominant playing spaces at Cambridge.

There are several Continental illustrations of cressets lighting stages set
up in the open air. A sixteenth-century French painting places two burning
cressets on long poles to either side of a simple platform stage (see fig. 20).
The painting is fairly crude, but its depiction of heavy clothing and a daytime performance may show that cressets provided warmth as well as light.
Considering that Cotgrave was translating the French word *falot*, he may, in
fact, have had such French utensils in mind.

Symmetrically placed cressets to the right and left of gates and stages built
for royal entries were also common in the sixteenth and seventeenth cen-

Fig. 20. Outdoor stage with cressets, sixteenth century.
Bibliothèque municipale, Cambrai.

Fig. 21. Gillis Coignet's *The Drawing of Lots for Bedlam*, 1592.
Amsterdams Historisch Museum.

Fig. 22. A *tableau vivant* on the Dam in Amsterdam, commemorating the beginning of the Twelve Years Truce. Engraving by J. C. Visscher after Verschuring, 1609. Graphische Sammlung Albertina, Vienna.

turies, whether the entries took place by day or night. Especially in Flanders, where a succession of Hapsburg rulers were welcomed in elaborate *blijde inkomsten*, cressets routinely stood to either side of ceremonial gates and platforms or were mounted to the right and left atop ornate facades.[51] During the same period, cressets sometimes lit the dialogues and *tableaux vivants* performed on stages built in the public squares of Amsterdam by various chambers of rhetoric (*rederijkkamers*). Figure 21 shows a 1592 benefit performance at night in such a square lit by two burning cressets to either side of the stage. A similar engraving by J. C. Visscher of a nighttime *tableau vivant* commemorating the beginning of the Twelve Years Truce (1609) shows a stage lit by two smoking cressets off to either side of a picture-frame stage and two cressets to the right and left of the spectators assembled in the Dam (see fig. 22).

Although some of the *rederijker* facades bear a rough resemblance to the architectural features of the Swan tiring-house, the *rederijker* presentations were rather different from English drama, insofar as their stages usually featured compartments at the rear of the stage in which static dialogues were recited, large paintings were revealed, or living tableaux in imitation of paintings were displayed, requiring that they be viewed from a vantage point closer to the centerline than was true in the London amphitheaters.[52] Hence, the placement of cressets off to either side of the stage ensured that the sight lines of the spectators viewing these pictures and scenes would not be obstructed by burning flames.

Theatrical references to the use of cressets under the Tudors and Stuarts are rare. W. J. Lawrence mentions an account of a play produced for a nobleman's wedding around 1550, where after supper, "*Iube the Sane*, a playe, with torch lyghts and cresset lyghts, lx cressets and c of torches, and a maske, and a bankett" were presented.[53] Sixty cressets and a hundred torches would light up the darkest night, but it is doubtful they were all used for the play, and there is no reason to suspect this special festival occasion established a precedent for the professional theaters in London. In a memorandum book found among Edward Alleyn's papers, there is an entry of ticket receipts from around 1614 or 1615, probably in Henslowe's hand, that records either a payment or receipt of threepence for "creset" under the heading "14 day the noble grandchild."[54] Given Henslowe's idiosyncratic spelling, I am not sure that this is a reference to burning cressets; but if it is, threepence is barely enough money to buy the fuel for an hour's burning of one average-sized cresset.

The only unmistakable evidence for cressets at a professional English playhouse was found by C. J. Sisson and later identified and analyzed by Herbert Berry in his exhaustive research on the Boar's Head. In 1603, John Mago, the builder of the playhouse, testified regarding his understanding of the running costs of the theater, including "rushes and cressett lights in Wynter w[ch] some weeks came to ten or twelve shillings a weeke."[55] Berry concludes that Mago's pairing of cressets with rushes implies that the cressets illuminated the stage, where rushes were sometimes strewn. This may be true, but rushes were also a fuel typically burned in cressets or by themselves in rush-holders. Mago's pairing of rushes and cressets more likely signifies only that they were purchased from the same source; hence, their juxtaposition cannot prove that cressets were placed near the stage. That certain weeks in the winter required more cresset lights than others suggests that one purpose for them may have been for heat, as the average winter temperature in London varies considerably more from week to week than the average amount of winter daylight. On the other hand, public establishments like inns and taverns sometimes had cresset lights burning near their doors so that torches for travelers could be lit,[56] and it is possible that playhouse cressets also served such functions for spectators apart from or in addition to lighting the stage or auditorium. Around 1595, Sir John Harrington tells of a noble lady climbing up "dark and privat staires" to an unidentified playhouse gallery when two thieves grab her and accidentally put out her page's torch; in the story, the page runs away and returns before much harm is done with "more store of light," whereupon the thieves flee.[57] Because the page reappears so quickly, there was likely a torch or cresset near the rear entrance of the playhouse.

Even if the function of the cressets Mago mentions was to light the stage, they cannot have produced a great effect. A few years later, Salisbury Court spent as much as ten shillings to supply only a few dozen candles for one performance,[58] whereas Mago says that the Boar's Head spent that much or a little more on both cressets and rushes during a particularly heavy winter week. What is more, this small amount of fuel would presumably have to service a much larger stage than at Salisbury Court. If cresset materials were employed in illuminating the Boar's Head stage, the disparity in the amounts of money spent on fuel at the two playhouses does not speak of brilliant results. While it is true that artificial lights may have been employed only toward the end of winter plays at the Boar's Head, the same is also true of Salisbury Court. If Salisbury Court lighted candles for the duration of the whole performance (as appears to be the case), then we cannot assume that the Boar's Head did not do likewise.

Keith Brown has revisited the issue of outdoor artificial lights and argues forcefully that showmen like the King's men must have known the theatrical value of bright light and that they chose to position their stage in the shadows of the southwest quadrant and cover it with a large stage cover in order to emphasize the sumptuousness of the artificial light that they could then introduce. He proposes that, in such reduced natural light, the King's men made substantial use of property lights to produce motivational and mood lighting, and Brown concludes that our hearing so little about cressets does not mean that they were not employed, because the need for them, at least toward sunset, is so obvious.[59]

Given the lack of clear evidence, it is impossible to say with assurance that artificial lights were or were not used at the ends of amphitheater performances. Still, we must consider the effect that the use of cressets or other large utensils would produce. To alleviate a problem of low light levels, we immediately think of resorting to strong light sources. But the lighting instruments at our disposal are very different from those accessible to Tudor and Stuart acting companies. The sources of brilliant light available to us can be concentrated, easily shielded, and, hence, all but ignored by spectators. The filaments of modern light bulbs are so small, in fact, that even without shielding our eyes from their glare we can see objects placed only a few degrees away from the filament (what lighting engineers call the glare angle). For two light sources of equal strength but different size, however, glare increases as the size of the source increases.[60] Because early lighting utensils strong enough to produce readily apparent rises in the level of light were inevitably quite large, it follows that spectators would find it difficult not to be blinded by them in overall dim light unless steps were taken to reduce glare.

Two possible solutions to such glare present themselves: cressets and torches could have been shielded from the eyes of the audience by means of shutters or metal coverings, or the lights could have been positioned such that they were not near the line of sight of the audience. Because none of the cressets preserved in the collection of the Victoria and Albert Museum has a shield, and because of the circular configuration of the amphitheater auditoriums, it is difficult to imagine a shade or shutter that could eliminate glare for much more than half the audience. As we shall see in our consideration of the stage lighting at court, Inigo Jones learned the trick of shielding the audience from the sources of general visibility light only on his trip to Italy in 1615 when he saw what could be done when the audience sat on only one side of the stage.

There were also only a few locations in which cressets could be placed so that they would not glare into the eyes or obstruct the view of large segments of the audience. In the Continental examples we have considered, cressets were placed beyond the stage floor to the extreme right and left of actors facing an audience sitting or standing before them. But in a theater that surrounded the actors with the audience, cressets placed immediately to either side of the stage would have blinded or obstructed the view of spectators sitting near them. Alternatively, cressets could have been placed on poles mounted on the tiring-house facade, but then the actors would fall into silhouette while the audience sitting or standing near the centerline would be forced to look directly into the naked flames. The best solution would have been to adopt a practice similar to the modern placement of spotlights high above the auditorium and stage. But as cressets need to be carefully minded and their fuel regularly replenished (figure 20 shows a boy doing just that), they would still have to be placed in locations where they were easily accessible. The columns of the topmost galleries or the columns supporting the heavens above the stage could have been constructed to support heavy cressets, and facilities for the necessary attendants to reach them could have been provided, but, as Gurr points out, there is no mention of such amenities in any of the extant contracts.

Apart from the safety problems involved in positioning conflagrations high above the stage or yard, the placement of cressets far from the lines of sight of a majority of the spectators would necessarily move the light sources so far from the actors that they would add little additional illumination onstage. If we assume that a cresset (producing, say, ten footcandles of illumination) was placed at either end of the Globe stage, each cresset would produce only approximately 0.025 of a footcandle at the center of the stage. The human eye can perceive this small amount of light, but only if it has become accustomed to relative darkness over a period of time in the absence of glare. The light emanating from such cressets could improve the visibility of actors standing center stage only if all other illumination on the players was equal to or less than the same order of magnitude as the light from the cressets; in other words, very dim indeed.

But on the summer days on which I took readings, the natural light on the new Globe stage at sunset ranged from 0.8 to 2.5 footcandles, which, although dim in absolute terms, is too bright for the average spectator to notice the light emanating from large artificial sources located at the two sides of the stage some twenty feet away. For a spectator accustomed to these levels of ambient natural light to discern a rise in visibility, the actor would have to move within six or seven feet of one of the cressets.[61] This proximity could be accomplished by mounting the cressets on the stage pillars closer to the center of the stage; but in such positions directly above the players, the cresset baskets themselves would tend to block out illumination directed downward on the players and exacerbate the problem of glare. As is frequently the case in early lighting systems, efforts to reduce glare and increase visibility worked at cross-purposes.

In estimating the effect of artificial light in the amphitheaters, the importance of brightness adaptation levels is crucial. The human eye is extraordinarily sensitive, able to see tolerably even in moonlight, but only if our eyes have become acclimatized to decreasing light over a period of time. Although the color-sensitive cones adapt themselves to low light fairly quickly, reaching full adaptation within ten minutes, the more important rods, which determine visual acuity, adjust themselves more slowly to the dark, approaching good sensitivity only after half an hour and not reaching maximum sensitivity until nearly an hour is passed in the dark.[62] An audience watching a play lit by natural light will gradually grow accustomed to the decreasing light and may easily find viewing comfortable well past sunset. Although individual perceptions will always differ, the waning daylight at the new Globe is entirely adequate for most modern spectators half an hour past sunset, and it seems reasonable to assume that early modern spectators would find such natural light equally or even more sufficient, unaccustomed as they were to modern incandescent lighting. In January 1569, in fact, the City banned plays "after the howre of v of the Clocke," which was an hour past sunset.[63] Although the level of illumination produced by natural light on the new Globe stage a half hour past sunset may seem dim to us, in terms of measurable illumination it was, in fact, approximately the same amount of light produced by the candles burning above the hall stages like that at Salisbury Court.

Having adjusted their eyes to twilight, spectators would find that the lighting of large cressets toward the end of a winter play would cause them to lose their accommodation to dim light and require a lengthy period of reorientation as they returned their focus onto the stage. Thus, if the amphitheaters did regularly light cressets, they probably did so not as dusk approached but from the beginning of the play. This was the procedure at the indoor theaters where candles were lit as the play was about to begin. But apart from the distraction of an attendant climbing up to light the cressets followed by their sudden ignition, the lighting of artificial lights in the final minutes of the play when natural light was waning would have abruptly raised the brightness adaptation level, destroying the spectators' acclimatization to low levels of light and making actors and properties, except those immediately beside a cresset, appear dimmer than before the cressets were lit.

Modern lighting designers make concerted use of this principle. For example, if a director does not want the actions of stagehands visible during a blackout, a competent lighting designer will make sure that the blackout was immediately preceded by bright light. Unless money is of little concern— as on Broadway or in the West End—the best way to ensure consistently high visibility on the modern stage is to employ as *low* a brightness adaptation level as is practical. In fact, strong lights, because they raise the brightness adaptation level precipitously, also raise the level of illumination below which everything seems black; that is, they raise the threshold at which we can see anything at all.

This principle applies as much to the auditorium as to the stage itself. Cressets near the stage would, in effect, make the recesses of the galleries and passageways farthest away from the stage seem even darker than they had appeared moments before the cressets were lit. The use of bright lights near the stage would therefore necessitate the lighting of artificial lights in other areas of the playhouse. If low light was of major concern, the most efficient way to increase visibility was not to light a few large cressets near the stage but rather to disperse many small sources of light about the acting area and auditorium. This, at any rate, was the procedure used in the indoor hall playhouses and at court.

Considering the size of the area to be lit, the desirability of using as many lights as possible, and the problems English weather might have caused in keeping them lit, I am skeptical that the artificial lights at the actors' disposal played a major role in the general illumination of the amphitheaters. Tiremen would have had to go about the stage and auditorium lighting and replenishing torches or cressets. And should any wind or rain come up, these same tiremen would have had to tend to vulnerable instruments. In the private theaters, there were act breaks during which such duties could be carried out without interrupting the performance. But the custom of inter-act music and act breaks did not spread to the public stages until shortly before Shakespeare's retirement.[64] Because the majority of references to late performances and their presumed need for artificial lights occurred well before then (especially before 1594), lights at the public playhouses would have had to be lit and attended to while the play was in progress.

Still more inconvenient were the dangers present with burning lights in the inflammable public playhouses. These theaters were almost entirely of wood, and it is not likely that the actors risked illuminating their theaters with fires that may not have been necessary. Lawrence takes Howe's description of the burning of the first Fortune at twelve o'clock midnight "by negligence of a candle" to refer to a candlelit performance at night.[65] But because we possess no proof of any amphitheater play continuing so late, it is more probable that a candle was simply left unattended by someone working after hours. If the Fortune fire in 1621 took place at a performance, I am amazed that the many reports of it failed to mention the fate of the audience. What is more, if artificial light were so prevalent, as Keith Brown would have us believe, it is puzzling that there is only this one incident that can be attributed to lighting utensils—the only other recorded fire involving burning cannon fodder at the first Globe, the fate of whose audience was indeed well recorded.

It is in the nature of things that we cannot dismiss the possibility that artificial lights were used outdoors. But we should recognize that the whole question of supplemental light never arose until early-twentieth-century scholars, accustomed to the carefully controlled stage illumination of their own era, began to worry about actors performing in the uncontrollable light and twilight of early modern London. It was assumed that the actors must have done everything in their power to correct the deficiencies of natural light, that they would attempt to perform in as consistently bright an environment as possible. Yet, the opposite seems to have been true. The occasional diminution of light does not appear to have bothered the actors. Indeed, their answer to the random fluctuation of light outdoors was the approximation of the reduced levels of light indoors. By placing the stage at the southwest, the actors were well shaded from the sun in the middle of the afternoon, while towards evening the audience could adjust to a lower brightness adaptation level because the canopy above the stage eliminated glare from the setting sun low on the western horizon. Practical men of the Elizabethan theater apparently wanted a stage protected from the elements, including sunshine. Dissatisfaction with a lack of brightness on their stage must be accounted a modern concern.

The general picture of the amphitheaters that emerges is one of a well-shaded stage with neither artificial light for general illumination nor the extreme contrasts of light and dark due to direct sunlight.[66] As an actor came forward toward the foot of the stage, the light would increase slightly because the cover overhead intercepted less light. The Swan sketch shows actors well forward on the stage throwing soft shadows toward the center of the arena. Since the conventions of shading in both amateur and professional northern Renaissance drawings, etchings, and wood blocks make it unlikely that de Witt or van Buchel added shadows *in front* of the actors for artistic reasons, we may take the shading as generally accurate and accept it as confirmation that the stage was placed so that light shone from behind the tiring-house. And apart from modern conjecture, there is little evidence of any concerted effort to introduce more light into the theaters. We read nothing of large windows, reflective interiors, habitual use of artificial lights for general illumination, or noontime performances but hear rather of painted imitation marble, stained oak, black hangings, and performances stretching into twilight.

Regarding the effect of twilight on the theatrical responses to the plays, we can be less sure of ourselves, dependent as such perceptions were on psychological reactions of the original audiences. But the use of the word "shadow" for what is elsewhere called the heavens in the Fortune contract and the few narrow windows we see in the various perspective maps of the Bankside theaters show that playhouses were not designed solely for the purpose of introducing light into them, however much it may have been one consideration. That the stage was not engineered to appear as bright as practicable is also supported by the frequent bringing on of stage-property candles and tapers, whose weak flames could not have made much of an impression on a stage flooded with bright sunshine.

Whereas modern stage lighting tends to be highly directional, emanating from two distinct positions to the front of the actor, Elizabethan lighting came from all around him. To the amphitheater audience, there was no impression of light focusing on the actor, no sense of light exposing him to the interpretive scheme of a lighting designer. In our modern theaters, Hamlet and Macbeth are examined under a blazing glare of spotlights, even if a pervasive gloom gathers around them and in the auditorium. English Renaissance actors moved in more natural surroundings. They performed in a pleasant, ungovernable light that shone on the tiring-house facade and spectators as well as on the actors. Like the bare, open stage, the overall illumination permitted not only flexibility in staging but also a sense of continuity between the stage and the auditorium, between the actors and their background. Shakespeare's audience viewed his plays by a natural, subdued light that, because it is as familiar to us as it was to them, helps us to recreate his plays in performance.

6

DAYLIGHT IN THE
INDOOR PLAYHOUSES

IN CONTRAST to the large amphitheaters that "lay partly open to the
Weather, and . . . alwaies Acted by Daylight," hall playhouses such as the
Cockpit in Drury Lane, Blackfriars, and Salisbury Court were "small to what
we see now, . . . had Pits for the Gentry, and Acted by Candle-light." So states
the *Historia Histrionica* of 1699.[1] The distinction it draws between the lighting systems at the two kinds of theaters is confirmed by several earlier sources
that mention artificial light in connection with the hall playhouses. But we
must take care not to make more of a distinction than was actually the case.
The *Historia* tells us the "public" playhouses employed daylight and the "private" playhouses candlelight; but it does not say that the private playhouses
"alwaies," that is, exclusively, employed artificial light, nor does it follow that
performances there regularly or even occasionally took place at night, as is
sometimes asserted.[2] In fact, references to the times of performances are consistently in the afternoon; the number of candles employed was apparently
not large; and such evidence as we have indicates the auditoriums were well
provided with windows, admitting substantial amounts of sunshine.

Performance Times

Early hall playhouses apparently abided by evening prayer prohibitions more
strictly than did contemporaneous amphitheaters. Although all but one of
the hall theaters lay outside the City's jurisdiction and could have ignored
such prohibitions, early hall theater companies were ecclesiastical in origin
and apparently felt no inclination to do so. These first companies were ec-

clesiastical in the sense that they were composed of boy actors drawn from the choir schools of St. Paul's and the Chapel Royal at Windsor, and their masters evidently felt compelled to obey orders promoting attendance at evening prayer. We know little about the playhouses they used, but times of performances can be fixed rather precisely in one case and inferentially in the other.

We are uncertain when the first children's playhouse, the theater at St. Paul's, began operations. By 1575, plays for the general public were performed somewhere within the church's precincts, because in December of that year the London Common Council gave notice to the dean of St. Paul's that plays and the resort of spectators attending them were inciting disorder within his jurisdiction.[3] Common Council minutes make plain that the real dissatisfaction was with the boys' master, Sebastian Westcott, who had refused to renounce Catholicism. But Elizabeth's approval of the company on the one hand and her religious tolerance on the other prevented them from objecting on such grounds. Lacking knowledge of any particular misdeeds, the City resorted to the vague charge of abetting disorder, the indefinite nature of which suggests that the company observed other regulations more or less scrupulously. If performances at Paul's were given at the time of evening prayer, the City fathers would undoubtedly have brought them to the dean's attention. As early as there are records, then, performances at Paul's were probably given after evening prayer.

Twenty-eight years later, this late starting time is confirmed by a "Note to the Master of the Children of Powles," which also mentions a six o'clock finishing time. The note was written by William Percy and accompanied several plays that he offered the reorganized Paul's boys in hopes of performance. Percy worried that his plays were "somewhat too long"; and with a mixture of complaisance and pride common to unproduced playwrights of all eras, he authorized cuts "if any of . . . these Pastoralls and Comoedyes . . . overeach in length (The children not to begin before Foure after Prayers, And the gates of Powles shutting at six) the Tyme of supper."[4] Not only does Percy make plain that plays lasted from 4 to 6 P.M., but his use of the proscriptive phrase "not to begin" rather than a descriptive one like "not beginning" implies that the time of the company's performances was established by official policy and not simply by custom. Times may have varied over the years, of course, but because we have evidence of late afternoon performances from the beginning and near the end of theatrical activity at Paul's, it is improbable that drastic changes occurred.

The next hall playhouse, the first Blackfriars, leaves us no useful information regarding its time of performance. Nevertheless, inasmuch as it was set up for boy actors who were joined by the Children of Paul's after Westcott's death in 1582, it may be that the Children of the Chapel at Blackfriars played at similar times. This joint boys' company disbanded in 1584, and Blackfriars went unused as a theatrical venue until James Burbage began to renovate another room for playing in the autumn of 1596. He intended to lodge the Chamberlain's men there, but his plans were thwarted when local residents complained to the Privy Council, which quickly put a stop to the enterprise. Although the troupe did not act there, the residents' petition indicates that performances were expected to coincide with evening prayer. The worried citizens predicted that the actors' drums and trumpets would disturb both parishioners and ministers "in tyme of devine service."[5] It will be recalled that two years previously, the Lord Chamberlain's men had requested permission to perform at the Cross Keys inn beginning at two in the afternoon. By 1596, the company's habit of playing during evening prayer had become so firmly established that Blackfriars residents expected nothing else.

In part because the boy actors delayed their plays until after evening prayer, the residents did not object when a new Children of the Chapel company began performing in Burbage's playhouse before 1600. In 1604, King James granted the company a patent as the Children of the Queen's Revels, but in February of 1606, they imprudently ridiculed the king's national origin in *The Isle of Gulls*. Two years later, after more unwelcome satires, the king angrily ordered them disbanded. As it happens, it is in the induction to *The Isle of Gulls* that we learn this third children's company also performed late in the afternoon. An actor posing as a stage-sitting spectator explains he can only see an act or two of the play because "I lay in bed till past three a clock, slept out my dinner, and my stomacke will toule to supper afore fiue."[6] Presumably, the play began around four o'clock (that is, after evening prayer) and continued until six or so in the evening.

The Lord Chamberlain's men finally took possession of this second Blackfriars playhouse in 1608 under their new name, the King's men. As befits the most prestigious theater in London, several contemporary documents speak to its time of performance. By 1619, for example, the popularity of the playhouse had caused logistical problems. In a letter to the Privy Council, neighbors protested that "multitudes of Coaches" clogged the streets and disrupted business "almost everie daie in the winter tyme . . . from one or twoe of the clock till sixe att night, which beinge the tyme alsoe most vsuall for Christenings and burialls and afternoones service."[7] Certainly the play did not last from 1 to 6 P.M.; it must have required at least an hour before and after the performance for the coaches to push through the traffic. And for spectators who came early to avoid the crowd, one-hour concerts were given to pass the time before the play began.[8] The plays themselves must have lasted from two or three o'clock until around five.

Under Elizabeth, the Privy Council might have listened to such a complaint, but the Stuart courts consistently sided with players in general and the King's men in particular. Under Charles, in fact, our information regarding performance times at Blackfriars is furnished by patrons from the highest classes—the gentry, nobility, and even the royal family. In 1628, the bishop of Salisbury acidly described how Joseph Taylor, the leading actor at Blackfriars, had won the admiration of Inns-of-Court lawyers and made "them Afternoones men."[9] On two separate occasions in the fall of 1633, the master of the revels, Sir Henry Herbert, found King's men's plays unacceptable and suppressed them "for that afternoone."[10] And from 1633 until 1640, Sir Humphrey Mildmay recorded six afternoon trips to Blackfriars in his account book and diary.[11]

From the same period, however, come suggestions that a few Blackfriars plays may have been presented at night for the enjoyment of the queen, Henrietta Maria. None of the six recorded performances the queen saw there is described as having taken place at night, but J. Q. Adams and G. E. Bentley arrive at this conclusion by reference to the type of remuneration the King's men received.[12] When the King's men performed at Whitehall near London, they received a standard payment of ten pounds. But when the company was obliged to travel to outlying palaces, they received an additional ten pounds because, as they stipulated in their bills to the lord chamberlain, "our day [was] lost at our house."[13] Because these bills record no extra payments for two of the queen's visits to Blackfriars (5 May 1636 and 23 April 1638), Adams and Bentley assume that no regular performances were lost and that the queen saw special performances that must, therefore, have been at night.[14] Indeed, several scholars have gone on to assert that performances for the public were also regularly at night.[15] As Adams and Bentley would admit, however, their argument for the queen's night plays is constructed of successively applied inferences, each of which is probably, but by no means absolutely, certain. Their argument thus barely supports itself.

The last children's theater, in Whitefriars, has left behind a starting time of "about" three o'clock. Whitefriars was leased in 1605, occupied by the Children of the King's Revels around 1608, and then continued until 1614 with a regrouped Children of the Queen's Revels and other boy companies. In 1611, a member of Prince Otto von Hesse-Cassel's entourage noted, "Das theatrum, da die kinder spielen, ist auf diesseit des wassers, spielen um 3 uhr, aber nur von michaelis bis auf ostern."[16] Because Whitefriars was the only children's theater in operation at the time, the Germans must have visited the Whitefriars playhouse around three o'clock.

The predominance of the King's men's Blackfriars playhouse was challenged in 1617 when a quondam member of the company, Christopher Beeston, remodeled the Cockpit in Drury Lane into an indoor playhouse, also performing in the afternoon. By the 1630s, Mildmay still preferred the Blackfriars to all other theaters but on at least one occasion was delighted with the "afternoone" play at the Cockpit.[17] It is surprising that Mildmay never noted going to the last private theater to be set up, the Salisbury Court playhouse (c. 1629). In consequence, we have no direct evidence as to when plays were acted there, although it is probable that its performances were presented at the same time as two public theaters. This can be deduced from a reference in the praeludium affixed to the published text of *The Careless Shepherdess*, which has as "The Scene. SALISBURY COURT." In it, a parsimonious citizen thinks better of paying the steep private playhouse admission price (one shilling) and decides instead to "go to th' Bull or Fortune, and there see / A Play for two pense, with a Jig to boot."[18] Because the Red Bull and Fortune presumably gave afternoon performances and because the citizen can go there or to Salisbury Court, this last hall playhouse seems to have hosted afternoon plays, as well.

Daylight and Candlelight

As it happens, the best estimate of the amount of candlelight employed indoors comes from a proposed article of agreement between housekeepers and hireling actors at Salisbury Court in 1639. In the agreement, the housekeepers promised to pay half the cost of the lights, "both waxe and Tallow, wch halfe all winter is near 5^s a day."[19] As will be discussed in the next chapter, it is from such a figure that we can make a more-or-less intelligent guess about the number of candles used at Salisbury Court in the winter. Depending on their size and the proportions of expensive wax candles to cheaper tallow ones, the total number works out to about two to four dozen candles for each performance—a goodly number, to be sure, but in actual brightness not even equal to the power of one sixty-watt light bulb.[20] The use of the phrase "all winter" suggests, in addition, that far from providing the principal source of illumination all year, candlelight was used primarily to help dispel winter darkness. For although some hall playhouses were used only in the winter (the King's men's Blackfriars, for instance), Salisbury Court has left behind records of a number of summertime plays.[21] A plausible interpretation of the facts is that summertime performances dispensed with much or even all artificial light and that wintertime performances relied on a mixture of natural and artificial light.

How such a mixture might have looked is shown in the familiar frontispiece to *The Wits, or Sport upon Sport* of 1662 (see fig. 23). In it, we see sixteen candles arranged in two branched chandeliers hanging above a small stage. The principal light comes from the actors' right, but not from the chandelier there, as the opposite chandelier casts no similar shadows. Apparently, daylight was plentiful from that direction. What kind of theater *The Wits* frontispiece purports to represent we do not know, but it provides some assurance that conjecture based on the 1639 Salisbury Court articles and on other evidence has not strayed too far from the possible.[22]

Window Light

That the actors took advantage of daylight to illuminate their permanent indoor theaters is attested to by Thomas Dekker, who noted specific exceptions to the practice. In *The Seven Deadlie Sinns of London*, Dekker describes a typical London nightfall, saying that he found that "all the Citty lookt like a private Playhouse, when the windowes are clapt downe, as if some *Nocturnal*, or dismall *Tragedy* were presently to be acted before all the *Tradesmen*."[23] Dekker was writing in 1606 when three early hall playhouses were in operation: St. Paul's, the second Blackfriars, and Whitefriars. The passage suggests several points about indoor lighting. It indicates that for some hall

Fig. 23. Frontispiece to *The Wits, or Sport upon Sport* (London, 1662). Reproduced by permission of The Huntington Library, San Marino, California (RB 107896).

playhouse performances, daylight was specifically blocked out. It also hints that playhouse illumination was used, not only for the sake of visibility, but also to reinforce aesthetic qualities of a play. Darkness is both metaphorically and technically associated with "dismall *Tragedy*," and there is the strong implication that afternoon performances of histories, comedies, romances, and even not-so-dismal tragedies would find the windows open.

What kind of windows were these that Dekker refers to, and how were they opened or "clapt downe"? We possess plans and sections of two indoor theaters that show the positions and sizes of their windows, and we know enough about medieval and Renaissance architecture to form an idea of the fenestration in the permanent private theaters for which we have no pictorial evidence. Further, the windows of several halls that were sometimes used as theaters stand today for our inspection. Of these, most interest attaches to the halls at Hampton Court Palace and the Inns of Court, since Shakespeare probably acted in them.

The Great Hall at Hampton Court was built by Henry VIII and continued as a favorite location for Christmastime plays until the Interregnum (see fig. 24). The King's men were frequent guests there and on at least one occasion performed in the afternoon.[24] The hall is 105 feet 6 inches long (including the screen passage), 40 feet wide, and 60 feet to the summit of the hammerbeam roof.[25] Its longitudinal axis lies east and west. A "minstrel gallery" at the west end defines the first of seven bays and is supported by a simple screen with two doors, which may occasionally have served as a tiring-house facade. Above the gallery is a window of seven lights, and higher still are two small windows treated almost as part of the roof. These windows are repeated in the east wall, where a dais for the king replaces the screen. In the north wall are seven mullioned windows high up above Flemish wall tapestries and moldings. In the south wall, six of these windows are repeated; in the seventh bay to the left of the dais is a tall, mullioned bay window divided into forty-eight lights, the purpose of which was to light the dais and to focus attention on it and the king.

The predominant effect, characteristic of all Tudor halls, is the soft, descending nature of the light. The sidewalls are paneled and draped to a height of over eighteen feet so that no direct sunshine is permitted to cross-light the room. Instead, the windows are set high on the walls with their sills nearly twenty feet above the floor. The windows are easily high enough that

Fig. 24. The hall at Hampton Court Palace.
Crown Copyright: Historic Royal Palaces.

only in the early afternoon at the height of midsummer does direct sunlight illuminate more than a narrow strip of the floor along the north wall. In winter, when Hampton Court was used as a theater, the sun is never high enough in the sky to light any part of the floor directly. Rather, a dim, gently diffused light descends from the warm-tinted glass and heavily mullioned windows and is partly absorbed and reflected by the arches, pendants, and corbels of the dark oak roof fretted with gold. Figure 24 gives a good idea of the indirect light near the front of the screen, even though the photograph was taken with direct midday summer sunlight flooding down from the south windows. In point of fact, even on the brightest days of summer with the sun at its highest altitude, the hall remains a relatively dim room whose windows admit less than a hundredth of the light available outside.

In overall plan, the Great Hall of the Middle Temple differs little from that at Hampton Court (see fig. 25). Constructed in the 1560s, it was used for a production of *Twelfth Night* on 2 February 1602. As at Hampton Court, the hall is oriented east and west and is divided into seven cross bays. In the first bay are the magnificent screen, two small windows, and a large end window. In the second through the sixth bays are square-headed windows, five on each side, with transoms and four elliptical-headed lights each. In the seventh bay, lighting the dais, are two large oriel windows.[26] The hall is the same width but some thirteen feet shorter in length than the hall at Hampton Court. Figure 25 again shows us diffused light filtering down from elevated windows. As at Hampton Court, light emanates from a band of veritable clerestory windows. Even on a bright summer day, the average level of illumination inside the hall is only about twenty footcandles.

In figures 26 and 27, the screens of these two halls have been sketched as if they were tiring-house facades. Stages have been placed before each, and by way of suggesting the direction of light from above, diagonal lines have been drawn from the center of the stage to the sills of the south windows. The diffused light typical of these halls seldom produces beams of light as distinct as these diagonal lines; they are meant only to indicate the lowest angles from which daylight, unreflected by the interior of the hall, could illuminate actors standing at the center of a stage.

For purposes of comparison, I print a similar sketch of the stage and galleries of the Swan, again based on Richard Hosley's reconstruction (see fig. 28). It will be seen that in both indoor and outdoor playhouses, light enters

Fig. 25. The hall of the Middle Temple. By permission of the Masters of the Bench of the Honourable Society of the Middle Temple.

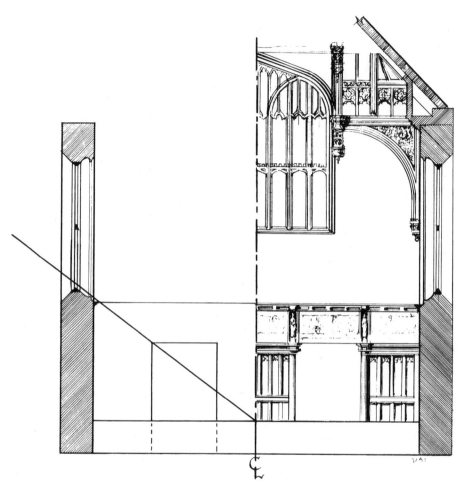

Fig. 26. Cross-sectional diagram of the hall at
Hampton Court with conjectural stage

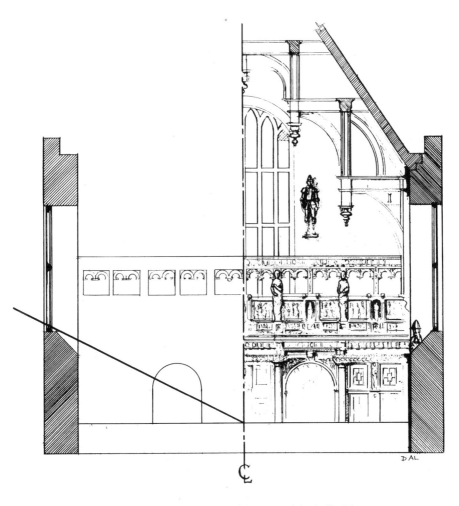

Fig. 27. Cross-sectional diagram of the hall of the
Middle Temple with conjectural stage

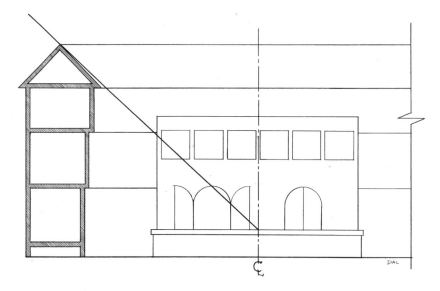

Fig. 28. Cross-sectional diagram of the Swan

from a relatively steep angle, crossing the stage from an altitude approximately equal to the height of the balconies above the stage. The angles of light from the hall windows are slightly lower than that in the Swan—thirty-two and forty degrees as contrasted with forty-eight degrees. But if one takes into account the lower altitude of the sun during the winter, late fall, and early spring when the indoor theaters were principally occupied, it is clear that the walls of both kinds of theaters do not permit direct sunlight to strike the stage. Rather, to an observer standing at the center of the stage, the angles are such that the afternoon sun is normally just below the hall windowsills in winter and just a few degrees below the top of the outdoor gallery roof in summer.

There are several reasons to suppose that the permanent private playhouses were set up in halls like these. For one thing, the resemblance between the early-sixteenth-century hall screen and the late-sixteenth-century *minorum ades* of the Swan implies that their chronological intermediaries—the tiring-house facades of the private playhouses of 1575 and 1576—did not differ widely from the seminal models. Moreover, the first private theater companies at St. Paul's and Blackfriars were originally founded for the purpose of entertaining Elizabeth in halls such as these. The boys' familiarity with such halls is likely to have been a factor in the sites chosen for nonroyal performances, especially since the boys claimed to play before the public only by way of "practicing" their craft "to yield Her Majesty recreation and delight."[27]

The similarity between Tudor halls and early private playhouses is also supported by the information we have pertaining to the kinds of buildings that were acquired for private theatrical productions. Two of these theaters, the second Blackfriars and the Whitefriars, were in fact called "great halls" in legal documents arising out of squabbles within their managements. Present thinking is that the hall Burbage bought in Blackfriars was the large (approximately one hundred feet by forty-six feet) Parliament Chamber on the second floor of the Upper Frater in the western range of the dissolved Dominican priory. Irwin Smith has shown that this was not a characteristic Dominican room but rather a hall typical of those made for the use of the court, with whom the medieval Mendicant friars enjoyed a close relationship.[28] The nearly equal dimensions and the similar uses to which these halls were put suggest that the Parliament Chamber and the several halls at court were built along the same lines.

In Burbage's deed for the second Blackfriars, we hear nothing of windows, although all the "glasse" belonging to the premises is included.[29] But in a lawsuit brought in 1609, a sharer of the Children of the Chapel mentions glass and wooden windows both above and below on each side of the premises: "in vitrio & in fenestris ligneis tam supra quam infra in vtrisque partibus premissorum."[30] The windows "infra," or below, do not concern the Parliament Chamber itself; they were in the ground floor that was also bought by Burbage. We do learn that the Blackfriars was through-lighted; that is to say, it had windows on both sides of the room, as do most Tudor halls. The theater itself seems to have occupied only part of the hall, because its dimensions were given, as sixty-six by forty-six feet, presumably including the tiring-house and stage. On the basis of the analogy between the Parliament Chamber and other halls, and considering these dimensions, we may guess that the second Blackfriars had fourteen side windows with ten in the auditorium itself, five on each side.[31] The south end-window or windows would have been obstructed by the tiring-house.

In a suit brought regarding an agreement between the original sharers of the Whitefriars theater, we hear again of a playhouse built within a "great hall." A deposition of 1609 states that the rooms leased were "thirteene in number, three belowe and tenne above, that is to saie, the great hall."[32] The hall at Whitefriars thus had formerly been divided into ten rooms and, like the second Blackfriars, was "above" other rooms. An early-seventeenth-century survey of the Whitefriars district survives in which "The Hale" is prominent,[33] and it is there that Chambers puts the playhouse. But this hall is unusually narrow for a Jacobean theater, only some sixteen or seventeen feet wide. As the sharers also rented "the kitchin by the yard," J. Q. Adams and Wickham assume the playhouse was set up in the old refectory that stood on the second floor of the south range and was approximately thirty-five by eighty feet.[34] The survey shows only the first floor of the south range, but the general lateral division comprises five units. If the division of the hall above into ten rooms was accomplished in respect to the architectural plan, then we may assume that ten windows pierced the walls of the Whitefriars playhouse, again probably five to a side.

Refectories, or fraters as they were sometimes called, were the halls in which religious orders took their chief meals together. Seeing that two important private playhouses were located in the old refectories of Mendicant friars, it is unfortunate that medieval English refectories are not better preserved for our examination. At Beaulieu in Hampshire and at Chester, two thirteenth-century monastic refectories have survived relatively unchanged. They display high, shafted lancet windows on both sides and large, pitched timber roofs quite similar to the great halls. One authority, the architectural historian Geoffrey Webb, believes that such refectories were the precursors of the great halls of the fifteenth century.[35] Because the preaching friars gravitated in the thirteenth century to the cities, where space, then and afterwards, was at a premium, no refectories of the Mendicant orders escaped the Dissolution unaltered. However, at Canterbury and at Gloucester, a few middle-thirteenth-century windows do remain in what were rather small friars' refectories. At Canterbury, the windows are double lancets about five by seven feet with plain quatrefoils above. The floor there has been raised, so it is difficult to confirm how high the windows were. At Gloucester, the surviving large end-window is fourteen feet above the original floor level, while the remains of the side windows are somewhat lower in a hall only twenty-five feet wide.[36] On the average, refectories of the Dominicans and the Carmelites were smaller than the halls of the Middle Temple and Hampton Court, but their proportions were similar, including the angles subtended by the windows. Windows were kept high in refectories not only in adherence to the Gothic style but also for the practical reason that an arcaded roof regularly jutted out from the exterior wall of the refectory to cover the obligatory cloister walk.

Written architectural theory in English before the Restoration is hard to come by, but what little there is supports this pattern of high windows on both sides of rectangular rooms. Eleven years after he saw the first Globe burn, Sir Henry Wotton published *The Elements of Architecture* (London, 1624), based largely on Vitruvian principles. Wotton was a member of the Middle Temple who spent a good part of his life as a diplomat in Venice, where he was influenced by neoclassical architecture. Still, he held the view applicable to most styles of architecture that the best light was "a descending Light, which of all other doth set off mens *Faces* in their truest Spirit" (N2). He allowed that Vitruvius "seems to have beene an extreame Lover of *Luminous Roomes*," but Wotton himself preferred not "to make a House (though but for civill use) all *Eyes*, like *Argus*" (G4). Especially in ecclesiastical buildings, "which were anciently darke, as they are likewise at this day," care must be taken not to distract the eye with too many windows.[37] Because all the private playhouses, excepting only the two Cockpits and Salisbury Court, were set up in former ecclesiastical buildings, it is not surprising that a pattern of clerestory illumination was observed.

The lighting of large rooms from both sides is endorsed by contemporary wisdom as well. In a short chapter on building, in *The Holy State*, published in 1642, Thomas Fuller (whose interest in theater extended to an early biography of Shakespeare) expresses the opinion that "[t]horow-lights are best for rooms of entertainment, and windows on one side for dormitories."[38] Fuller does not refer specifically to theaters, of course, but it may be that he had them and other halls and refectories in mind when he spoke of "rooms of entertainment." With both contemporary practice and theory calling for high windows on both sides of such rooms, it seems likely that when the actors sought permanent indoor theaters, the illumination available to them resembled that of the halls they had so often played in as guests.

Figures 26 and 27 represent the use of halls as they stand today and presumably stood in the seventeenth century without any elaborate theatrical preparation. Only simple, low stages have been introduced. But there is another aspect of the physical arrangements that may have affected the quality of the light: the seating of the audience. We know from several sources — particularly Office of Works accounts — that halls were normally furnished with "degrees," or tiered scaffolds for the seating of the spectators. In the 1603–4 holiday season at Hampton Court, for example, carpenters were paid for "making of the stage and setting up degrees and p[ar]tic[i]ons for the playe in the hall."[39] The degrees at court were high, bleacher-type affairs (typically of seven rows of benches) that were probably only of one order. But in the private playhouses, where spacious magnificence gave way to questions of profit, it is likely that two or perhaps three orders of galleries lined the auditorium walls.

Jones Playhouse

If we turn to the theaters for which contemporary architectural drawings exist, we can understand how such galleries might affect the auditorium lighting. In the collection of drawings by Inigo Jones and his disciple John Webb at Worcester College, Oxford, are two sets of designs, one of an unidentified indoor theater and the other of renovations for the Cockpit-in-Court. The Cockpit-in-Court plans and elevation were identified as long ago as 1913, but it was not until G. E. Bentley studied them that it became clear that they reflected Office of Works records of substantial remodeling to turn the old Cockpit, which had only occasionally been used for plays, into a permanent, active theater for professional actors. In 1969, D. F. Rowan represented the other set of drawings by Inigo Jones as a "missing link" between the Elizabethan and Jacobean private theaters set up in preexisting ecclesiastical buildings and the Palladian style of the Caroline Cockpit-in-Court and later Restoration theaters.[40] More recently, John Orrell has argued that these unlabeled drawings represent Jones's ideas for Christopher Beeston's conversion of the Cockpit in Drury Lane into a permanent playhouse in 1616.[41] Orrell's case is strong but circumstantial; caution suggests that we refer to these unidentified plans as the "Jones playhouse," following the lead of the International Shakespeare Globe Centre, which is reconstructing it in Southwark. Whatever the auspices of the drawings, the information they reveal is substantial, for they largely corroborate independently derived reconstructions of the hall playhouses—particularly Richard Hosley's reconstruction of the second Blackfriars. It is manifestly not that theater, but its discovery reassures us that recent conjecture has not gone too far astray.

The arrangement of the windows in the Jones playhouse confirms the pattern of the clerestory lighting of the Tudor halls but shows signs of adaptation as well (see fig. 29). The playhouse is a little smaller than the halls at Hampton Court or the Middle Temple; but, again, the proportions are similar. Six elliptical-headed windows are placed around the auditorium high above the stage in the second gallery, while no light at all enters from below. The cross section shows that a similar row of windows could easily have been accommodated in the lower gallery but that none was needed. Only narrow-slit windows (similar to those in views of the outdoor public theaters) light the otherwise dark passageway beneath the first gallery.

The windows in the upper gallery are unusual architecturally, and they suggest, I think, how Tudor halls were converted into private playhouses. Both native English and Continental proportions would have required such windows to be nearly twice as tall as they are wide. But Jones has apparently cut off their lower halves, leaving the remaining tops of the windows too small and too high on the exterior walls. Why the sills have been raised is explained, of course, by the position of the second gallery. As may be seen in the cross section through the stage, the stepped gallery would have obstructed light entering from the bottom half of a normally proportioned window. The height of the windowsills above the ground has consequently been determined by extending a line intersecting the center of the stage and the gallery benches through the exterior wall. The rake of the gallery (about forty-three degrees) thus equals the lowest angle at which unreflected light may strike the center of the stage.

To exemplify how the height of the Jones playhouse windows was determined, I have placed the Jones playhouse galleries at the stage-level of the Middle Temple (see fig. 30). It will be seen that the second gallery blocks out the lower portion of the side window, producing, in effect, a smaller, higher window.[42] The similarity between this partially obscured hall window and the permanently reduced windows in the Jones playhouse is unmistakable. If early private theater galleries were set up in halls with windows similar to those in the Middle Temple or Hampton Court, then the reduced size and

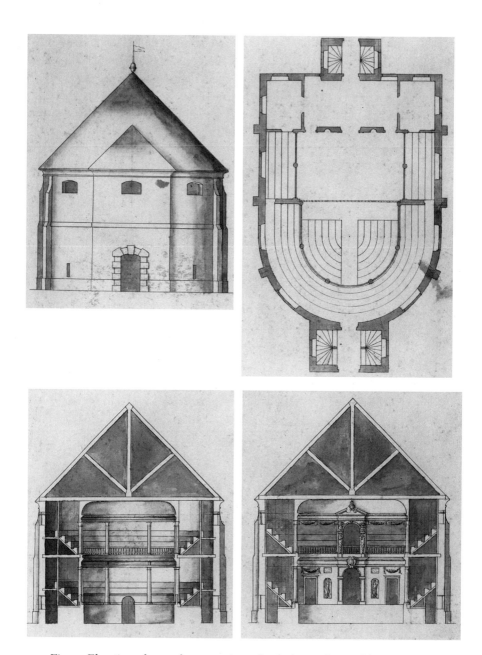

Fig. 29. Elevation, plan, and cross sections of a playhouse designed by Inigo Jones.
The Provost and Fellows of Worcester College, Oxford.

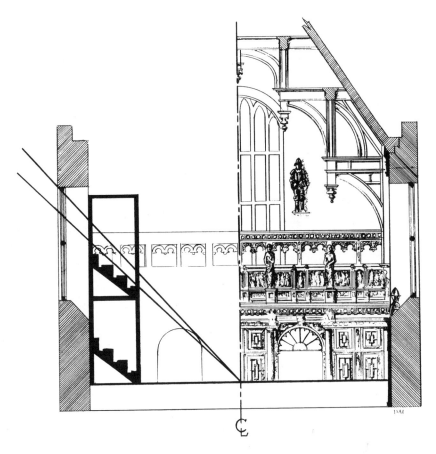

Fig. 30. Cross-sectional diagram of the Middle Temple
hall with Jones playhouse galleries

elevated position of the resulting openings would match the shortened and
raised windows of Jones's drawings. All Jones has done is to make the obstruction permanent.

In figure 30, a second line has also been drawn intersecting the top of the
window and the center of the stage. This upper diagonal line gives an idea
of the apparent width of the band of light from the side windows. To imagine the total effect of natural light from all the windows, one should think
of this band as revolved about a perpendicular axis, producing a cone of light

with its apex at the center of the stage. Were all windows the same size and evenly spread around the hall, light from the windows opposite the stage would be less bright and lower than from the sides owing to the rectangular nature of the hall and the consequent greater distance of the windows opposite the stage. But in actuality, light from all directions descends at virtually the same angle and intensity because the windows opposite the screens in rooms such as the halls at Hampton Court and the Middle Temple and in the refectory at Gloucester are higher and larger than the side windows, thereby compensating for their greater distance.

In figure 31, a heavens has been added to the Swan section and similar diagonal lines have been drawn, the upper one intersecting the roof above the stage. The total impression of this amphitheater illumination may likewise be estimated by revolving this band about a vertical axis. The impressions created by the cones of natural light at the indoor and outdoor playhouses are thus roughly similar. In both kinds of theaters, tall sidewalls eliminate frank sidelight, while a roof above the stage eliminates overhead

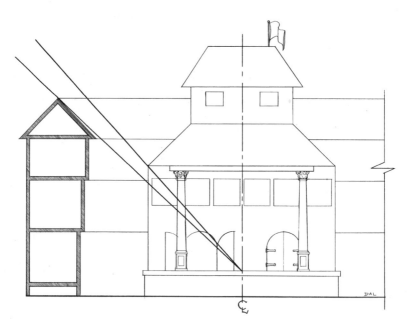

Fig. 31. Cross-sectional diagram of the Swan

light. Primary illumination is rendered by a circle of indirect light emanating from an angle of about forty or fifty degrees above the horizontal plane of both indoor and outdoor stages.

Although the date and provenance of the Jones playhouse plans are uncertain, the plans appear to represent either the extensive remodeling of a preexisting building or the design of a new theater, intended from the start for the production of drama. If the second decade of the seventeenth century is correct for the date, then the design of the windows may well have incorporated changes made less permanently in the private theaters around the turn of the seventeenth century. The owner of the first Blackfriars, let it be noted, complained that when the Children of the Chapel vacated the premises in 1584, his windows were "spoyled." And in 1609, a sharer of the reorganized company testified against his former colleagues that, again, the second Blackfriars had been left "dilapidated . . . and unrepaired, namely . . . in the window glass and in the wooden windows."[43] A recurrent expense after Cambridge theatricals was also the repair of windows. Nearly every year in one college or another, glaziers were hired to fix "windowes wch were broken dowen at the plaies."[44] Perhaps galleries rising above the window level were set up along the walls and their scaffolds fastened to the window jambs, or spectators in the top row of the galleries leaned or were pushed against the window glass. In either case, some portion of each window would be obstructed by the gallery itself, by modifications to the casements or shutters for the protection of the windows or by the spectators sitting in front of them.

Cockpit-in-Court

At first glance, the Cockpit-in-Court seems to contradict this pattern of angled illumination from above and the enclosure of the performing space by high, solid walls. An exterior view of the Cockpit painted by Hendrik Danckert around 1675 shows not only two rows of square-headed windows circling the theater but also a small lantern atop the castellated walls (see fig. 32). Although the upper windows are in a position similar to those in the Jones theater, the lower windows would allow sunlight to flood lower portions of the auditorium while the lantern would introduce light from overhead. Perhaps an exception was made to the standard pattern of theater lighting, because the building Jones was converting into a playhouse was not a typical hall and, moreover, was not often employed for daytime performances. But based on an analysis of the vertical dimensions of the Cockpit-in-Court and the placement of the windows in Danckert's painting, John Orrell has argued that the Cockpit-in-Court may have accommodated only one gallery circling the auditorium, thus occluding light from the lower order of windows.[45] Moreover, pertinent Office of Works accounts also suggest that some of the windows were covered and that much of the light from the lantern was obstructed by a false ceiling above the stage.

The plan for the Cockpit-in-Court shows that Jones hit upon the notion of placing his stage within three sides of the original octagon with the auditorium comprising the remaining five sides (see fig. 33). But Jones encoun-

Fig. 32. Exterior of the Cockpit-in-Court after the Restoration. Detail from "Whitehall & St Jame[s]'s Park" by Hendrik Danckert, c. 1675. Berkeley Castle.

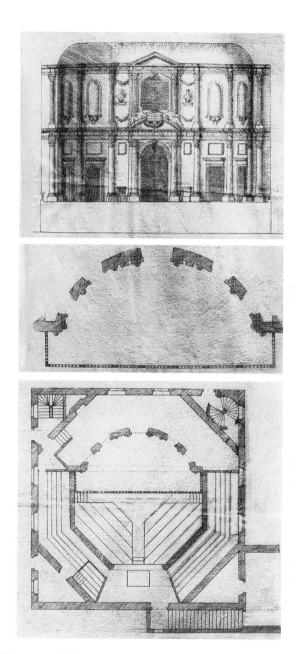

Fig. 33. Elevation and plans for renovation of the Cockpit-in-Court, Whitehall,
c. 1630. The Provost and Fellows of Worcester College, Oxford.

tered problems in fitting such an arrangement into the small space available. To make room for the tiring-house and stage, Jones pushed the stage forward into the hall, obliging him to join the walls extending from either side of the *scaena frons* not to an angle of the octagon but to one of its faces. It will be seen that the proscenium wall to either side of the stage joins each side-wall of the auditorium at the unfortunate position where there were preexisting windows. Because these proscenium walls presumably extended from the stage floor to the top of the *scaena frons*, it is unavoidable that the outside edge of the proscenium not only joined the sidewall itself but also abutted against the two windows, one above the other, on each side of the auditorium.

These intersections of the proscenium walls and side windows would have been awkward at best. The walls would have obstructed light entering the auditorium and created architectural problems of what to do with the window openings and how to support the proscenium walls that must somehow be attached to these windows. The only satisfactory solution would have been to board up the window bays, make them flush with the interior walls, and then properly join the proscenium to the now-solid sidewalls. However the conjunction was accomplished, the auditorium windows near the stage must have been modified in some way so as to accommodate the joining of the extensions of the *scaena frons* and the sidewalls of the auditorium.

At one of the stage-right windows, for instance, Webb has indicated a doorway communicating with the tiring-house and gallery. Were the doorway and window on the same level, their intersection would have been even more ungainly both structurally and visually, because the door jamb (represented by a small dot) would have been unsupported and exposed while it ran up the interior face of the open window bay. At the stage-left window, a similar difficulty arises. Here Webb also indicates what appears to be a doorway in the proscenium wall next to the side window, but he has treated the opening differently, inking in the outline of the door, perhaps to indicate that it was to be newly framed or boarded over as well. Again, the architectural and aesthetic problems arising out of two apertures abutting each other in a corner imply either that the opening in the proscenium wall was not at the same height as the window bay or that the window bay was indeed walled up and made part of the sidewall. Orrell argues for the first solution, but if the vertical dimensions of the windows and their heights above ground-level are taken into account, it is unlikely that a door that communicates between the galleries and the upper tiring-house could be positioned so as to avoid abutting either the lower or upper windows near the stage. Since Danckert shows the distance between the top of the lower windows and the bottom sills of the upper windows in the north wall (the stage-right wall of the auditorium) as no more than three or four feet, there would simply not be enough room for a doorway to be placed vertically between them.[46]

It is not surprising, therefore, that Office of Works accounts both before and after the Interregnum speak of painting over and boarding up windows in the Cockpit-in-Court. The renovation accounts of 1629–30, for example, list a payment of thirty shillings to painters for "payntinge like glasse xx[ty] panes w[ch] had bin Lightes."[47] We do not know which windows were painted. Twenty panes suggest that only a few windows were involved. But the motive for painting panes to look like glass is logically explained only by the circumstance that the windows had been boarded up on the inside of the building, making them look strange from the outside. The painting was thus probably not for the benefit of the interior decoration but a means by which the now-blank windows could be made presentable to passersby in St. James Park. After the Restoration, when the theater reopened, Office of Works records mention similar practices. In January 1662, carpenters were paid for "bourding vp 2 windowes," and the following April two sets of shutters were installed when joiners were hired for "making shutting windowes for y[e] Cockpit playhowse," which were four feet three inches wide and four feet ten inches high.[48] Some of these boarded-up windows and shutters may have been intended for the tiring-house, but the measurements (when compared to the scale of Webb's elevation) appear to rule out the three small windows in the corners of the building. That not all of the windows were walled up is attested to by a payment to plasterers in October 1661 for "poynting [applying mortar around] the glass in three windowes at the cockpit playe house." Perhaps these were the three corner windows lighting the stairways and the public entrance.

An alternative to boarding up windows that could no longer serve their purpose was to move them. John Astington has noted that Danckert shows the two lower windows on the stage-right of the auditorium as considerably higher on the wall than the corresponding windows behind the stage.[49] He concludes that these stage-right lower windows were raised so as to be clear of ranked seating in the gallery. If this is so, then it speaks of an effort both to maintain the presence of daylight in the theater and to raise the angle from which the daylight descended. All we can say for certain is that, at some time before 1675, the lower stage-right windows were at a different height than their counterparts behind the stage.

The lantern above the pit must have been an original or very early addition to the Cockpit. A drawing by Wyngaerde, dating from the mid-sixteenth century, shows a large polyhedral cant roof adorned with an impressive lantern.[50] But when the building was remodeled into a permanent theater in the early 1630s, overhead facilities were constructed that would likely screen out daylight from the lantern. In the 1629–30 accounts, artisans are described as setting up posts to support a ceiling and "cutting fitting and soweing of Callicoe to couer all the roome ouer head wth in the Cockpitt." This cloth false ceiling, garnished with many "Starres of Assidue," was suspended by "a great number of Copprings [copper rings? metallic decorative pieces?] to Drawe the cloth to and fro." At the same time, a property maker was paid for "hanging the Throne and Chaire in the Cockpit wth cloth bound about wth whalebone packthred and wyer for the better foulding of the same to come downe from the Clouds to the Stage." Orrell assumes that this descending throne was positioned upstage close to the *scaena frons*; this is possible, but because the cant roof began its steep ascent toward the center of the building at just this point, it seems more likely that the hoisting machinery was located farther downstage. I take it that when the building was converted into a permanent theater, the space immediately below the lantern became a hut to house machinery. Below this hut and "to couer all the roome ouer head," a cloth heavens was hung by rings and wires. But this heavens, or part of it, could be drawn aside so that the throne could be lowered through the cloth. With all this paraphernalia intervening between the lantern and the stage, one wonders how much, if any, natural illumination could descend from above.

It remains to be said that neither the boarding-over of windows nor the use of cloth false ceilings was unusual, architecturally or theatrically, indoors. Court theaters as early as 1522 had been completely covered by large, star-studded cloths, well described by John Orrell in *The Human Stage*.[51] In the second Jacobean banqueting house at Whitehall, completed in 1622, where today one can see two orders of windows, Jones boarded over the lower windows, turning them into "bastard wyndowes," as John Webb later called them.[52] In his study of this famous building, Per Palme demonstrates that at least eight of the fourteen lower windows were either walled up, converted into niches for statuary, or covered with rich tapestries.[53] Here, for ceremonial occasions particularly, but perhaps also for afternoon plays, Jones emulated the English hall tradition of illumination from high above the main floor, while the king's state was brilliantly lit by a great window in the end wall.

Shuttered Windows

When Dekker speaks of windows that could be "clapt downe" and Alexander Hawkins of "wooden windows," they do not refer to the common sash windows we know, sliding sashes not having been invented until late in the seventeenth century.[54] Even wooden casement windows that could open outwards from a vertical hinge were uncommon in England until Inigo Jones made them fashionable after he returned from the Continent.[55] Thus, the windows in the old ecclesiastical buildings at Blackfriars, Whitefriars, and St. Paul's were probably framed by heavy stone tracery and not by wood. If these windows could be opened at all, they would not have worked up and down but would have incorporated several small lights whose iron casements could be swung outwards like a door. The windows Dekker and Hawkins refer to must have been wooden shutters or "shutting windows," as they were called. Most early English windows had no shutters, but when they did, the shutters were normally on the interior side of the window and could be opened inwardly from the sides or top or—less frequently—slid horizontally back and forth in grooves across the window.

We have no specific evidence of windows being closed at the professional indoor theaters, although records of "wooden windows" in the second Blackfriars undoubtedly refer to wooden shutters rather than to wooden window frames.[56] We do know that for a few afternoon performances at Cambridge and Oxford, halls were darkened by closing such shutters.[57] Dekker's reference to "clapt downe" suggests that the shutting windows he knew were hinged to a transom, but an allusion by Ben Jonson to Jones's theatrical "windows" in the second Jacobean banqueting house, masking house, or perhaps even the Cockpit-in-Court may imply sliding shutting windows. In the 1631 or 1632 poem "To Inigo Marquess Would Be," a corollary to the scathing attack in "An Expostulation with Inigo Jones," Jonson contrasted a true architect's achievements with Jones's theatrical "shopp / Wth slyding windowes, & false Lights."[58]

Dekker also makes clear that when shutting windows were employed, they were closed before the beginning of the performance. Their being clapped down "if some *Nocturnal*, or dismall *Tragedy* were presently to be acted" means that they could not have been used to indicate darkness, say, in any illusionistic sense as the scene of the play changed from day to night. Someone would have had to sit beside each window and open and close the shutters on cue as the time of the play was supposed to change. I venture to say the expense of hiring apprentices to perform this duty would have eliminated the practice from normal consideration. Since the shutting windows were clapped down at the beginning of the play and since their closing was associated with the overall mood of the play rather than with the specific times of the play's action, the darkness Dekker alludes to is artistic, compositional lighting rather than realistic, motivational lighting.

Dekker tells us the shutting windows were also closed for "nocturnals," but what kind of shows these were is not recorded. W. J. Lawrence describes the nocturnal as a subgenre of comedy in which darkness causes the major complications.[59] He finds a half-dozen plays from both the public and private theater repertories that fit his descriptions—among them, A *Midsummer Night's Dream*, *The Merry Devil of Edmonton*, and *The Dutch Courtesan*. But not one of the plays he cites was ever called a nocturnal in contemporary documents, and other evidence regarding the nocturnal hardly supports Lawrence's theory. In an undated Jacobean prospectus for a mammoth, but unrealized, amphitheater, plans were announced to present "NOCTURNALLS of vnexpressable [that is, mute] *Figures*; Visions, and *Apparitions Figureing deepe Melancholly* and vnusuall Representationes."[60] These nocturnals were apparently sad dumb shows rather than comedies.

In another pamphlet, Dekker implies that nocturnals were more solemn than tragedies. Under the rubric *"Play-houses stand empty,"* in his *Worke for Armorours*, Dekker describes the plague of 1608–9, when the playhouse doors were locked and "the *Players* themselues did neuer worke till nowe, there *Comodies* are all turned to *Tragedies*, there *Tragedies* to *Nocturnals*, and the best of them are all weary of playing in those *Nocturnall Tragedies*."[61]

Now if comedies became tragedies during the plague and tragedies became nocturnals, then it seems nocturnals must have been melancholy indeed. Since Dekker states that the regular playhouses were empty, these nocturnals and nocturnal tragedies must have been presented elsewhere. We know that the King's men, Queen's men, Prince's men, and the Queen's Revels children of Blackfriars all performed during the 1608–9 winter season at court and that the King's men received special remuneration "for their private practise in the time of infeccon."[62] Does Dekker mean by "the best of them" performing "*Nocturnall Tragedies*" during the plague that these companies played at night for royalty and the nobility? Marston's *Antonio and Mellida* (London, 1602) mentions "nocturnall court delights" (E3), which might reinforce such a construction. Does he imply by "the *Players* themselues did neuer worke till nowe" that the actors were so hard put to earn a living that they performed whenever and wherever they could and that, in consequence, their plays became sad and melancholy like nocturnals? Or does he mean that, in plague time, all that was fitting to be performed at night were sad songs or poems, like John Donne's touching "Nocturnal upon St. Lucy's Day, being the Shortest day" (1631), or the later ecclesiastical reading where "Fryeries . . . say the Offices for the dead, and cause a Nocturnal to be rehearsed"?[63] At all events, the nocturnal appears to have been a very minor dramatic form judging by the dearth of theatrical references to it. A larger corpus of drama may fairly be designated "dismall *Tragedy*"; but when Dekker associated closed windows with both types of plays, I wonder whether he was pointing to an essential difference or similarity between them. In the latter case, "dismall *Tragedy*" as used in *The Seven Deadlie Sinns of London* would be synonymous with the "*Nocturnall Tragedies*" in the *Worke for Armorours*, and we could assume that private plays were rarely performed with the shutting windows closed.

Moreover, there is the possibility that the closing of the shutting windows had little to do with reducing the amount of daylight. All Dekker may mean is that when plays were performed nocturnally (that is, at night), the windows and shutters were closed. People tend to close shutters and drapes at night to cover the black holes in the wall, to keep out night vapors, and to prevent passersby from peeping inside. For the Pyramus and Thisby play in *A Midsummer Night's Dream*, for example, Bottom makes the startling suggestion that the window casements of the hall be opened so that real moonshine might light the scene (3.1). Actors performing surreptitiously at night during the plague in taverns would certainly have closed the windows, if for no other reason than to prevent nonpaying patrons from watching performances or officials from reporting them. At any rate, the closing of windows and shutters was probably more a function of the comfort of the audience and actors than of the aesthetic environment. In the depth of winter, windows and shutters might be closed to keep out the cold; but owing to the smoke and fumes of the candles, I imagine they were not habitually closed the rest of the year. After the Restoration, Pepys mentions open windows at Killigrew's Drury Lane several times, but always in the spring.

Before turning to the artificial illumination of the private theaters, we should have some notion of the amount of natural light that such windows introduced into the playhouse auditoriums. We can physically measure light in extant halls, but the calculation of natural light within a building no longer standing is obviously inexact, depending on the varying power and changing direction of light from outside (including obstruction from neighboring buildings, buttresses, and the like), the location and size of the windows, the type of glazing, and the reflectance of the room's interior. By assuming the presence of an average overcast sky (a standard established by the Commission Internationale de l'Eclairage) and by using protractors for the determination of daylight factors from architectural drawings (available from the Building Research Station of Great Britain), along with other simplifying conveniences, however, one can estimate the percentage of light from the sky that a building's windows will admit inside.[64]

In the Middle Temple hall, the many large windows permit roughly two percent of the total light from the sky to reach the stage. If the sky is brightly overcast, the luminance onstage equals about eighteen footcandles but decreases to around two or three footcandles on dark winter days at 3 P.M. On the other hand, the few small windows of the Jones playhouse will introduce less than half as much light, the quantity onstage ranging from under one footcandle on dark afternoons to seven or eight footcandles on bright, overcast afternoons. The Cockpit-in-Court with its two orders of windows would have been a little brighter, reaching approximately nine footcandles on bright, overcast days at 3 P.M., assuming for the moment that none of the windows was boarded up.

These levels of brightness are lower than the average illumination measured at the new Globe. Candles supplemented the natural light indoors, of course, but it should be borne in mind that all these levels represent measurable, not apparent, brightness. A brightly lit location outdoors will have a level of illumination between one thousand to three thousand footcandles, while windowlit papers on a desk typically reflect only three to eight footcandles.[65] Yet observers can comfortably accustom their eyes to viewing both after only a few minutes. The range of human visual adaptation is thus easily more than one thousand to one. Because the ratio of natural light at the amphitheaters to that at the hall playhouses was at most thirty to one, the adaptation required to see both stages as equally bright falls well within the possible human range. In consequence, we must not think of the adult private theaters as dim, at least not in the early afternoon. On the contrary, we may imagine them as satisfactorily lit even by our own standards and entirely adequate by medieval and early modern standards.

7

THEATRICAL LIGHTING
AT COURT

L ONG BEFORE they established professional indoor playhouses, troupes of
adult and boy players had acted frequently before Tudor monarchs
under artificial light in the halls of state. By the time of Queen Elizabeth, re-
sponsibility for the lighting of these performances fell primarily to the Revels Office in the queen's household, and since many of its accounts survive,
we can reconstruct a good deal of typical lighting arrangements at court. Undoubtedly, these accounts give us clues as to what professional private theater lighting was like, but we cannot assume that court methods inevitably
filtered down (or up) to the playhouses catering to the general public. I offer
a summary of the artificial light at court by way of describing court lighting
techniques and contemporary theatrical equipment and in hopes that Revels Office records will place the more scattered references to professional
playhouse lighting in understandable contexts.

Performance Times

The extensive use of artificial illumination at court was primarily a function
of the wintertime season and late hours at which most performances were
given. Under both Tudor and Stuart monarchs, plays and masques at court
normally began around 10 P.M. and routinely stretched well beyond midnight. Tarleton is said to have acted before Elizabeth until one o'clock in the
morning, and foreign ambassadors occasionally complained of 10 P.M. starting times and revels extending until 1:30 and 2 in the morning. When Jon-

son's *Pleasure Reconciled to Virtue* ended early on the morning of 17 January 1618, for example, Orazio Busino, chaplain to the Venetian embassy, grumbled about wending his way home at 2 A.M. "half disgusted and exhausted."[1]

Given the lack of complete records, however, Chambers's conclusion that "court performances were always at night" may be too categorical and, at any rate, does not apply to late Jacobean and Caroline practice, which fell beyond his scope.[2] According to later accounts, the King's men performed Fletcher's *Rollo, Duke of Normandy* at the Cockpit-in-Court during the "day time at Whitehall" on 21 February 1631 and Lodowick Carlell's *1 Arviragus and Philicia* at Hampton Court on the "Afternoon" of 26 December 1636, for example.[3] How many other Caroline plays and masques had daytime presentations at court is difficult to say because the best source of information in this regard, the master of the revels, Sir Henry Herbert, did not always bother to note the times of performances precisely. Of the nearly six dozen plays and masques at court mentioned in his office book, Herbert indicates that 52 percent were at "night," 5 percent on a given "day," and 2 percent on an "afternoon," while 42 percent of his records give no indication of the time of performance.[4]

Other sources, like the Declared Accounts of the Chamber, also rarely list performance times at court, but they occasionally indicate two separate performances on the same day. For instance, the King's men performed twice on both 6 and 17 January 1608.[5] Because most of these multiple performances were in February, matinees may or may not have been performed after sunset, which occurred around 4:45 P.M. at the beginning of the month and after 5:30 P.M. at the end. The first performance of a play on 1 January 1604 must have started early enough to allow not only for another play (presumably *A Midsummer Night's Dream*) but also for a masque and banquet afterwards.[6] And because both plays were acted by the same company (the King's men)—who would have required some sort of break between performances—the first play may well have been performed before sunset.

Although most court productions in the winter must have been performed without benefit of natural light, we should nevertheless recall that the halls in which these productions came to life were, as a rule, generously fenestrated. We have already noted that the hall at Hampton Court is illuminated by sixteen large and four small windows. The Elizabethan banqueting house at Whitehall had at least sixty-three casement windows in addition to two great bay windows.[7] The walls of the first Jacobean banqueting house were pierced with forty-six double-casement windows in two orders, and Jones's surviving banqueting house is magnificently lit by twenty-eight large side windows, also in two orders.[8] That some of these windows were occasionally covered with tapestries or boarded over, however, suggests a partial diminution of natural light, even if the reason for covering windows had more to do with the mechanics of placing of degrees in front of them than with aesthetic considerations. On the other hand, we find a reference in the accounts of the Office of Works to the apparent elimination of daylight in the hall at Whitehall. In 1625, carpenters were paid for "[b]oarding vpp all the wyndowes in the Hall, setting vpp rayles, and boardes vppon the Degrees and fitting the Hall for Playes," implying daytime performances there that emulated a nighttime atmosphere.[9] But because there is only this one explicit record of boarding up all the windows, we can imagine that natural light normally mingled with candlelight when performances began before sunset.

Lighting Equipment

Extant Revels Office accounts frequently tell us what sorts of lighting instruments illuminated the audiences, actors, and masquers at court. But because the accounts run by the season, it is difficult to distinguish between the facilities made available for the various kinds of entertainment that the Revels Office supervised. Rarely can individual expenditures be linked to specific masques, plays, dates, and locations to provide detailed pictures of given performances. Instead, we must settle for a general idea of standard Elizabethan lighting equipment and procedures before Inigo Jones made several important changes in court lighting.

Judging by the Revels Office accounts, the principal light in Queen Elizabeth's halls came from candles mounted in what were called branches. The candles were generally of tallow, not wax, and were purchased in three different types—wick, cotton, and white. Wick candles had wicks of flax or rushes; they were cheaper than the others but were bought infrequently. Cotton candles were made of tallow impregnating cotton strands and were by far the most popular type. They came in various sizes but were often quite large, typically weighing a pound apiece. White lights were used less often and were rather small. Their name derived from the bleached tallow used in their manufacture.

The branches so frequently mentioned in the accounts were candelabra usually suspended above the hall as chandeliers. In halls with high-pitched roofs, branches were not hung directly from beams or rafters but from wires stretched across the hall from one wall to another. For "Braunches that bare the light*es* in the hall at Hampton Coorte," for example, the Revels Office bought "Wyer to strayne crosse the hall & to hang the braunches with the light*es*," while carpenters supplied vices and winches "to draw the wyers tighte whereon the light*es* did hang crosse the hall."[10] We know that one play by Leicester's men (of whom James Burbage was a member) and another by the Merchant Taylors' children, as well as two short masques, were performed under these hanging lights on 21 and 23 February 1574. The following Christmas, when the Children of the Chapel and Leicester's and Lincoln's men acted, "Wyer of the greate sorte" was again purchased "to hang or to strayne crosse the hall at *Hampton Coorte*." In a canvas and lath banqueting house at Whitehall, twenty-four branches and "Wyer to hang them by" as well as "Great wyers that went cross the hall" were provided for a June 1572 masque.[11] Similar entries pertaining to the halls and temporary banqueting houses at Whitehall, Windsor, and Greenwich for plays by such troupes as Warwick's, Sussex's, Chamberlain's, and the Children of St. Paul's and the Chapel demonstrate that hanging branches were common for professional plays at court.

The number of branches used in Elizabeth's various halls falls within a narrow range—normally twenty-eight or twenty-nine. At Whitehall in 1572, there were only twenty-four, and at Richmond in 1575, only nineteen.[12] But by the 1580s, the quantity had increased, and the branches were furthermore numbered in two distinct sizes, regularly designated in the accounts as great and small. At Windsor in 1583, twenty-six small branches and three great ones lit the hall where the Lord Chamberlain's men played. At either Greenwich or Somerset (the accounts are not clear), there were twenty-four small and four great branches in the 1584–85 season.[13] While varying slightly over the years, the numbers at Whitehall show how standardized the Elizabethan arrangements were. In February 1579, fourteen small branches were mended, and eight small and three great were newly purchased. For Christmastide entertainments in 1579–80, there were twenty-six small and three great, and again the following Christmas, twenty-six small and three great.[14] Jacobean arrangements were more generous. In 1611, the Revels Office increased the number of large branches in the first Jacobean banqueting house to twelve.

A year later, thirty-six large branches were ordered; these must have supported a large number of candles, but as some thirty plays were performed that season in various locations as well as two masques in the banqueting house and one in the hall at Whitehall, it is impossible to estimate the amount of light for any one performance.[15]

How the branches were arranged about the English halls cannot be determined from the accounts. But the Venetian chaplain who saw Jonson's *Pleasure Reconciled to Virtue* through to the bitter end in January 1618 happens to tell us that there were "two rows of lights" in the banqueting house, the small branches apparently having been eliminated entirely.[16] Under Elizabeth, the three or four great branches were probably hung over the stage or the center of the hall while ten or twelve small branches were distributed to each side, perhaps mounted as branched sconces. Light may have been concentrated near the actors, but evidence for such a practice is not forthcoming until late in the period. Indeed, because so many Elizabethan arrangements were obliged to serve for both plays and masques, in which large dancing areas needed to be lit, we can assume that a relatively even distribution of light prevailed.

Some of the branches could be lowered by wires and pulleys so that the candles could be lit, snuffed, and extinguished. Lines, ropes, and pulleys are frequently mentioned in the accounts, but there are only a few explicit references to the raising and lowering of lights. In 1576, wiredrawers supplied "Ten pound of wyer for the Coming vp of the small lightes" at Whitehall, and in 1612 "8. new Pullyes for the Branches" were purchased.[17] Special utensils mentioned for the management of light include "A long staf to reache vp & downe ye lightes" for Whitehall plays or masques in 1574 and "Dowtes [doubters, that is, extinguishers] for Candells" and "snuffers vj paire" in 1579–80.[18] Such utensils are not habitually mentioned, however, and I assume that these were used as stage properties by torchbearers in masques. The 1527 accounts for the building and decoration of the banqueting house at Greenwich list "4 great cans or [of?] reeds to light the candles"; perhaps such utensils remained relatively simple over the years.[19] In the early Jacobean accounts, the master wiredrawer normally charged expenses for six assistants working both day and night immediately before each performance. By 1633, five men were required to work six days and six nights each to hang branches in the hall at Whitehall.[20] The wiredrawers saw to the installation, decoration, and repair of the lights rather than to their being lit and snuffed, duties that were handled by servants of the hall or chamber.

Only occasionally do the accounts indicate how many candles were supported by each branch. In June 1572, a wiredrawer was paid "for white Rownde plates turnde in with a crest for xxiiij braunches eche bearing iiij (for lightes)."[21] With only four candles on each branch, I presume these are what the accounts elsewhere call small branches. For the 1604–5 season, however, eight "Gre[a]tt Branches to holde fiftingreat Lightes Apece" were acquired presumably for the great chamber in Whitehall.[22] If these figures for small and great branches are typical, then we may estimate that the average total number of candles for court performances from 1576 to around 1588 was forty-five in the small branches and ninety-six in the great branches, or a total of 141 candles.

Jacobean averages are larger. In 1605, the great branches supported 120 candles, and the small ones at least thirty-two, probably more. In 1611, when twelve new branches "of the largest sort" were purchased, there was a minimum of 180 candles in all shining overhead.[23] It was under this particular splendor, we know, that early productions of *The Tempest* and *The Winter's Tale* were given. The next year, the Revels Office purchased thirty-six great branches containing fifteen lights each for various halls. By the end of James's reign, however, the size of the branches also seems to have grown: in 1621, branches that held fifteen lights were called "ordinary" in contrast to more expensive "greate" branches that were garnished with gilt and crowns.[24]

That the great branches held ninety-six candles in 1572 is confirmed by the purchase of ninety-six corresponding "plates," which is a common, though somewhat ambiguous, term throughout the accounts. The term "plate" seems to have been used in at least four senses: (1) shallow pans beneath the candles to catch drippings; (2) metal sheets placed above the candles to protect the ceiling from burning; (3) mountings for wall brackets, perhaps reflective; and (4) gilt or silver plating on branches, candlesticks, or wall brackets. Since one plate was often provided for each candle, one purpose was to prevent tallow drippings and charred wicks from falling on the spectators and players below, as was true at Greenwich in 1520 and 1527 when large branches stood in gilt basins attached to the tops of posts serving as part of the degrees accommodating the audience.[25] For Christmastide plays and masques at either Hampton Court or Greenwich in 1572–73, there were

"Rownde plates for socket*tes*" and "wyer to hang them by," implying that one plate was attached to each candle socket.[26]

At other times, however, plates were attached to the ceiling, not above each candle but above the entire branch. In 1605, for example, one large plate was provided for each of the eight branches at Whitehall "to kepe ye Greatbranches for [from?] bur[n]inge ye Roufe of ye Chamber."[27] Perhaps the great chamber at Whitehall had a dangerously low ceiling. Even the brick banqueting house built in 1607 required similar protection; there is no mention of plates for its ceiling, which presumably was high, but in 1612 four dozen large "pastbord*es* to save the Colloumes" were ordered.[28] Apparently the "two rows of lights" in the banqueting house were attached to columns arising from each side gallery to support the roof. If the older banqueting houses had horizontal ceilings as the present banqueting house does, plates could easily have been attached to their painted canvas ceilings. But this method would have been unnecessary in halls with high-pitched roofs. Jones's banqueting house certainly did not have plates attached to its ceiling, as a constant fear was that smoke from the candles would damage Rubens's paintings there. In fact, Charles I was obliged to build a wooden masquing house in 1637 because, as one courtier explained, "the King will not have his Pictures in the Banqueting-house hurt with Lights."[29]

Branches usually required round plates, but other kinds of plates were associated with wall brackets and candlesticks. For autumn rehearsals in the great chamber at St. John's of Jerusalem in Blackfriars (where the Revels Office itself was located in 1580), eight inexpensive "Plates for to hange vpon Walles to sett .v Candells in" were procured.[30] These must have been five-branched wall brackets with plates protecting the walls. Other plates bought by the Revels Office are specified as "for pillers," for "Boordes," "for walls," and "for hatt*es*."[31] This last reference to "Plates with holes for hatt*es*" has been taken to imply a lantern-like utensil in which a candle, secured to a flat plate, was surrounded by a cylindrical "hat" attached to the plate through holes.[32] Something like this is possible, but such an interpretation is based entirely on a modern use of the term "hat" (from "stovepipe hat," a nineteenth-century coinage) to describe the reflective shields around gas footlights and early electric spotlights.

Plates were also acquired for use with simple candlesticks. We hear of "Plates for small Canstick*es*" in 1573 and "Plates for the Candlestick*es*" the following year. There are also records of "Dubble plate candlestick*es*" in 1572 and 1573 and of "Branches maied of Dobll whit Plat" in 1611.[33] These probably refer to drip pans or to plated, that is, gilded or silver-plated, branches. Other extravagancies included three Caroline "Cristall" branches and a Jacobean branch or branches trimmed with forty dozen "Looking glasses," that is, small mirrors or crystals.[34] On the other hand, the decoration of other branches, even those lighting the auditorium, was essentially theatrical: a good deal of trouble was taken to garnish branches with inexpensive metal foil called arsedine, cut into intricate shapes such as roses, tassels, and pendants in order to make them appear more rich.

True candlesticks were purchased in a large variety of styles—hand, stock, small, high, vice, and prick. Some of these names explain themselves: hand candlesticks were carried; prick candlesticks supported candles not in sockets but impaled on metal spikes. I assume high and small candlesticks stood on floors and tables respectively, but other explanations are possible. I can offer no precise definitions of the attributives "stock" and "vice." In 1579–80, twelve stock candlesticks were acquired "for painters" who often worked late into the night finishing the garnishings for the halls.[35] Probably they were simply made of wood. Vice candlesticks were the most expensive, costing a shilling apiece. The word "vice" may describe a method of securing the candles by side pressure, but it more likely refers to screw clamps of some sort, by which the candlesticks could be fastened to railings, scenery, cornices, and the like.

Small and stock candlesticks were bought in large numbers, sometimes as many as four dozen in one holiday season. High, vice, hand, and prick candlesticks were bought in smaller quantities, usually less than a dozen at a time. For any given season, however, only two or three styles were purchased. In 1572–73, for example, the Revels Office obtained four dozen small but only twelve high and twelve vice candlesticks. The next year, the number of high candlesticks was decreased to six. The following year saw the purchase of four dozen stock and six vice but no small or high candlesticks. Hand and prick styles were bought only twice each in the Elizabethan and Jacobean years for which we have records.[36]

The uses to which these candlesticks were put varied. Some were used as stage properties, as one obviously was in 1574 when a "silk tree for A devise in one of the Candellstick*es*" was made for a Candlemas play or masque at Hampton Court. A wax chandler also provided six ornately decorated candlesticks and six "sweete lightes of white wex," presumably for the masque, since it was described as a "Maske of Ladies with lightes being vj vertues."[37] Other candlesticks may have been carried by the torchbearers, who regularly accompanied the masquers.

Although the Revels Office purchased such utensils for masques, it seems likely that professional actors supplied some or all of their own property lights. But even for the masques that it produced, the Revels Office does not seem to have recorded payments for all the lighting equipment and material necessary. At least that is one way of interpreting the remarkable consistency with which the Stuart Revels Office spent precisely three pounds each season, year in and year out, "for Torches, lights, and Candles, as hath beene accustomed."[38] One might have thought, because some years witnessed considerably more entertainments than others, that a good deal of variation in the amount of chandlery goods purchased would reflect variations in the number of lights required. But although the number of candlesticks and branches ordered each year varies greatly, the amount spent on candles and torches does not. Three pounds would normally buy approximately eight hundred tallow candles and several dozen torches, which would provide sufficient lighting for perhaps six or seven modest entertainments along the lines of those under Elizabeth.

But the early Stuarts regularly enjoyed many more evenings of revels than six or seven and apparently viewed them under more ample light. Hence, the figure of three pounds is much too low to account for all the lighting required. In one of the years for which the Revels Office recorded purchases of only three pounds for lights, we are fortunate to have a separate memorandum, dated 31 December 1631, on the back of one of Jones's designs for *Albion's Triumph*, requesting the purchase of four dozen torches, three dozen "ordinary" torches, sixteen dozen wax lights for the branches, and two hundred sises, or small devotional candles.[39] The memorandum does not give the cost of these lights, but by itself this order would use up nearly half the yearly lighting allotment of the Revels Office. Even more brightly lit (and undoubtedly the most extravagant masque of the era) was James Shirley's *The Triumph of Peace* (performed at the banqueting house, 3 February 1634, and repeated at the Merchant Taylors' Hall, 13 February 1634). Although the Revels Office again recorded a payment of only three pounds for lights that year, the combined resources of the benchers of the Inns of Court spent no less than £142 on torches for the two events.[40] Such a sum could purchase nearly a thousand torches and some fifty flambeaux for each presentation, although many of these must have been deployed for a "shew through the streets," which Sir Henry Herbert found "glorious."[41] We are left to surmise that the Revels Office provided lighting for general illumination of plays and masques but that many of the torches carried by the torchbearers and at least some of the special lighting arrangements associated with Jones's increasingly elaborate scenery were paid for by other court funds, by the sponsors of masques, or (less likely) from Jones's own fees. Perhaps an unstated distinction about who was responsible for the illumination of the earl of Salisbury's 1607 *Entertainment of the King & Queen at Theobalds* lies behind the equivocal comment in the inventory of expenses that "Mr Iones hath all the waxe lightes torches and candlestickes."[42]

It is reasonable to assume that the responsibilities for payment may have been determined by the different purposes to which various lights were put. After the Restoration, lighting expenses are clearly divided among such categories as (1) tallow candles for the players' rehearsal and dressing-room needs; (2) wax candles for the branches in the hall; (3) torches for guards, porters, and waiters; (4) yellow wax lights for the scenes; and (5) wax lights for the king's and queen's presences.[43] The pre-Interregnum Revels Offices do not furnish us this sort of detail, but Oxford records occasionally provide more particular categories of expenditures. For two nighttime plays before Charles I at Christ Church in August 1636, for example, Jones purchased some twenty-three dozen wax lights to illuminate the hall and scenery but purchased only less expensive tallow candles for the music rooms and tiring-rooms and "for the Backe part of the Sceenes."[44] After the Restoration, the "vsual allowances" for lights were proportionally similar: in 1679, the lord chamberlain gave orders stipulating, in effect, that 34 percent of the lighting expenditures be for the hall, 63 percent for the scenes, and 3 percent for the dressing rooms and backstage areas.[45]

Whatever the pre-Interregnum accounting procedures, the memorandum for *Albion's Triumph* and the Middle Temple warrants for *The Triumph of Peace* demonstrate that by the early 1630s, large numbers of wax lights illuminated Jones's spectacles. With the literary inhibitions of "Ben Jonson being . . . discarded," as one court gossip put it, Jones could accomplish his goal of making masques "nothing else but pictures with Light and Motion."[46]

Stage Lighting for Masques

Before returning to the professional playhouses, we should contrast the theatrical illumination typical of the Tudor court with the more elaborate illumination that Inigo Jones arranged for Stuart masques. At the time that adult actors began to inhabit the private hall playhouses, Jones introduced important innovations in stage lighting for the sophisticated amateur performers in masques. These innovations concerned the color, placement, and movement of light on his scenes. Jones usually experimented with all three of these aspects at once, but early in his career, colored light seems to have fascinated him most. In Jonson's *Masque of Beauty*, for example, performed in the banqueting house at Whitehall on 2 February 1609, Jones created a *"tralucent* Pillar, *shining with seuerall-colour'd lights"*; and in the next year, the friezes of the House of Fame in the *Masque of Queens* "were filld w'h seuerall-coloured Lights, like *Emeralds, Rubies, Saphires, Carbuncles,* &c."[47] For a few years, colored light shining through architectural scenic elements was the rage: the *Masque of Flowers*, performed by the gentlemen of Gray's Inn at the banqueting house on 6 January 1614, featured pyramids *"glistering with transparent lights, resembling carbuncles, saphires, and rubies."*[48] These effects may have been accomplished by placing lights behind colored glass or colored oiled paper. In the second book of his *Regole generali di architettura* (Paris, 1545) and again in the English translation of 1611, the Italian designer Sebastiano Serlio suggests placing lights behind glass, paper, or painted cloth in his comic scene so that "all the roundels and Quadrans which you see in the Buildings, they are artificiall lights cutting through, of diuers colours."[49] Jones frequently made whole pieces of scenery glow by this method. In *Oberon* (1 January 1611, banqueting house, Whitehall), after the customary scene with a dark rock, a glorious palace is discovered *"whose gates and walls were transparent"*; this palace, in turn, opened to reveal fairies bearing lights, which, presumably, furnished the illumination that radiated through the transparent shutters.[50]

To strengthen the effect of color, Serlio recommends placing special bottles or glasses filled with colored water in front of lamps to act as lenses. These glasses were then placed so that they projected through small holes cut in the scenery. Thus, in Jonson's *Entertainment of the King & Queen at Theobalds*, 22 May 1607, after the opening gloomy scene lit by only one light, a glorious shrine is discovered, in the columns, frieze, and cornice of which *"were placed diuers Diaphanall glasses, fill'd with seuerall waters, that shew'd like so many stones, of orient and transparent hiewes."*[51] The next year, Jones jotted down a list of expenses on the verso of a design for another murky scene, charging three shillings eight pence *"for glasses for y*[e] *Rocke,"* apparently also for colored light in a masque to entertain James in the library of Salisbury House in the Strand, May 1608.[52]

One of the few discussions of early modern stage lighting was occasioned by a minor debate about whether lamps or candles burned behind these bottles to illuminate Jones's scenes. Basing his view on Italian practice and the English translation of Serlio, Allardyce Nicoll maintained that "lamps were more conveniently adapted" than candles "for back-stage work," but C. F. Bell asserted that oil was never used.[53] Bell's argument is the stronger: his analysis of Serlio's influence on Jones is well informed and judicious, and there is no evidence of any widespread use of lamps outside the kitchen in Stuart England. Moreover, the Revels Office accounts clearly demonstrate that candles supplied the principal illumination of both auditorium and stage.

All the same, Bell may overstate the case. For one thing, he makes no distinction between the utensils providing overall illumination of the stage and those positioned in openings in the scenery to produce colored light. He leaves the impression that most of the light onstage passed through bottles, whereas the actual number of instances in which glasses are called for is small and confined to the years from 1607 to 1614 or so. To clinch his argument against the use of lamps, Bell cites the 1631 memorandum, already referred to, requesting sixteen dozen wax lights for branches in addition to torches and sises. He reasons that "the expenditure of such a great quantity of wax can scarcely be accounted for unless candles alone were in use for lighting both stage and auditorium."[54] But chandeliers or branched wall sconces would be unsuitable for projecting colored light through the scenes, and, at any rate, the Revels accounts for that holiday season make it clear that most of these branches were not special theatrical instruments but rather standard utensils carted down to Whitehall from Denmark and Somerset Houses. Indeed, the sixteen dozen wax lights were undoubtedly intended for the sixteen dozen "Wallers" and "Prickers," that is, wall brackets and spikes on which to impale large candles.[55] By confusing general lighting with specially colored light, Bell argues that, because payments for lamps and oil are "entirely absent from the Revels Accounts," wax must have burned behind Jones's vials. But Bell's assertion notwithstanding, there is at least one reference to "lamps & Vialles" in the Elizabethan Revels accounts, and on the auditorium plan that John Orrell suggests represents the 1605 theater at Christ Church, Oxford, is a note that "many lights or lamps of seueral coulers may be placed" on a portico near the king's state.[56] After the Restoration, lamps were also occasionally hung above the scenes, as Serlio and Nicola Sabbattini had suggested, although not apparently behind the scenes.[57]

The Revels Office accounts indicate no purchases of oil, and the single record of the use of lamps does not imply heavy use. This record, in a long summary of expenses for the 1581–82 season, reads in part, "Candles links Torches lightes lamps & Vialles."[58] That lamps were placed near the end of the list after the inclusive "lightes" suggests these lamps were not major expenses. In fact, their juxtaposition with vials clearly suggests that they were used in special colored-light effects. Certainly, the use of lamps rather than candles in conjunction with vials would have solved one practical problem. The difficulty in using a candle to shine through a glass vial is that, as the candle burns down, the angle at which the light is projected by the condensing vial will change, casting the beam of colored light gradually higher as the candle grows shorter. Given a substantial reservoir of oil, however, the position of the flame of a floating-wick lamp remains more or less stationary, and, hence, the colored light emanating from the glass vial can be focused in a particular direction with less fear that the direction will change as the masque wears on. Italian practice indicates that lamps were found most useful in positions where it was inconvenient to attend to the lights. For example, Sabbattini, who equipped the Teatro del Sol in Pesaro around 1636, employed lamps behind the top of his proscenium arch where they could be left to burn, but because the lamps smoked profusely, he preferred to place candles near his scenes where they could conveniently be trimmed.

The use of paper, fabric, and glass bottles to create colored light would, of course, tend to decrease the brightness produced by any one flame. Apparently, some colors occluded more light than others. In his essay "Of Masques and Triumphs" (1625), written after years of observing and even supervising masques, Francis Bacon advised, "Let the scenes abound with light, especially coloured and varied," but admitted that not all colors worked well: "The Colours that shew best by Candle-lights," he wrote, are "White, Carnation, and a Kind of Sea-Water-Greene," in short, relatively unsaturated colors.[59] Effects produced by shining light through liquids of deeper hue—blues, purples, and reds—were apparently less successful.

To produce a striking effect with colored light, then, the general illumination must be kept dim, as the Italian designer Leone di Somi recognized by the mid-sixteenth century.[60] Apparently, this was not the direction in which Jones wanted to go. Though Jones was fond of dark scenes at the beginning of his masques, his colored lighting effects were more frequent in brightly illuminated scenes than in scenes of gloom. And indeed, over the years Jones relied less on colored lighting effects and more on sheer brilliance; at least, there are fewer and fewer references to colored light in the texts and descriptions of his Caroline masques. It may be that colored light was so common by then that it went unreported or that, because we are missing so many descriptions of the "bodily part" of masques from the 1620s, we simply do not possess the relevant data. Still, even when Jones himself seems to have provided the description of the *mise en scène* (as for *Tempe Restored*, 1632), we hear nothing of colored light. Perhaps Jones took less interest in color for its own sake; he certainly drew fewer color renderings as the years went by.

In emphasizing brilliance, Jones also experimented with the concentration of light onto particular objects and areas. Nicoll and Bell assume that much of this concentration was accomplished by glass vials, and it is possible that condensing glasses were used for this purpose. But spherical condensing glasses will focus light only at a distance equal to the distance of the flame from the glass and, hence, could not illuminate an object situated more than a foot or two from the glass. A globe flattened on one side, like a modern convex lens, would throw light farther, of course; Serlio mentions that "if the bottels . . . on the side where the light stands were flat, or rather hollow, it would show the clearer," but his conditional mood causes one to doubt if even his proximity to Venetian glassmakers could regularly supply him with such instruments.[61] Certainly the early *bozze* glasses found at the Teatro Olimpico and prominently discussed by Nicoll are all spherical. The purpose of Serlio's vials—like Jones's—was clearly less to focus light onto particular scenic elements than to provide decorative highlights on the scenes themselves.

To effect brilliance by concentrating light, Jones simply used the methods he had adopted for his scene changes—the *machina versatilis* and the *machina ductilis*. Jones had learned that to produce an effect of glowing brightness, he should hide the sources of light, place the utensils close to the scene, and make the objects to be lit as reflective as possible, hence Jones's reliance on metallic fabrics and metallic sequins, or what Felice in *Antonio and Mellida* (1602) calls "glistering copper spangs, / That glisten in the tyre of the Court" (E3). In *The Masque of Queens*, for example, the brilliance surrounding the queens in the House of Fame came not only from the friezes with "seuerall-coloured Lights" but also from the reflection of those and other lights on the queens' costumes, or, as Jonson puts it, "The reflexe of w^{c}h, w^{t}h other lights plac'd in ye concaue, vpon the *Masquers* habites, was full of glory."[62] Jones found such "concaues" useful not only as turntables but also in concentrating the light onto a relatively small area. Thus, *The Haddington Masque* (9 February 1608, banqueting house, Whitehall) relied on an "*illustrious* Concaue, *fill'd with an ample and glistering light*" in which the masquers were discovered in a turning eighteen-foot silver sphere.[63]

The lights in these concaves were sometimes hidden behind reveals, casting their light toward the center of the concave. The "great concaue shell" in the masque *Blackness* (6 January 1605, banqueting house, Whitehall) "was struck with a *cheu'ron* of lights, which, indented to the proportion of the shell, strooke a glorious beame" on the masquers.[64] Presumably, these indentations provided support for the utensils and served to shield the sources of light from the eyes of the audience, as they did in George Chapman's *The Memorable Masque* (in the hall at Whitehall, 15 February 1613), where a "rich and refulgent Mine of golde" featured

> lights . . . so ordered, that though none were seene, yet had their lustre such vertue, that by it, the least spangle or sparke of the Maskers rich habites, might with ease and cleerenesse be discerned as far off as the state [of the king].[65]

Like his use of colored light, Jones's techniques for concentrating light evolved over the years. Early on, Jones was content to concentrate light on relatively small areas (shells, caves, mines, and the like), usually within a *machina versatilis*. After his return from Italy in 1615, Jones was inclined to spread brilliance over an entire perspective scene, an effect he apparently had admired at the Teatro Olimpico in Vicenza. In Jones's copy of the 1601 edition of Andrea Palladio's *I Quattro libri dell' architettura*, Jones records his impressions of the Teatro Olimpico, which he visited on 23 September 1613. There he saw three three-dimensional perspective alleyways disappearing into the distance behind the ornate *scaena frons*. He was particularly impressed by the placement of the lights in the side alleys: "On the Passages of the sides all the lightes wear Placed," he noted, presumably meaning that in addition to the relatively dim general-purpose illumination of the stage and *cavea*, many lights were placed behind the *scaena frons*, brightly illuminating the passageways built in forced perspective.[66] Jones can hardly mean that "all" the lights for the stage were placed in the side alleys, but because lights in the alleys could be placed much closer to the scenery, it may well have appeared so. When the *machina ductilis* supplanted the *machina versatilis* as the way of changing scenes, Jones could more or less duplicate the lighting he had admired in Vicenza by placing lights behind the sliding shutters or proscenium arch to produce brightness over the entire scene. Thus, in *The Golden Age Restored* (1 January 1616, Whitehall), shutters are drawn aside to discover a "Scene of light," and in *Tempe Restored* (14 February 1632, banqueting house, Whitehall), a similar "Lightsome *Scene* appear'd."[67]

The wonder so often expressed by spectators at Jones's lighting effects comes in part from this placement of light but also from his technique of moving and turning, not the lights individually, but the whole structure on which the lights were mounted or on which the object to be viewed was displayed. The text of Daniel's *Tethys' Festival* (5 June 1610, banqueting house, Whitehall) quotes Jones's own description of one of these effects: "*First at the opening of the heavens appeared three circles of lights and glasses, one within another, and came down in a straight motion five foot, and then began to move circularly.*"[68] Here the rings supporting the lights and glasses could not only be lowered but also be revolved to produce a shimmering illumination that distracted the eyes of the spectators sufficiently to hide the method of changing the scene. Similarly in Campion's *Masque of Lords*, a sky is revealed with eight large stars moving. The stars vanish and clouds give way to "artificial fires, with severall circles of lights in continual motion."[69] Such effects continue throughout Jones's career, and W. A. Armstrong correctly reminds us that Jonson's ridicule of Jones's

ffeat
of Lantern-lerry: wth fuliginous heat
Whirling his Whymseys

refers not to a distaste for gorgeous light as such but to "lights and machines which *moved* before the spectators' eyes."[70] Still, in Jones's defense, we may note that over the years his experiments with moving light became less abstract than they were originally. In the early masques, we often see circles of light turning, more or less gratuitously, on or within *machinae versatiles* with little or no connection to the illusionistic or even the allegorical environment. In the later masques, lights still move, but they tend to do so as part of a pictorial representation of a place, however imaginary. Instead of revolving circles, most of the moving lights in the Caroline masques accompany floating clouds and refulgent glories surrounding *dei ex machinae*, as in *Tempe Restored* (1632), *Cœlum Britannicum* (1634), and *The Temple of Love* (1635).[71]

Although masque scenes were common in plays produced at the professional theaters, there is little evidence that this sort of spectacle devolved to the professional hall playhouses.[72] All the same, John Orrell has underlined Jones's personal and professional associations with the adult players, and Jones may well have designed Beeston's Cockpit—and certainly designed the Cockpit-in-Court at Whitehall, at which adult companies were regular tenants.[73] As we consider the artificial light at these and other private theaters, then, Inigo Jones's (and our) knowledge of theatrical illumination at court may help us to understand the less well-documented practices in the indoor hall theaters.

8

ARTIFICIAL LIGHT IN
THE INDOOR PLAYHOUSES

Having considered the availability of daylight in the private playhouses and the use of artificial light at court, we can now attempt to make sense of the sparse references to artificial light at the private playhouses. I distinguish between artificial light and natural light at these indoor playhouses for convenience and for the practical reason that contemporary descriptions did so, too. But for the present, I do not take up the question of artificial lights carried by the actors as stage properties.

These principles of organization are open to criticism. Certainly, they tend to disintegrate the total visual effect into distinct elements that the audience never saw except in relation to others. But because the light produced by daylight, chandeliers, and stage properties could not be easily controlled, each source of light remained more or less independent from the others, sometimes producing disparate effects and even participating in apparently contradictory theatrical conventions. We have seen evidence, for example, that daylight was reduced for certain somber tragedies by absorbent black hangings outdoors and perhaps by window shutters indoors. But there is no evidence that candles were dimmed or even could be dimmed for similar reasons. In fact, in Fletcher's *The Queen of Corinth* (c. 1617, Blackfriars), burning tapers are explicitly associated with tragedy. The heroine has shut herself up in her room after having been raped and has obstructed all the window light with black hangings, we are told. But she has many tapers lighting the room, which her friend finds unhealthy. The friend counsels

out with these Tragick Lights,
And let day repossesse her naturall howres:
Teare downe these blacks.[1]

The conventional uses of daylight and candlelight thus attend opposite effects.

Artificial Light in the Afternoon

Because the early children's companies waited until after evening prayer to begin their plays, little natural light could have illuminated their halls in the depth of winter. In a commendatory verse to Fletcher's *The Faithful Shepherdess,* for instance, which had been unsuccessful at its premiere by the Queen's Revels boys at the second Blackfriars in 1608, Ben Jonson described the unreceptive spectators as "rank'd in the darke."[2] The phrase is a fusion of double meanings: "rank'd" suggesting both social rank and tiered seating, "darke" referring both to the putative ignorance of Fletcher's audience and to the literal darkness in which they sat. As the Queen's Revels boys performed only from around Michaelmas (29 September) until Easter, natural darkness inevitably accompanied many of their performances.[3]

A comment by a German tourist visiting the second Blackfriars six years earlier may or may not imply that no daylight illuminated the children there. A diary entry of Frederic Gerschow, tutor to the duke of Stettin-Pomerania, says that the children's performances were "Alle bey Lichte Agieret, welchs ein grosses Ansehen machtt"—all acted by lights, which makes a great effect.[4] It is unclear if by "Alle" he meant that the illumination was furnished *exclusively* by artificial lights, or if he was saying the children used lights at *every* performance, or if he simply meant that the whole event was artificially illuminated, in contrast to the amphitheaters. Considering that the visit was on 18 September when the sun set at a little before 6 P.M., one would be surprised if no sunlight illuminated the entire performance. To have produced a "great effect" throughout the large Parliament Chamber would have required many candles indeed. In all likelihood, the audience sat in window light for the most part, while candles were placed as near the actors as possible to emphasize the splendor of their costumes, with which Gerschow was much taken.

Although the children's troupes were most active in the winter (preparing for and repeating their January and February entertainments for the monarch), we cannot say that artificial light was absolutely necessary throughout each performance. In fact, the induction to *Michaelmas Term*, performed at St. Paul's around 1604, suggests that nightfall occurred near the end of the play. Middleton confirms the two-hour duration mentioned at about the same time by William Percy (4 to 6 P.M.) but in legal metaphors appropriate to his theme promises the audience that "wee dispatch you in two howers, without demure; your Suites hang not long here after Candles be lighted."[5] The phrase "not long . . . after Candles be lighted" might refer to playhouse candles lit near the end of the performance, but it more likely means that the play would not detain the audience much past candle-lighting time for the City in general—apparently around 6 P.M. at that time of year.

Hence, darkness may not have been the sole reason for the use of artificial light. The children's companies were accustomed to acting under the queen's candlelight and may not have foregone its refined associations, no matter how much daylight poured through the windows at their own theaters. As late as 1636, candlelight was advertised as a measure of theatrical distinction and refinement, even though it had become commonplace long before that.[6] On the basis of the children's troupes' attention to such matters as touched on their reputations (the adoption of the word "private" to describe thoroughly public performances, for example), we may surmise that early troupes used candlelight not just for the sake of visibility but in hopes that its sophistication would contribute to their good report. Early masques, mummings, and disguisings had for centuries been performed to artificial lights, whether or not the light they provided was necessary. Because of extreme heat in the banqueting house at Whitehall in June 1610, for instance, torchbearers were omitted at the last minute from Samuel Daniel's *Tethys' Festival* without complaints about darkness.[7] For Sir Henry Unton's wedding masque, torchlight graced the festivities even though strong sunlight came through the windows, brightly lighting the room. Visibility was undoubtedly the principal impetus for introducing candles, but it may not have been the only reason.

Lighting and Extinguishing the Candles

Several playhouse inductions mention or show us the lighting of playhouse candles. The earliest comes from Marston's *What You Will*, acted at St. Paul's in 1601. At the opening, there is the authorial stage direction *"Before the Musicke sounds for the Acte: Enter Atticus, Doricus, & Phylomuse, they sit a good while on the Stage before the Candles are lighted, talking together."* Immediately following is the stage direction *"Enter Tier-man with lights,"* whereupon Doricus exclaims, "O Fie some lights, sirs fie, let there be no deeds of darknesse done among vs."[8] We need not take his reference to darkness literally, of course, but the stage directions make clear that spectators finding their seats or waiting for the play to begin did so without the benefit of artificial light, at least near the stage. Instead, candles were lit only just before the play was to begin. Reference to a single tireman also indicates that one person could attend to the candles quickly and conveniently because, as Atticus explains, "the Stage is so very little."

We get a glimpse of tiremen lighting candles at an adult hall playhouse in Jonson's *The Staple of News* (London, 1631), performed around February 1626, when the King's men occupied Blackfriars.[9] In the induction, four lady gossips decide that they will sit on the stage like their male counterparts. But when *"The Tire-men enter to mend the lights,"* the Prologue must calm them: *"Nay, start not Ladies, these carry no fireworkes to fright you, but a Torch i' their hands, to giue light to the businesse."* At the same time, we hear the Book-holder (probably from within the tiring-house) giving the tiremen directions: *"Mend your lights, Gentlemen. Master Prologue, beginne."*[10] While the theater at St. Paul's was small enough to require only one tireman, the prestigious Blackfriars some twenty years later lavished two or more men to attend to the lights. Yet, the use of the word "mend" here may imply that some of the candles were already burning before the prologue began. Whether daylight or minimal candlelight illuminated the auditorium, it must be true that there was enough illumination to permit spectators to find their seats and admire each others' clothes as well as to allow the actors to begin the induction without a full complement of candlelight. The ladies in *The Staple of News* enjoy a lively conversation and the gallants in *What You Will* sit *"a good while"* before the candles are lighted, and one doubts such actions took place in utter darkness.

At court, where money was of less concern, most of the candles were also not lit until the play or masque was ready to begin. When Orazio Busino went to Whitehall in January 1618, he arrived two hours before the king was due to appear because he wanted to view the ladies at his leisure. When he entered the first Jacobean banqueting house around 8 P.M., "there was little light, as if it were the twilight of dusk or dawn," he recalled, because the two rows of lights "were to be lit [only] at the proper time."[11] If the court did not squander money on artificial light at night, then one doubts that the King's men were lavish with candlelight in the early afternoon before their plays began.

The corresponding extinction of candles is called for by a stage direction in a collection of three plays published after the Restoration as the *Gratiae Theatrales* (London, 1662).[12] In the epilogue to the first play, *Thorney-Abbey*, the death of the hero is associated with the putting out of candles. We are reminded that "death betides to Men, and Tapers too," after which, in a footnoted stage direction, it is explained that " *Here the Candles are putting out*" (*6ᵛ). Given the vagaries of the epilogue's auspices, we cannot claim it necessarily refers to either pre- or post-Interregnum playhouses. Whatever the venue, the practice of quickly putting out the candles at the conclusion complements the lighting of candles immediately before the play was to begin and, moreover, speaks to the probability that there was sufficient window light or, in the depth of winter, sufficient numbers of wall sconces left to burn in the auditorium and exit passages to ensure that spectators could make their way home without tripping over each other in the dark.

Regarding the kinds of lighting utensils used, private playhouse lighting does not seem to differ much from that provided by the Elizabethan Revels Office. Surviving playtexts, inductions, preludes, and epilogues mention only candles and the general term "lights" in regard to artificial illumination for visibility. These references are not plentiful, but with corroboration coming from the Revels Office accounts, they take precedence as evidence over vague allusions to torches, lamps, and cressets in an even smaller number of non-playhouse sources. In Francis Lenton's satiric pamphlet *The Young Gallant's Whirligig*, for example, we hear that the penniless hero has sold the fine clothes that once "glistred in the Torchy Fryers."[13] But the phrase "Torchy Fryers" has obviously been compressed to fit the iambic pentameter and to rhyme with the preceding line. It probably connoted no more than an artificial—that is, a burning—method of illumination. Similarly, a phrase like "lamps, which at a play," found in George Wither's *Faire-Virtue*, may privilege poetic rhythm over careful classification of lighting utensils.[14] Oil was so expensive that even the wealthiest homes regularly did without lamps; even at court we have seen that their use was confined to occasional colored lighting effects, effects that were not reproduced at the private playhouses.

Management of Artificial Light

Another description of a young gallant in the playhouse mentions candles and apparently refers to two chandeliers over the stage. In one of Thomas Overbury's popular character sketches, published around 1615, a stage-sitting "Phantastique" shows off his clothes, "and when the Play is done, if you but mark his rising, 'tis a kind of walking Epilogue between the two Candles, to know if his Suite may passe for currant."[15] Since stage-sitters entered and exited through the tiring-house and not from the pit,[16] Overbury is making the point that the gallant is ostentatiously parading over the stage instead of modestly retiring directly through the tiring-house wall. In fact, the gallant brazenly walks to the place from which the epilogue was spoken, presumably downstage center and "between the two Candles." There are several possible interpretations of the passage. Perhaps candlesticks or wall sconces were positioned to the sides of the stage, and the area "between the two Candles" was simply the stage itself. W. A. Armstrong takes the scene in *The Changeling* (London, 1653) where De Flores stabs Alonzo as proof of such sconces.[17] De Flores induces his victim to turn his back by inviting him to "take speciall notice of that Sconce before you" (D4). But Armstrong has misunderstood the passage: "The Sconce," as Alonzo himself later comments, is part of the "impregnable Fort" he is touring, which can be seen through a window (D3ᵛ).[18] In fact, the term "sconce" was not applied to wall brackets until the Restoration. The Revels Office called such equipment "plates for walls," "wallers," and the like, and other references to sconces in such plays as *The Malcontent* ("*Enter* Mendoza *with a sconce*" [C4ᵛ]) refer not to permanent wall mountings but to a kind of portable lantern. We cannot be sure wall brackets never lit the stage, but it should be pointed out that sconces in the Restoration theater were relegated to the walls of the auditorium and only later and on special occasions placed near the stage. Congreve described a brilliantly lit gala performance at Dorset Garden in 1701 that "was all hung with sconces of wax-candles, besides the common branches of lights usual in the playhouses."[19]

The remaining interpretation of Overbury's "two Candles" is that two chandeliers hung symmetrically above the stage and that actors speaking epilogues downstage center would thereby be standing "between" them. This arrangement is corroborated by *The Wits* frontispiece but by no other pre-Restoration source. Still, the interpretation of Overbury's candles as stage chandeliers meets with less countervailing evidence than does thinking of them as floor candlesticks or wall brackets and is supported by the Revels Office's persistent use of three or four great branches hanging above early court performances.

The Wits frontispiece (1662) shows two branched chandeliers suspended by long wires over the left and right edges of a narrow thrust stage (see fig. 23). Each chandelier supports eight candles with drip pans beneath each socket. The chandeliers appear to hang rather low to the stage, but the artist has handled the perspective crudely. While the vantage point of the drawing and the position of the chandeliers would seem to indicate we are looking down on the branches, they are nevertheless drawn from the point of view of someone looking up at them. It may be that the branches were actually higher than is shown but that the artist lowered them so as to simplify rendering the gallery above the stage. The principal light comes from the actors' right but, judging by the shadows, not from the branch there. Apparently, daylight was plentiful from that direction. Crosshatching indicates that the rear of the stage was dimmer than the front, but the six double-wick lamps serving as footlights are not, again from the shadows cast at the characters' feet and on the hostess's gown, very bright in comparison to the sunlight. The relevance of *The Wits* frontispiece to pre-Interregnum playhouses is uncertain. In his edition, J. J. Elson concludes that the drawing was "purely a work of the artist's imagination" and not a rendering of "the actual setting in which some furtive Commonwealth shows were given."[20] John Astington has recently traced several iconographic sources for the picture and concludes that, while it was probably based on pre-1660s theatrical style, it should not be considered evidence for any particular theater.[21] Although no trace of English footlights predates *The Wits* frontispiece, its articulation of sunlight and candlelight is congruous with what we have conjectured was typical of pre-Restoration hall lighting.

We get a notion of the personnel required to tend to burning candles in the masque scene of *The Two Merry Milkmaids* (1620). Lodwicke is seen reviewing the arrangements just before his private masque is to begin. He orders his gentleman usher, "Pray haue a care those lights be not offensiue vnto the Ladies, they hang suspiciously." By "offensiue," he means not only that the candles could fall or drip on the audience but also that leaning candles smoked profusely, creating an unpleasant odor. The gentleman usher delegates the job to an usher; "Looke to those lights I pray," he says, "my Lord is very angry, fearing they might do trespasse." The usher in turn repeats the order to a groom, whereupon the groom replies, "They shall sir, where's the fellow heere shud looke vnto these lights, things are done so vntowardly." After a short while, we get the stage direction, "*Enter* Ferdinand [the gentleman usher], Groomes *with Torches.*"[22]

At the height of its financial success in 1624, the King's men boasted twenty-one hirelings, most of whom were actors and musicians. When not required onstage or in the music room, some may have been pressed into service as candle-snuffers, but a citation from the praeludium to *The Careless Shepherdess* implies only a few attendants — or even one — regularly saw to the candles at Salisbury Court around 1638. Commenting on the poverty of most playwrights, a citizen opines:

> I do not think but I shall shortly see
> One Poet sue to keep the door, another
> To be prompter, a third to snuff the candles.[23]

Considering the disparity in available personnel, the private theater companies could rely on only a fraction of the number of lighting attendants at court and in noble houses. Other troupes had even fewer hirelings at their disposal than the King's men. It is unlikely, therefore, that enough attendants were present to watch lights spread generously throughout the entire theater.

Because the major concern was the dripping of hot tallow, lights hanging over spectators were probably avoided. It would have been awkward and distracting to raise ladders or to lower branches in the auditorium to snuff smoking or dripping candles during the performance. At his Italian court theater, Sabbattini assigned to each chandelier in the auditorium one "reliable person" equipped with "two poles long enough to reach the candle tops." "On one of the poles is a taper for lighting," he explains; "on the other pole is a sponge soaked in water . . . to extinguish a candle that begins to drip because it is not burning evenly."[24] As it is unlikely that the Jacobean private theater companies could spare this many attendants to watch branches hanging above the pit, it is improbable that the twenty-eight branches common to early court plays were transferred *en masse* to the private playhouses. If there were artificial lights in the pit, they were more likely to have been placed to the sides and near the boxes. This arrangement, at any rate, was the practice after the Restoration: at Wren's Drury Lane (1674), the scenes behind the proscenium arch were lit by four branches (each with twelve candles), the apron stage by two similar branches, and the house by approximately sixteen sconces, holding two or four candles each, which were probably placed on the pillars supporting the galleries.[25] Indeed, there is no evidence of a chandelier hanging above the pit in London until Garrick's tenure at Drury Lane in the mid-eighteenth century, when less troublesome wax candles were used.

The candles burning above the stage would also have required attention during performances. The tiremen who lit and extinguished the lights at the beginning and end of the play presumably would also emerge from the tiring-house to trim or extinguish sputtering candles during act breaks or even during the action. Or the actors, who would have been the unhappy targets of falling candle drippings, may well have mended bothersome candles themselves. We have no specific reports of actors performing this chore before the Restoration, but after it there are occasional references to the players snuffing the candles even while they acted.[26]

Salisbury Court

We are fortunate in that, for Salisbury Court in 1639, we can compare the total amount of money spent on lighting with that spent at court. In 1849, Peter Cunningham published a transcription of a series of articles endorsed "Instructions Touching Salesbery Co^rt Playhouse, 14 Septem., 1639," which contrasted an old and a new system of dividing the playhouse's expenses among the housekeepers and the actors. One of the articles explains that, while the housekeepers had formerly not paid anything for illumination, they now agreed to pay "Halfe for lights, both waxe and Tallow, wch halfe all winter is near 5^s a day."[27] Since it is clear the articles were drawn up to convince the actors how generously the householders were going to treat them, we may assume that "near 5ˢ a day" is a generous, even an inflated, figure. In the following calculation, I adjust this half-expense to four shillings a day to allow for the householders' exaggeration. Because we know the average price of candles in the late Caroline period (sixpence a pound for tallow, two shillings a pound for wax) and their total cost (eight shillings), we can make a rough estimate of how many candles lit Salisbury Court if we make several assumptions as to the size and type of the candles used.

In allotting costs, I set aside two shillings of the daily total to account for backstage and rehearsal lights and for the torches that lit the candles and served as properties, as well as for miscellaneous expenses such as property lanterns, torches, squibs, matches, flints, tinderboxes, snuffers, douters, and general replacement and upkeep. If Salisbury Court replaced its equipment as often as the court did, two shillings would not be sufficient. The private playhouses gave as many as one hundred more performances a year than the court did, running up expenses day in and day out, after all. On the other hand, actors were not obliged to buy new branches every year, as the Revels Office often did. Since torches cost over a shilling apiece, two shillings is not too much to ascribe to miscellaneous lighting expenses.

In estimating the size of the candles employed at Salisbury Court, we may note that, although the Revels Office acquired several different sizes over the years, most candles at court weighed fourteen or sixteen ounces each. Given the budget at Salisbury Court, only three wax candles of this weight could have been purchased each day. But they would not have been completely consumed during a single performance. Presuming that as little wax and tallow was thrown away as possible, we may estimate a *maximum* number of sources of light by settling on the average size of candles that would be efficiently consumed during any one performance. A wax or tallow candle weighing six in the pound will burn for nearly four hours if it is well trimmed. But if left to gutter and drip, a good half of the fuel is wasted, and the candles will burn less than two hours. Therefore, I take it as the smallest candle that would have been practical in the private playhouses. A candle weighing six in the pound is a little more than ten inches long and almost three-quarters of an inch in diameter. The candles in *The Wits* frontispiece are apparently close to this size.

By means of such assumptions, then, we may calculate the approximate number of candles at Salisbury Court. If all the candles were of wax, general illumination was provided by a maximum of eighteen candles. If three-quarters were of wax and one-quarter tallow, then there would have been fifteen wax candles and five tallow candles for the same amount of money. But if the number of wax and tallow were equal, then there could have been fourteen candles of each. And if only one-quarter were of wax and three-quarters tallow, then there could have been as many as ten wax candles and thirty tallow ones.

The 1639 articles do not record the shares of wax and tallow at Salisbury Court. Since wax had largely supplanted tallow in the overhead branches at court some seven years earlier, we might guess that more than just a few wax lights were employed and that the total number of candles was, therefore, closer to twenty or thirty than forty. The articles' specification of lights, "both waxe and Tallow," suggests more than a token use of wax candles. But our modern inclination toward finding evolutionary processes everywhere may lead us astray in accounting for a shift from tallow to wax. As early as the premiere of Fletcher's *The Faithful Shepherdess* at Blackfriars in 1608, his friend Beaumont deplored spectators who based their opinions of plays on such ephemera as whether "the wax-lights be new that day."[28] Beaumont confirms that large wax candles could be reused, but I do not know that we can take him to mean that wax was regularly used at the early children's playhouses. That candles were reused shows that economy was an important consideration in the lighting. Beaumont's point is that the new wax lights were special enough to sway an uncritical spectator's judgment, especially at the premieres of plays. As late as 1667, Thomas Killigrew reported to Pepys "[t]hat the stage [of the remodeled Theater Royal, Bridges Street] is now by his pains a thousand times better and more glorious than ever heretofore. Now, wax-candles, and many of them; then, not above 3 *lb.* of tallow."[29] Three pounds of tallow makes only about eighteen candles of six in the pound, slightly less than appears to have been used at Salisbury Court in 1639 and slightly more than in *The Wits* frontispiece of 1662. To what period Killigrew was referring by "heretofore" and "then" is not beyond doubt. The Bridges Street theater was built in 1663 but closed by the plague and the great fire from 1665 to 1666, during which time Killigrew made the improvements he described to Pepys. He probably meant that tallow was used from 1663 to 1665, but he may be casting his mind back to the pre-Interregnum theaters he wrote for as a young man. The Bridges Street theater was approximately the same size as or a little larger than the average pre-Interregnum hall theater.[30] Killigrew obviously thought three pounds of tallow insufficient for a playhouse of these dimensions, but he nonetheless illustrates that large numbers of wax candles were not standard equipment before 1667.

Whatever the proportions of wax and tallow, it is plain that Salisbury Court employed only about one-tenth the number of candles used at the Caroline court—roughly thirty, say, as contrasted with over two hundred. We do not know the exact dimensions of the theater at Salisbury Court, although according to a 1629 indenture, the playhouse sat on a plot of land 42 by 140 feet; a chamber built over the old theater in 1660 was 40 feet square.[31] If its width were something close to 40 or 42 feet, then this dimension would approximate the widths of other halls and theaters—Hampton Court (40), Middle Temple (40), second Blackfriars (46), Jones's playhouse (42), and Whitefriars (35). Given the similarity in sizes, one can best explain the reduction in the number of candles from court to private theater practice by assuming that the candles were concentrated near the stage and that the professional playhouse auditoriums made do with window light or minimal candlelight.

A further implication of the Salisbury Court article is that candles seem to have been used in the winter but not necessarily in the summer. The article speaks of lighting expenses incurred "all winter," but we have records of plays produced there in the late summertime.[32] In fact, there is reason to believe that the occupants of Salisbury Court at that time, Queen Henrietta's men, performed there regularly during the summer because they had no alternate outdoor venue and do not seem to have made provincial summer tours.[33] We are left to assume that summer plays required few or no artificial light at all. If the windows at Salisbury Court were anywhere near as large as the windows in surviving halls, artificial light would certainly not have been necessary in the summer. In winter, early sunsets and overcast days were so frequent, evidently, that candles were lit daily as a matter of course.

We should like to have as detailed figures of lighting expenditures for other theaters. Perhaps some weight can be given to the fact that in enumerating the various categories of expenses, legal documents connected with both the second Blackfriars and Whitefriars mention lights near the end of their lists. In a lawsuit between the sharers and hireling actors employed by the King's men, for instance, the cost of running both the Globe and Blackfriars in 1635 is given as nine hundred or one thousand pounds a year, including "wages to hired men & boyes musicke light*es* &c."[34] Similarly, in the articles of agreement between the sharers of the Whitefriars signed 10 March 1608, the playhouse's expenses are listed as "gatherers, the wages, the Childrens bourd, musique, booke keeper, tyreman, tyrewoman, lights, the Maister of the revell's Duties, and all other things needefull."[35] From these we can say that lighting was not the major expense of the companies.

Cockpit-in-Court

We have no records of day-to-day expenses for candles at the Cockpit-in-Court at Whitehall, but for its renovation in the early 1630s we have detailed Office of Works accounts that mention the fixtures in which candles were placed. Although it had long been a venue for professionally produced drama, the Cockpit-in-Court apparently reopened in November 1630 with new facilities, but the first we hear of its lighting arrangements occurs the following May when the Revels accounts mention removing and then hanging branches. In accounts for the year October 1631 through September 1632, no less than fifteen candelabra or chandeliers are mentioned. John De Critz, His Majesty's Sergeant Painter, was paid "for diuers times Cullouring in Gould cullo:^{r} the Braunches of xv^e Candlesticks in the Cockpitt."[36] Of these fifteen branches, twelve were placed near the stage and are again differentiated as small and great: "tenn smaller and twoe greater then thother about and before the Stage." An unspecified number of great branches—perhaps the remaining three of the fifteen De Critz painted—were placed "in the front of the stage." The ten new fixtures were "Candlestickes of Iron," beautifully garnished at a cost of thirty shillings each. But the heat or dripping of the candles obliged De Critz to regild all the branches several times. The next year, the Office of Works purchased two very expensive chandeliers with "diverse branches for the Cockpit" at a total cost of over thirteen pounds. I gather these replaced either the "twoe greater" branches "about and before the Stage" or the unspecified number of "great Braunches in the front of the stage." But in the very next year, 1633–34, the Revels Office again ordered two great branches at a cost of sixteen pounds.

The distinctions, if any, between "about," "before," and "in the front of" the stage are rather fine. Small branches could have been attached to the *scaena frons* or the proscenium wall and have been considered spread "about" the acting area. In November 1660, when the Cockpit was again refurbished, "twenty faire gillt Branches wth three Socketts in each for Candles and Six Sconces for the Passages that are darke" were ordered.[37] If these Restoration fixtures resembled pre-Commonwealth ones, we could estimate that the ten small branches held thirty candles and that the two greater ones held perhaps another thirty, with three more branches lighting other parts of the theater. Perhaps these last three branches lit the auditorium, but the first we specifically hear of lights near the audience is in the 1634–35 Revels accounts, which call for twelve relatively inexpensive "great wallers for y[e] gallery at y[e] Cockpitt" as well as "24 Platts made for y[e] Cockpitt for wax lights." The positioning of large lights in the gallery suggests that it was poorly lit by lights near the stage and by the four windows piercing the gallery walls (see fig. 33).

If two galleries encircled the Cockpit auditorium, one is inclined to put six wallers in each gallery, although, because each gallery was divided into only five bays, the placement of six fixtures would have been arithmetically inconvenient. Perhaps the bay for the king's state had special lighting utensils; elsewhere in the accounts for that year we hear of two "Candlesticks for y[e] State," although they are not related specifically to the Cockpit. On the other hand, if most of the ambient light in the theater came from chandeliers overhead, the lower gallery would lie in deeper shadows than the upper gallery and would require more fixtures.

Articulation of Light

Several descriptions of court lighting tell us that the hall was "as bright as day," or words to that effect. But in terms of measurable illumination, a hall cannot accommodate enough candles to equal the strength of average daylight. Because subjective brightness is a function of the cube root of actual brightness, the number of candles necessary for even small increases in perceived brightness increases geometrically. To double the apparent brightness of an actor, one needs to light him with eight times as many candles (from the same distance).[38] The difficulty in attempting to equal the strength of sunlight by means of candlelight lies, therefore, in the physical limitation that a hall would need to be literally filled with candles. Apart from leaving little room for the actors or audience, so many burning candles would quickly deplete the oxygen and the candles would go out of their own accord and leave the audience gasping. What the simile means, of course, is that compared to the artificial light common to most seventeenth-century rooms, the light on the theatrical scene at court was much brighter.

As we saw in the consideration of artificial light in the amphitheaters, differences in the perception of brightness are functions of the average level of light to which one has adapted. Unlike modern light bulbs, candles flicker and yield varying amounts of light. These variations occasionally distract our attention, but, more important, they make it difficult for the pupil of the eye to adjust to one comfortable and efficient aperture. The eye can adapt to the brightest extreme of a variable light source within seconds, but it cannot adapt to the lowest extreme unless variations are eliminated and a low level of light is sustained for many minutes. In fluctuating light, then, the eye will adapt to the greatest and not the least amount of light. In consequence, a flickering source of light will appear dimmer than its average strength would suggest, especially when the number of candles is small and the fluctuations are greater. The more candles there are, the less pronounced the variation and the better the eye can adapt to its most efficient light-gathering capability. Conversely, when candles are lit in a room where sunlight is plentiful, the pupil of the eye will not dilate so as to perceive the candlelight efficiently but will close down to an aperture at which it may comfortably view the brighter sunlight. This is why candles seem so much dimmer during the day. An assertion that candlelight is as bright as daylight can only be made at night, therefore, when there is no daylight to reduce the size of the pupil.

In the private playhouses we have been investigating, daylight was more powerful than candlelight except after sunset. If we assume that thirty-two candles hung in chandeliers ten feet above the Jones playhouse, then the ratio of stage light from artificial and natural sources on a typical overcast afternoon at 3 P.M. in autumn is around one to twenty. That is to say, the window light was, on average, twenty times stronger than the candlelight in terms of measurable brightness. The contributions of each to the overall illumination may be imagined by replacing the candles with the more familiar light bulb. Comparisons between candles and electric filament lamps are not especially productive unless the candles are relatively close together and the light bulbs are small. One sixty-watt light bulb will produce a light flux nearly equal to that of one hundred candles. But while the light near an electric lamp will be brilliant, ten feet away the light will be only one-hundredth as strong. The same principle holds true for candles, of course, but the large number of candles required to equal a single bulb can be spread over an area of some size, producing a low but evenly distributed articulation of light. Shakespeare needed no light meter to appreciate this phenomenon. The brightness of Juliet's cheek, he says during the balcony scene, would shame the most beautiful stars just "[a]s day-light doth a lampe" (*Romeo and Juliet*, Q2 D2). To him, even moonlight can outshine a candle. Nerissa in *The Merchant of Venice* remembers "when the moone shone we did not see the candle," from which instance Portia generalizes with her lawyer's gift for tautology, "So dooth the greater glory dim the lesse" (Q2 13). And while Wither's playhouse "lamps" were probably not true lamps, he nonetheless makes clear that they could add no luster

> To what Titan gaue before,
> Neither doth their pretty beamings
> Hinder ought his greater gleamings.[39]

The adaptation that permits the eye to become accustomed to a wide range of brightness also controls our ability to detect differences in brightness once the eye has adapted to a particular level of illumination. In bright daylight, this ability to perceive contrasts is great: the eye can see differences in brightness amounting to less than 1 percent of the average brightness to which it has adapted. But in the less brilliant light of the private playhouses, the eye perceives differences in brightness only when they are greater than 10 percent of the average level of illumination. Thus, while the eye can readily adapt to the darkness indoors, it cannot see details as efficiently. As the average level of brightness decreases arithmetically, one's ability to see contrasts and to differentiate brightnesses decreases geometrically, and objects of various colors, shapes, and reflectances tend to merge together in a monotonously undifferentiated gray picture. In darkness, as John Heywood retold the old saw,

> The faire and the foule, by darke are lyke store.
> *When all candels be out, all cats be grey.*
> *All thyngs are then of one colour, as who say.*[40]

In the hall playhouses where the amount of daylight was at best only 10 percent of the amount at the amphitheaters, the flames of the candles replaced the highlights that the eye could not normally find indoors. The candles afforded relief from the monotony of the interior, just as "accent lights" lend refreshing contrasts to contemporary rooms without raising the general level of illumination. The candles in the private playhouses served not so much to duplicate as to imitate the more varied light outdoors.

In experiments conducted in various Tudor halls, I found that one hour before dusk, the amount of natural light on a four-foot-high stage placed near one end of a large hall was less than ten footcandles. At sunset, the average level of illumination onstage was less than one footcandle. In such dim light, actors on a stage could clearly be made out; but as the light waned, their faces lost definition and quick movements became blurred. Indeed, it was relatively easy to let the eye wander away from the actors, and a test audience reported that they sometimes found themselves looking elsewhere or attending only to the words.

An hour before sunset, several dozen candles burning overhead did not add appreciably to the *perceived* amount of brightness onstage, but they nevertheless created a warmer, more pleasing atmosphere and helped to focus the gaze of the spectator toward the stage, where the candles burning overhead served to "frame" the playing space and invite spectators to focus their attention toward the actors. Something very similar to this effect also occurred at the amphitheaters, where, as I have noted, a pleasing orange glow often surrounded the heavens at dusk. In the waning natural light in the hall playhouses, artificial light from above helped to define the outline of each actor, especially by articulating the shape of the players' heads, hats, and shoulders. The importance that Andrew Gurr has recently attached to Shakespearean hats as a means of conveying vital information to the audience was underscored by these experiments, which showed how much each hat, when lit from above, could define a character's physical presence onstage even in dim light.[41]

Near the conclusions of many performances in the depth of winter, the candlelight inevitably took on a larger burden of the illumination, and in my experiments I attempted to duplicate various configurations of artificial light at the hall playhouses after sunset. The variables were the number and placement of the candles, the size of the hall, and the reflectivity of the interior walls and ceiling. In a very small hall (thirty by forty feet) with light-colored walls and with three dozen candles arranged near the front of the stage, an entirely adequate, even beautiful, illumination prevailed. But in a larger hall with high, stained-timber ceilings and with only two dozen candles burning ten feet above the stage, measurable brightness decreased to fractions of one footcandle after sunset. Only large, slow gestures could be clearly read from the auditorium. A half-hour past sunset, the actors on the stage appeared to modern eyes as so many presences rather than persons.

Apart from the number of candles, the reflectance of the ceiling above the stage and its distance from the candles were most crucial. A light-colored roof or cloth stretched above the stage but still fairly close to the candles could increase the amount of light on the actors by as much as 10 to 20 percent. Apart from any iconographic functions, cloths and ceilings could serve to reflect candlelight and alleviate glare, especially in theaters and banqueting houses intended largely for nighttime presentations.

The higher the branches were hung, the less glare but also the less light on the actors—indeed, the less light by the inverse square of the increased distance. We do not know how high the branches were hung in the professional playhouses, but the wires that were stretched across the hall at Hampton Court must have been eighteen or nineteen feet above the floor if they were attached to the cornices running along the sidewalls. Assuming that the candles hung a few feet below these wires and that the stage was four or five feet high, then the maximum height of the candles above the stage floor was eleven or twelve feet. Corroboration of this estimate came in my experiments, where the optimum height of the candles also fell within this narrow range. Because raising the branches from ten feet to twelve feet, say, reduced the amount of light on the actors by nearly 30 percent but reduced glare for spectators by less than 10 percent, it became clear that it was inefficient to hang the branches much higher than twelve feet above the stage floor.[42] With the branches lower than nine feet, glare reduced visibility by upwards of 50 percent.

One of the most interesting results of these experiments concerned the placement of the candles and its relationship to the movement of the actors. To achieve the best visibility, one might have thought that the candles should be positioned as close as possible to the actors, directly over the middle or front half of the stage. But it was clear that a better location for the branches was a yard or two forward of the front edge of the stage, just as in the modern theater, where the principal light emanates from instruments hanging above the audience and projecting down at a forty-five- to sixty-degree angle to the stage.

In one experiment with thirty-two candles burning in four chandeliers placed ten feet above the front of the stage (and supplying the only light in the hall), it was found that the actors' faces were best seen when they stood approximately two yards upstage of the hanging branches. When they stood directly underneath the branches, where one would have expected the best light, only the tops of their heads and shoulders were clearly seen while their faces and the fronts of their bodies lay in shadows. This poor illumination directly underneath the branches was due not only to the perpendicular angle of the light but also to the excessive amount of light that was obstructed by the branches, the bodies of the candles themselves, and the drip pans beneath them. Thus, narrow cones of shadow, with their apices at each flame, descended perpendicularly down from the candles, making the area directly below the branches one of the worst locations to stand if one wanted to be well illuminated.

Moving a yard or two upstage brought an actor out of this shadow and retained enough top light to define his silhouette. But as actors moved still farther to the rear of the stage, they began to disappear in darkness. At only three yards upstage of the lights, measurable brightness on the actors decreased by half and perceived brightness by more than two-thirds, because the steady glare of the candles made them seem dimmer by contrast. When candlelight served as the only mode of illumination, therefore, certain limitations in the range of the actors' movements imposed themselves. Whereas in the mixed natural and artificial light before sunset, the actors were adequately lit wherever they moved onstage, the elimination of general natural light obliged the actors to remain relatively close (but not too close) to a hanging chandelier in order to be seen. Even adding chandeliers farther upstage did not appreciably alleviate this problem, because these instruments only added backlight and produced yet more glare.

This limitation on an actor's mobility could be temporarily alleviated by his carrying a hand-held light illuminating his face, and it may be that early modern actors employed this trick toward the end of their nighttime performances, as when, for example, the sleepwalking Lady Macbeth carried a candle during a nighttime performance of *Macbeth* that was likely given at Hampton Court on 7 August 1606. At the daytime playhouses, on the other hand, the actor playing Lady Macbeth was free to move wherever he wished. Thus, the artificial lighting and time of performance affected not just the atmosphere of the playhouse but also the movements and, in a certain sense, the acting style of the players.

Given the widely accepted progression from what is usually described as an older, presentational style of acting to modern realism, we tend to assume that seventeenth-century acting was likely presentational. This may well be true, at least in comparison to the acting we know, but the general, overall lighting that prevailed in most seventeenth-century playhouses may give indirect evidence of a more natural style than is sometimes thought. The gradual delay in performance time by the early eighteenth century and the resulting elimination of all daylight in the theaters necessitated a different playing style near the chandeliers and (eventually) footlights than had been true in the early seventeenth century, when a more widely diffused light allowed actors to be seen no matter where they stood onstage. When Denis Diderot asked Madame Riccoboni of the Paris Théâtre Italien in 1758 why actors could not move all over the stage in the bourgeois settings he advocated, she replied that the faces of the actors were not visible three feet from the lamps.[43] But by the end of the eighteenth century, the introduction of more and more lights about and over the stage allowed the actors once again to move away from the footlights. One of the reasons Mrs. Siddons's famous innovation with Lady Macbeth's taper was possible was that, by 1785, Drury Lane boasted seventy-two footlights and dozens of candles illuminating the stage, both from above and from the side wings. In the early eighteenth century, Mrs. Pritchard had been obliged to carry Lady Macbeth's taper with her while she sleepwalked the gloomy recesses of the stage. But citing the "impracticability" of washing out a damned spot while juggling a candlestick, Mrs. Siddons caused an uproar by putting the candle down—business made possible, in part, by the increased visibility she enjoyed wherever she walked, particular at either side of the stage.[44] The evenly distributed illumination at the end of the eighteenth century was, in effect, a return to the diffused illumination at both the public and private playhouses in the early seventeenth century.

In the absence of window light, however, the movements of Jacobean and Caroline actors would, in one respect, have appeared more artificial to us than for later actors. If the only light shining on the actors came from branches above them, then the actors would be obliged to hold their heads high in order to be seen. In my experiments, as actors moved closer to the hanging branches, they had to tilt their heads back lest their faces disappear in shadows, creating an effect (at least for us) of theatrical posturing. Later seventeenth-century theaters attempted to solve this problem by the introduction of footlights and, in the eighteenth century when nighttime performances became the rule, by light emanating from the side wings. Both these methods of introducing artificial sidelight were simply a way of replacing the gently angled window light of pre-Interregnum afternoon performances.

Although the stage would be nominally brighter that the rest of the playhouse after sunset, we must not think of the stage as a modern showcase where the audience's attention was drawn toward beautiful pictures behind a proscenium frame. Except for some costumes and properties, the environment more nearly approximated that of a lecture room today, where overhead artificial light normally supplements the window light. In comparing hall playhouse lighting with our own theatrical illumination, we must remember that our psychological associations with candles were not shared by Renaissance Londoners. There was nothing quaint, old-fashioned, or romantic about candles to them. For us, the flickering subtlety of candles may call up feelings of poignant sophistication or natural warmth or exquisite loneliness. But to the spectators at the private playhouses, the effect was rather the reverse. Insofar as the candles were few in number, the audience found itself in the dreary, dull light they saw every day in their homes, businesses, and inns. But insofar as the candles at court, say, were many and provided bright, overall illumination, early modern spectators could be deeply impressed. But even at court, there was nothing exotic about the brilliance. At most, it struck the spectators as rich and extravagant, sometimes gorgeous, but never precious or theatrical. In modern theaters where stage light is produced by instruments especially designed for the purpose, private playhouse illumination cannot be duplicated by placing spotlights or even chandeliers in plain view of the audience. These lights have different connotations for us than they did for Shakespeare's public.

Comparing Hall and Amphitheater Illumination

In imagining the effect of the illumination systems indoors and outdoors, we may tend, perhaps, to make more of a distinction between them than is borne out by the evidence. In fact, the two lighting systems shared many similarities. Daylight entered each kind of theater from approximately the same angles and directions. Just as a spectator standing in the yard at a public playhouse would perceive a bright glow of light above the heavens, so also would a spectator at the private playhouses perceive bright light emanating from the branches hanging above the actors. The top and back lighting shining into an amphitheater toward sunset was thus duplicated in the hall playhouse by either the hall's end window above the screen or by chandeliers glaring over the stage.

In consequence, I do not see that we must attribute any shift in dramatic style solely to indoor lighting when the King's men began taking up winter residence at Blackfriars in 1609. The King's men had been accustomed to performing indoors long before that. From 1594 to 1608, in fact, when we think of the company as playing outdoors, we have records of ninety-three indoor performances and at least twenty-eight more probable indoor performances in the provinces. In contrast, we know of only thirteen recorded performances outdoors—three at the Globe and ten at Newington Butts.[45] Although Andrew Gurr has defined some intriguing differences in the repertoires, rhetoric, and use of swordplay typical of the two kinds of playhouses, there is little to indicate that these differences were caused by distinct modes of illumination.[46] Nor can we necessarily lay any increase in subtlety or refinement in the acting to the charge of the candlelight. The strength of light indoors was on average less than that at the amphitheaters, and the flickering shadows in the hall playhouses can hardly have made it easier for the audience to catch subtle gestures than in the sunlight outdoors. If there was any difference in the acting styles, it may be attributed to the smaller size of the auditoriums, not the kind of lighting there.

But while we cannot argue any simple cause-and-effect relationship between candlelight and the style of the children's and later adults' indoor plays, we can think of such light as occasionally answering the needs of the drama. Especially at the conclusions of some indoor plays, one feels that the candlelight may have complemented the less profoundly tragic or comic resolutions that begin to take hold as the drama moved into the late Jacobean and Caroline periods. In the early outdoor plays, the waning sunlight can sometimes be construed as underscoring the finality of the hero's destruction in tragedy and the culmination and dissipation of the day's intrigue in comedy. The sun literally sets on the lives of Faustus and Lear and on the lovers' quarrels in *The Comedy of Errors* and *Friar Bacon and Friar Bungay*. But as tragedy moves indoors, there is, perhaps, a less profound feeling of loss or of the victory of the powers of nature over man. We may doubt that a prevalence of artificial light caused such shifts in tone, but we must consider the degree to which artificial light may have contributed to that new tone once it had been established. As for indoor comedy, we might say that the coming of night in many plays signals not so much the consummation of the lovers' desires as the satiric and self-conscious victory of the wits over their dupes, of artifice over nature. Of course, any new styles in playwriting were undoubtedly the result of social, intellectual, and political fashions rather than of particular theatrical ambiences, but it is easy to imagine such new plays making their points particularly well by candlelight.

But even if such generalizations apply to more than a few new plays written for the hall theaters, the old outdoor plays were frequently revived indoors. Thus, the lighting systems were obliged to fit a wide range of plays, and we would expect that the technical capabilities and dramatic conventions of the two lighting systems were not so very different from each other, except that indoor illumination was theoretically susceptible to more control than outdoor illumination. A 1638 woodcut from Nicola Sabbattini's *Pratica di fabricar scene e machine ne' teatri* shows two tin cylinders supported by cords and pulleys that can be raised and lowered over stage candles "[w]hen it is desired to darken the whole stage in a moment" (see fig. 34), but I have been unable to find any evidence confirming the use of such equipment in England, even at court.[47] No playtexts indicate that candles were dimmed or extinguished to give the impression of darkness or night, nor, conversely, that additional lights were lit to present brightness. As we have seen, changes in brightness at court were effected by the opening and closing of shutters, not by lighting and putting out candles.

Although candles could have been extinguished entirely in the indoor playhouses, there were several obstacles to the regular use of such a method for obtaining darkness. First, the putting-out of lights would not have pro-

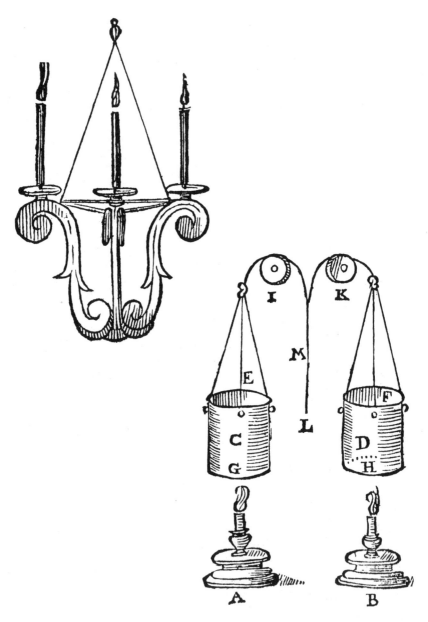

Fig. 34. Branched chandelier and a device for dimming candles. Prints of illustrations from Nicola Sabbattini, *Pratica de fabricar scene e machine ne' teatri* (Ravenna, 1638). University of Illinois Theatrical Print Collection.

duced a significant difference in the amount of light until near sunset or unless window shutters were also closed. Sunlight shining through the windows would have obliterated the effect. Second, a tireman would have had to come out of the tiring-house and then lower and extinguish the candles while the play was in progress. And when the "dark" scene was finished, he would have had to enter once again and relight them. If the night scenes lasted for entire acts, the extinction and relighting of the candles could be performed during the act breaks. But Caroline night scenes begin and end in the middle of acts or spill over into the next just as often as they coincide with act breaks. Moreover, no stage direction or prompter's marking in any text, printed or manuscript, even hints that the candles in the branches were put out or lit during the course of the play's action or its act breaks. The earliest English allusion to the extinction of lights for the sake of a play's mood comes after the Restoration when the Prologue to Dryden's *The Rival Queens* (1664) tells the audience that "reforming Poets of our Age . . . blow out Candles to give Light to th' Plot," an indication that the practice was new and not carried over from the Caroline theaters.[48]

Still another objection to the extinction of candles is that the wicks smolder for several minutes after they have been put out. The hot wicks continue "frying" the tallow, as Sir Fopling Flutter puts it, creating a disagreeable odor and not a little smoke. I assume candles could be more pleasantly extinguished after the Restoration because wax was by then the principal fuel above the stage. Before the Restoration, night scenes were suggested by properties associated with night and by pantomime—methods that worked as well indoors as out. Thus, while Thomas Heywood had the Greeks climb out of the Trojan horse *"as if groping in the darke"* at the Red Bull around 1612, Richard Brome could likewise direct a boy actor at the Cockpit in Drury Lane in 1639 to tail after another character *"as in the darke."*[49] There is a handful of stage directions calling for dimmer light in plays performed at the professional theaters, but these are associated with property lights and not with the general illumination. Jonson's *Catiline* (1611), for instance, contains the rubric, "A *darknesse comes ouer the place.*" Thinking of performances at both the Globe and Blackfriars, W. J. Lawrence guesses that darkness was effected by emitting smoke through a stage trap on the authority of a narrative description in the argument to the third act of Jonson's unfinished *The Sad Shepherd*: "There ariseth a mist sodainely . . . darkning all the place."[50]

Unfortunately, there is no evidence that *The Sad Shepherd* was performed anywhere, and there is no confirming stage direction in the text, which is so replete with stage directions that one would expect it. The rubric in *Catiline* sounds like a masque effect, and it corresponds in date to the masque scene in the King's men's *The Maid's Tragedy*, performed at Blackfriars, where the figure of "Night rises in mists."[51] But while mists might have accompanied a few night scenes, they perhaps represented night more by symbolism than illusionism. Mists might not have indicated night without a character named Night to point out the identification. The darkness in *Catiline* was also likely suggested rather than realized, because Jonson provides a convenient signal of darkness when, at the moment the argument calls for darkness, the text indicates that a "*vestall* flame" goes "out."[52] A modern lighting designer would lower the amount of light onstage at the same time the vestal flame goes out, but the next chapter will show that the general illumination of the theaters and the illumination emitted by property lights sometimes worked quite independently of each other.

The articulation of light in the hall theaters, then, could easily approximate that at the amphitheaters. A steady, diffused light without strong shadows emanated from high above the stage at nearly the same angles as it did outdoors. Despite the addition of a few dozen candles over the stage and perhaps a few in the darkest corners of the auditorium, the major component of the illumination was natural and, therefore, largely ungovernable. Artificial light may have lent a sense of refinement to some productions, but not necessarily so. Candles lit the gracious entertainments at court, to be sure, but as frequently they lit barroom revels in taverns and surreptitious "private" performances by some of the poorest companies of the period. The use of candles was neither something new in the history of theatrical production nor a technical improvement that enlarged the palette of artistic choices open to the actors and playwrights. Artificial light served to attenuate the extremes of the fluctuating daylight, but it made possible no major effect that could not be achieved by daylight alone. Instead, the candlelight represented a continuation and exploitation of long-standing theatrical traditions as well as a canny adaptation to the mutable fashions of early modern English playgoing.

9

PROPERTY LIGHTS AND
SPECIAL EFFECTS

BESIDES THE GENERAL ILLUMINATION of the playhouses, various kinds
of lighting utensils and fireworks were used as practical stage properties and in special effects. Stage directions call for familiar candles, tapers,
lanterns, and torches as well as such curiosities as suns, moons, blazing stars,
strokes of lightning, and burning cities. Many of these have been described
by W. J. Lawrence, Lee Mitchell, and others, together with assessments of
their functions as stage images.[1] It is not my purpose to go over the same
ground again. Rather, I wish to focus on the relationship between property
lights and the overall illumination in the playhouse. Further, I should like
to examine whether playwrights used property lights differently in the public and in the private playhouses. For unlike many stage properties, hand-
held lights and special lighting devices were more or less dependent upon
the general theatrical environment for their effect, and a dramatist's expert-
ise in using such property lights cannot be measured without reference to
the ambient light onstage.

In taking up such questions, difficulties arise that make definitive conclusions elusive. The most troubling problem is that we do not always know
which plays may be considered public and which private. The assurance
on a title page that a play was acted indoors or outdoors cannot be ignored,
of course, but at the same time, it is not proof that a printed stage direction
calling for a property light does not derive from a promptbook prepared for
a different venue. For example, W. A. Armstrong has taken the stage direction in Henry Chettle's *The Tragedy of Hoffman*, "*Enter as many as may be*

spar'd, with lights," to imply that the general illumination was not strong at the indoor Cockpit in Drury Lane, where the title page of the first edition says it was acted.[2] But who wrote this stage direction, and to what time and place does it refer? The tentative phrase *"as may be"* suggests it was written by the author and not by whoever prepared the authorial text for production. We know from Henslowe's diary that the Admiral's men paid Chettle for the play as early as 1602.[3] In this case, the stage direction may reflect production at the outdoor Fortune theater, that is, if Chettle was thinking of a certain theater in the first place.[4] On the other hand, the play bears evidence of revision, no doubt for its revival indoors at the Cockpit around 1630. Did the reviser write this stage direction, taking poor indoor light into account? One is inclined to doubt it, because he presumably would know the resources available and not have been so vague. And in any event, the stage direction does not necessarily point to a desire for more illumination. These lights are brought on for a formal scene of mourning at night, only forty-two lines long, near the end of the play. The *"as many as may be spar'd"* may signal only a wish for ceremony and spectacle while the lights themselves represent an attempt to indicate pretended darkness on a daylit stage.

A better example for Armstrong comes from Marston's *What You Will*, almost certainly written for the Paul's boys around 1601 and published in 1607. In the last act, a stage direction reads, *"Enter as many Pages with Torches as you can."*[5] But again, the theatrical situation reveals that Marston was primarily employing torches as signals for the coming of night and for the preparations preceding the play-within-a-play about to be performed. These lights are brought on only some 150 lines before the end of the play. One would think that if the playhouse illumination was consistently so dark as to warrant extra stage lights, they would have been introduced sooner. These torches may have compensated for waning daylight, but one searches in vain for a pattern of children's plays that brought on lights at the end. Had locutions like "so many as may be" regularly referred only to torchbearers, one might view their purpose differently. But such phrases often occur without any mention of lights. A stage direction for a wedding procession in Robert Armin's *The History of the Two Maids of More-clack, "Enter . . . some other women for shewe,"* gives a simpler reason for the employment of the largest cast possible.[6]

Functions of Property Lights

Thus, we encounter another problem in dealing with property lights—namely, we cannot always tell what their functions were supposed to be. Did the author of these stage directions want more light onstage, or did he merely want more characters and paraphernalia there? Was it the torchlight that produced the sense of ceremony, or only the large number of attendants holding lighting utensils? I doubt that Marston, Chettle, or Chettle's reviser saw any need to differentiate these functions, but for our purposes, we may distinguish among three roles that property lights played in relation to the general illumination—roles that I shall call illusionistic, realistic, and emblematic.

By illusionistic, I refer to stage light that attempted to duplicate lighting in the real world: dark for night, bright for day, artificial light for indoors, natural light for out-of-doors. The criterion here is whether the playwright attempted to approximate images the audience would recognize. By realistic, I refer not to verisimilitude of the illumination but to the use of property lighting instruments as realistic detail. In this second role, torches or tapers did not accomplish their theatrical purpose by means of light but by their appropriateness to the scene and the authenticity with which the actors used them. Whether or not Lady Macbeth's taper accurately reproduced the lighting of a castle at Dunsinane, for example, it nevertheless "realistically" signaled such information as the time of the sleepwalking scene (night), the place (indoors, since tapers were rarely used outside), and even the circumstance that her walk was unplanned, since she is not accompanied by the usual retinue of attendants lighting her way. By emblematic, I refer to uses of property lights not strictly verisimilar but figurative. Extensions of this category would include various iconographic associations—Lady Macbeth's taper construed as a token of her loneliness, for example—but mainly I have in mind the use of such lights as suns, moons, stars, and comets as signs of night and day, order and disorder, and the like.

Sometimes property lights serve theatrical purposes in two or three of these modes at once. In scenes of pomp, for instance, the introduction of many richly garnished lights could throw enough artificial light on the scene to create the illusion of the artificial light at a noble entertainment in a hall.

The lighting instruments themselves could contribute to the realistic decoration of the scene. And one might argue that, in some cases, the glittering torches emblematized the artifice and unnaturalness of the courts, for example, during such ironic masques as those in *Women Beware Women* (5.2), *The Maid's Tragedy* (1.2), and even the Mousetrap play in *Hamlet* (3.2). In these scenes, illusion, realism, and emblems work together to produce a concert of visual meaning. When torchbearers entered "so many as may be," the playwrights wanted both brilliance and a crowded stage, as well as some of the sophistication associated with torchlight.[7]

But in the more prevalent use of stage lights as a means of evoking darkness, the three modes can work against each other. Light emitted by the instruments brought onstage to add realistic detail obviously prevented the illusionistic depiction of night. Although this convention had been adumbrated in the daylit theaters of antiquity,[8] the remarkable aspect of the use of property lights in both the amphitheaters and hall playhouses is that indications of darkness were effected by the introduction of more, rather than less, light onto the stage. Light paradoxically represented darkness and as such must be accounted not illusionistic. But in another sense, the deployment of property lights was very realistic, because real people do light candles and torches when it gets dark. In other words, the action onstage was real enough, even if the illumination onstage was not. When torches and tapers were carried onstage to indicate that a scene was supposed to take place at night, the theatrical statement was that an *instrument* of light had been called into use. It was the instrument, or rather the imaginary need for the instrument, and not the light it produced that represented the darkness. Perhaps the actors sometimes carried unlit utensils, because the light they might produce would add little to, indeed would work against, the evocation of darkness. An experiment at the new Globe playhouse showed that while the flame of a candle was visible in daylight, its light flux was not. On windy days especially, the actors might even have had difficulty in keeping open-flamed candles lit. Even a good, modern candle blew out more than once as I walked across the new Globe stage.

Conventions of Indoor and Outdoor Illumination

Yet in the hall playhouses, one would think that the illumination provided by stage lights was sometimes illusionistic, because it was the same light that illuminated all halls at night. W. J. Lawrence, for one, was convinced that the "rear stage" was in such an obscure position that the audience's "inconvenience . . . almost invariably demanded the bringing in of lights at the commencement of all inner [stage] scenes." Later, Lawrence changed his mind and admitted that lights were brought on just as frequently for what he calls "outer" scenes. But he continued to argue that the inner stage and tiring-house wall made the artificial illumination emanating from these brought-on lights look more real.[9] Similarly, Harley Granville-Barker thought that Imogen's taper in the bedroom scene of *Cymbeline* was doubly effective because it not only helped to symbolize her chastity but also joined with the candlelight already present to produce the illusion of the intimate artificial light in her bedroom.[10]

But the general illumination of any playhouse had to shine on both indoor and outdoor scenes. If we follow Lawrence's and Granville-Barker's theory to its logical conclusion, then we should have a situation where indoor scenes were played illusionistically at Blackfriars and conventionally at the Globe, while outdoor scenes were played illusionistically at the Globe and conventionally at Blackfriars. There is a marginal increase of indoor scenes in children's theater drama but no inkling of a reversal in the conventions of lighting as the actors performed indoors. Distinctions in location were effected by what I am calling realism, not by illusion. When a scene was supposed to take place indoors, lights designed for indoor use were brought on. By far the most common lights introduced into scenes Lawrence calls "inner" were tapers, which were typically used as night-lights in bedrooms and tents. Like Imogen and Lady Macbeth, Evadne (*The Maid's Tragedy*, 5.1), Clarinda (*Lovers' Progress*, 3.1), and Merione (*The Queen of Corinth*, 3.2) have tapers by their beds. When Cassius meets Brutus in his tent, they sit near a taper that, after Brutus retires and Caesar's ghost appears, grows dim— "How ill this Taper burnes" (F 2288).[11] When the scenes shift to outdoors, torches and lanterns replace tapers. In the first two scenes of *Othello*, we get no less than three calls for torches as the characters hurry to the council chamber; once inside, the action is accompanied only by "lights." At the end of the play, as Alan Dessen points out, Iago carries a torch in act 5, scene 1, indicating an outdoor scene, whereas Othello carries a candle into Desdemona's chamber in act 5, scene 2.[12] Whether the audience was to think of the scene as indoors or outdoors was determined by the *type* of lighting utensil, not by its light. In using the shape of the utensils rather than the quality or quantity of the light they produced to help set the scene, the actors were consequently free to use the same staging in whatever general light they found themselves.

Depending on how it was described, a lighting utensil could signal multiple locations, and dramatists could emphasize the atmosphere of first one and then another location. For example, Dessen has also noted the inconsistency that, although the monument scene of *Much Ado about Nothing* (5.3) begins with an entrance of *"three or four with tapers,"* indicating an indoor monument, later, when day breaks, Don Pedro orders, "put your torches out" (Q 12ᵛ), indicating an outdoor location.[13] But here Shakespeare is employing a secondary association of tapers—their connection with religious locations and ceremonies. Thus, identical lighting instruments are called tapers when Shakespeare emphasizes their sacred character but are called torches when the mood turns romantic. Similarly, in act 3, scene 1, of *Antonio's Revenge* (1600, Paul's), tapers accompany Andrugio's hearse to church; but once his son Antonio plots revenge, pages reenter with torches instead of tapers. The one Shakespearean example of tapers used in a simple outdoor scene occurs in 2 *Henry VI*, when the barefoot Eleanor carries a burning taper in "open penance" (2.4), but here the taper's association with religious ceremony takes precedence over its more typical use as a signal of place.

In the hall playhouses, then, where one might have expected that lights carried onstage were used to amplify the existing light, the same practice of indicating darkness by the occasional introduction of property lights took hold. Blackfriars plays such as *The Elder Brother* (4.3), *Love's Pilgrimage* (1.2), *The Fair Maid of the Inn* (1.1), *The Maid in the Mill* (1.3; 4.3), and *The Knight of Malta* (4.2), as well as a host of probable Blackfriars plays like *Alphonsus of Germany* ("Enter Alphonsus *the Emperour in his night-gown, and his shirt, and a torch in his hand*"),[14] use stage lights to indicate darkness, not to increase the sense of brightness in the play or the theater. So too, Cockpit plays like Shirley's *The Maid's Revenge* (3.6), *The Witty Fair One* (4.4), *The Wedding* (4.4), and *The Lady of Pleasure* (3.1) employ stage lights exactly as they are used in the outdoor theaters—to represent darkness. The interesting corollary to this conclusion, moreover, is that despite the attempt to suggest darkness, there had to be enough light onstage for the audience to see what kind of lighting utensil was brought on as well as to see other important signals of time, place, and character that had nothing to do with light.

Corroboration that the evocation of darkness was not illusionistic comes from Shakespeare's satire of the mechanicals' naive representational expectations in act 3, scene 1, of *A Midsummer Night's Dream*. In preparing for their play, Quince points to the major obstacle for an illusionistic presentation: "that is, to bring the Moone-light into a chamber: for you know, *Piramus* and *Thisby* meete by Moonelight." Snug, Bottom, and the others are literalists; they insist on consulting an almanac to learn whether the moon will be shining on the night of their play. When they discover that the moon will indeed be out, Bottom finds the solution to the problem simple: "Why then may you leaue a casement of the great chamber window (where we play) open, and the Moone may shine in at the casement." Bottom contends that moonlight may best be represented by the real thing, but Quince, who has had more experience in these matters, believes that the emblematic approach is better. He suggests, "[O]ne must come in with a bush of thorns and a lanthorne, and say he comes to disfigure, or to present the person of Moonshine" (F 858–72).

The joke rests in part on the fact that no one champions the method of representing night that Elizabethan playwrights used most often—the realistic mode. No one suggests that a few token properties associated with night be brought onstage. Bottom proposes an illusionistic technique that is patently absurd. But although we may find Quince's emblematic solution just as ludicrous, there is reason to believe that the Elizabethans found it less so, or at any rate considered a man holding a lantern only a little less sophisticated than other emblems for night—representations of moons and stars, for example.[15]

Moons and Stars

Such emblems as moons and stars were most popular before the turn of the century, but they continued throughout the period. Among the Admiral's men's properties, inventoried in 1598, for example, was "the clothe of the Sone & Mone."[16] What this was is not clear: it may have resembled the costumes that dressed Phoebus and Persephone in Thomas Heywood's *Ages* plays for Queen Anne's men,[17] or it may have been some sort of painted emblem of day and night along the lines of the Admiral's men's own "sittie of Rome." In the last act of *1 Troublesome Reign of John*, Philip the Bastard casts his eyes up "to heauen" and sees "Fiue Moones reflecting, as you see them now." Were these moons only imaginary? To make it explicit, we get the stage direction, "There the fiue Moones appeare."[18] The play is early, Chambers assigning it to the Armada period of 1588, but we cannot say definitely that it was performed indoors or outdoors.[19] When Shakespeare wrote the same scene for outdoor production in his *King John*, however, these physical moons were eliminated and their appearance only narrated.

We are left wondering, though, what these moons looked like. There were utensils called "Moons" in early modern England; according to the antiquarian Thomas Wright, they were globe-shaped lanterns.[20] George Kernodle is positive the effect in *1 Troublesome Reign of John* was produced by "a machine which made one moon whirl about the others, to symbolize England and her scorn of popish lands," on the authority of such machines in Continental *tableaux vivants*.[21] Of these possibilities, neither the Admiral's men's cloth nor Kernodle's machine can be thought of as lighting effects as such, because they emblematize night in pictorial rather than in luminary terms. Wright's moon lantern and Quince's lantern are true lighting utensils, but unless they were employed in darkened halls, they too might achieve their effect less by light than by symbolism. Like realistic property lights, to the extent that successful emblems of night did not depend on light alone, they afforded a flexible means of indicating night, which worked as well outdoors as indoors.

Other important emblems associated with night were the star and blazing star or comet. These may be traced back to the nativity stars in medieval religious drama, many of which produced their effect in broad daylight. But stars were also featured in the Chester Cathedral in liturgical plays. Late churchwardens' accounts there list several payments for stars, including "a pully to the starr & setting it vp 4^d^" in 1558.[22] The London Cordwainers had three "greatt stars" for their Bethlehem pageant "with iij^re^ glasses and a cord for the same steris."[23] Similar stars on cords were used at Yarmouth in Norfolk from 1462 to 1512. Churchwardens' accounts there include "leading the star" and "a new balk line to the star and ryving [pulling] the same star."[24] With the Reformation, nativity stars went out of fashion, but I doubt that stars on lines and pulleys did. Some of these stars may have been painted effects rather than burning lights. We read nothing of tallow or wax for them, and one would think it dangerous to pull burning lights along lines suspended above the parishioners. The Cordwainers' stars with "glasses" might be some sort of lamp, but "glass" more likely refers to a mirror or crystal. Probably pieces of glass glittered on the stars, reflecting back the existing light.

Most of the stage directions calling for stars in the professional theater occur early in the period and would, therefore, often refer to open-air productions. In a dumb show in *The Battle of Alcazar*, performed around 1589 by the Admiral's men, there is thunder and lightning as Iris descends from the heavens. Then comes the stage direction, *"Heere the blazing Starre."* The Presenter of the dumb show elaborates: "Now firie starres and streaming comets blaze," after which another stage direction calls for *"Fire workes,"* and the Presenter continues, "Fire, fire about the axiltree of heauen, / Whoorles round."[25] *The Birth of Merlin*, ascribed to Shakespeare and Rowley on its title page, gives a similar description of a blazing star. Again, thunder and lightning precede the climactic moment when the *"Blazing Star appears,"* and a fire-breathing dragon appears out of a "flaming ring" from which also emanate seven smaller "blazing streams."[26] Rowley seems to have written or revised the play in 1608 while he was working for Queen Anne's men at the Red Bull, but even though the Red Bull was famous for its special effects, one wonders whether all the fire Rowley describes was real, painted, or imaginary.[27]

Because blazing stars are so often associated with pyrotechnics, one explanation of them is that they were a kind of fireworks representing comets. Unfortunately, no Renaissance handbook or list of fireworks mentions blazing stars. John Bate's *The Mysteries of Nature and Art* has a short chapter explaining *"How to make Starres,"* but these, we learn, were merely small, round firecrackers. From their ingredients, moreover, it is clear that Bate's stars would not create much light, despite their name, but only a loud report.[28] Bate also describes a "flying Dragon"—a dragon's body attached to a rocket that ran along a line—which might explain the dragon's head in *The Birth of Merlin*, while that play's flaming ring may be a girandole whirling about the blazing star. Because blazing stars were so popular at the Rose, it is disappointing that Henslowe's inventory does not include one, although his list is by no means complete. The trouble with fireworks is that they are dangerous and cause unpleasant odors. These problems may have raised little concern at the outdoor theaters, but indoors it was otherwise. The Prologue to Shirley's *The Doubtful Heir* proclaims that, as the play was intended for Blackfriars, there would be no squibs in it. In *Northward Ho!*, a Paul's play of 1605, improvident gallants are compared to "squibs that run vpon lynes."[29] A similar metaphor in Marston's *Parasitaster*, a Blackfriars play of the same year, also refers to "squibs running vpon lines" that "Stink."[30]

If blazing stars were fireworks, we might tentatively conclude that they could be used only outdoors. Such is the opinion of Inga-Stina Ewbank, who, in the continuing controversy over the authorship of *The Revenger's Tragedy*, offers the blazing star in act 5, scene 3, as evidence that the play was written for outdoor production at the Globe and, hence, cannot have been written by Middleton for the children at Blackfriars.[31] Her argument for attribution to Tourneur turns on Chambers's remark that in comparison to the Red Bull and its elaborate fireworks, "The Globe, with its traditional 'blazing star,' is left far behind."[32] She takes Chambers to mean that blazing stars were more characteristic of the Globe than anywhere else. But Ewbank has misunderstood Chambers. By "traditional," he meant only that blazing stars were old devices and that in the competition for new spectacle, the Globe had not kept pace. He does not mean that blazing stars were unique to the Globe; indeed, I have been unable to find one play, other than *The Revenger's Tragedy*, that contains a blazing star and is associated with Globe production.[33]

Although most blazing stars are associated with the Rose and Red Bull, we cannot entirely discount their use indoors. Both the manuscript and quarto versions of Thomas Goffe's *The Courageous Turk* call for blazing stars, and the manuscript states that the play was acted 21 September 1618 by students of Christ Church, Oxford, presumably indoors.[34] The stage history of *If You Know Not Me, You Know Nobody* is confused, but there is a strong possibility that the second part (or sections of it) was performed at the Cockpit in Drury Lane around 1630.[35] Quartos published before and after this revival include stage directions calling for blazing stars. At the Globe on 23 May 1633, Sir Humphrey Mildmay saw Fletcher's *Rollo, Duke of Normandy*, whose text describes a descending "bright starre" that may or may not have been actually shown. But the text of 1636 can as easily reflect court performances in 1630, 1631, or 1637.[36] According to the *Historia Histrionica*, a performance of *Rollo* was in progress at the Cockpit in Drury Lane when that playhouse was raided in 1648.[37] It may be that some hall theaters resorted to less combustible methods of showing stars: as a gloss to the question "How many starres . . . ?," a stage direction in the undated manuscript play *Timon* calls for "the signe of the 7 starr[es]."[38] We do not know for whom this play was written, but its frequent quotation of Greek proverbs and other pedantries imply a student performance indoors. On the whole, we may say that blazing stars may have been presented less elaborately and less often indoors, but any decline in their popularity may as easily be traced to the Jacobean distaste for the naive emblems of the Elizabethans as to a Jacobean fondness for indoor theaters.

In regard to the general illumination, it is interesting to note that most blazing stars occur late in the action of the plays. I give their positions in redacted acts and scenes: *Battle of Alcazar*, 5; *Captain Thomas Stukeley*, 5; *The Birth of Merlin*, 4.5; *The Revenger's Tragedy*, 5.3; 2 *If You Know Not Me*, 3; *Rollo*, 5; *The Courageous Turk*, 5. Could it be that blazing stars were meant to look more real in the gathering darkness at the end of the play? Or were they simply delayed so that the rise in dramatic tension was paralleled by an increase in spectacle? An appearance of three suns early (2.1) in the bad quarto of 3 *Henry VI* (*The True Tragedy of Richard Duke of York*) might argue likewise that suns would look more natural in the bright afternoon light. In the first folio version, Edward exclaims, "Dazle mine eyes, or doe I see three Sunnes?" while Richard gives a long description of "Three glorious Sunnes" coming together to become "but one Lampe, one Light, one Sunne" (F 678–83). But in the quarto, Richard's narration is trimmed, and a stage direction is added: "Three sunnes appeare in the aire" (Q B3ᵛ). What these suns looked like is even more difficult to imagine than what moons looked like. It seems unlikely that the English had any lights at their disposal that could have produced convincing suns out-of-doors.[39] Perhaps something on the order of the Admiral's men's "clothe of the Sone" was employed, a technique effective in nearly any theatrical environment.

Other Fireworks

Outdoors, and perhaps indoors, fireworks were often employed for their own sake without regard to associations with night and day. *Doctor Faustus*, performed at the Rose and Fortune, is familiar evidence. Not many serious plays nowadays employ fireworks, and we perhaps need to rethink their appropriateness to certain kinds of drama that were never intended to be taken realistically. For example, the sober academicians of Vicenza used fireworks extensively at the Teatro Olimpico in 1585 for their revival of *King Oedipus*.[40] A modern theatergoer, used to scenic illusionism, might speculate uneasily about which moments of the play were deemed most appropriate for fireworks.

But even if fireworks did not support the imaginary time or place of the play, one still wonders how effective fireworks were in the daytime, whether indoors or outdoors. Fireworks are clearly better at night. The conjecture that certain plays may have been performed late in the day because they included fireworks suggests itself but without conclusive evidence. We do know that at the Beargarden in Southwark (c. 1584), fireworks concluded the day's games.[41] And a look at *Doctor Faustus* shows six uses of fire and fireworks with a distinct progression of more and more elaborate spectacle toward the end. For this play, perhaps, Marlowe may have been aware that it might be wise to delay the big lighting effects until the sun was beginning to sink. Thus, through the first four acts of the 1616 B text (Greg's divisions), fireworks are used only to frighten people—the Pope, his Cardinals, and the soldiers. This fright can be accomplished by the noise of the fireworks alone, for we should remember that Elizabethan fireworks did not produce the long-lasting, brilliantly colored displays we enjoy. In *The Broken Heart*, Ford makes the point that fireworks produced their effect mostly by noise, not by light:

> So squibs and crackers flye into the ayre,
> Then onely breaking with a noyse, they vanish
> In stench and smoke.[42]

But in the final scene of *Doctor Faustus* when *"Hell is discouered"* (apparently the "Hell mought" included in the Admiral's men's 1598 inventory), we know that something more than noise was resorted to.[43] Probably the audience saw none of what the Bad Angel describes (an ever-burning chair, damned souls being tossed on forks, bodies broiling in lead) except in their mind's eye, but the Admiral's men did not leave everything to the imagination, either. We are fortunate to have two contemporary accounts of the play's catastrophe. In *Astrologaster*, John Melton tells of a performance at the Fortune before 1620: "a man may behold shagge-hayr'd Deuills runne roaring ouer the Stage with Squibs in their mouthes, while Drummers make Thunder in the Tyring-house, and the twelue-penny Hirelings make artificiall Lightning in their Heauens."[44] And in a satire on warfare, *Worke for Armorours*, Thomas Dekker mentions that in one battle, "wilde fire flew from one [army] to another, like squibs when Doctor *Faustus* goes to the diuell."[45] Much or all of the effect of the burning in hell might have been represented by fireworks or smoke (medieval devils are frequently pictured with bellows), although neither Melton nor Dekker mentions smoke.

Artificial lightning from the heavens could have been produced by a number of methods. Both flames and strokes of lightning were sometimes produced by powdered rosin thrown or blown past a burning torch. This technique was popular early in the period but, like the blazing star, fell into some disrepute later, even though it was cited as the correct method for making lightning in the 1611 English edition of Sebastiano Serlio's *Architettura*.[46] In 1599, the King's men's A *Warning for Fair Women* disdainfully recalled the crowd-pleasing entrances of vengeful ghosts when "a little Rosen flasheth forth, / Like smoke out of a Tabacco pipe, or a boyes squib."[47] As late as 1636, Richard Lovelace in the epilogue to *The Scholars*, a Whitefriars play, was still complaining about some of the audience's love for rosin lightning flashes.[48] Lovelace is not quite clear on the matter; evidently rosin flashes could also be used indoors at Whitefriars, although he certainly disapproved of them. Similar disapproval was voiced regarding lightning produced by squibs running on lines. In some quarters, at least, both these effects were considered less refined and less safe than various Continental techniques for representing lightning, which nevertheless did not become popular in England.[49]

Fire Effects

Most fires were represented simply by smoke. Literary stage directions of descents into hell mention fiery exhalations and the like, but it would have been dangerous to have real flames emanate from beneath wooden stages. In Robert Wilson's comedy *The Cobler's Prophecy*, written before 1594, the Priest tells us, "The Cabbin of Contempt doth burne with fire," but we know from the stage direction that the effect was actually more modest. In a playhouse stage direction, the tireman was ordered, "*[F]rom one part let a smoke arise.*"[50] One of the rare playhouse distinctions between smoke and fire is made by stage directions in John Fletcher's *Bonduca*. In act 3, scene 1, we witness a Druid sacrifice during which ceremonies are performed at an altar. A stage direction calls for "*[a] smoak from the Altar,*" and Bonduca duly notes that "[t]he fire takes." But his sister is upset that "no flame rises." More prayers are offered, a stage direction reads, "*A flame arises,*" and Bonduca happily announces that "[i]t flames out."[51] Bibliographical analysis of the text shows that these stage directions originated in the playhouse and not simply with Fletcher, who might only have imagined that the difference between smoke and flames could be demonstrated onstage. From the cast list appended to the play, Chambers can date it to either the 1608–10 or 1613–14 season when the King's men were performing at both Blackfriars and the Globe.[52] Probably a similar trick altar was used at about the same time for the King's men's Blackfriars play *The Two Noble Kinsmen*, in which Emilia puts a hind upon an altar and sets fire to it, whereupon the hind disappears and in its place a rose tree ascends (5.1). Or again, a play performed "nine days together at the Globe," Middleton's *A Game at Chess*, requires an altar from which "flames aspire," tapers "set themselues afire," and statues move in a dance.[53] Clearly, the use of such altars both indoors and outdoors suggests that playwrights could rely on the audience's readily understanding the same lighting conventions in a variety of lighting environments.

Luckily, we have an example of how such altars could work. The English magus Robert Fludd described a trick altar in his *Technical History of the Macrocosm* (Oppenheim, 1618). It worked by emitting smoke and fire through a hole in the top of the altar that could be opened and closed by a sliding plate (see fig. 35) Fludd explains the apparatus this way:

Houses can be burned, sacrificial altars can burst into flames, trailing and bearded comets made to appear, brimstone effected, and many other special effects of this kind by the use of a triggering mechanism . . . if a candlestick with a lit candle is set in the hollow of an altar out of view, in such a way that the burning flame touches a sheet of copper covering a sort of opening in the top surface of the altar. By the movement of a lead weight or of water at a certain time, the sheet will be secretly removed, and the flame, issuing through the opening, will kindle whatever it finds over the altar that is combustible.[54]

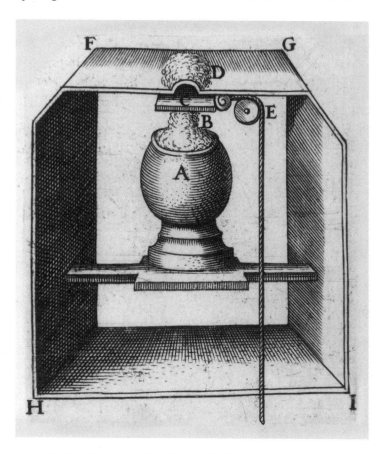

Fig. 35. A trick altar. Illustration from Robert Fludd, *Utriusque cosmi maioris scilicet et minoris metaphysica, physica atqve technica historia*, Tomus Primus, Tractatus Secundus: *De naturae simia seu technica macrocosmi historia* (Oppenheim, 1618). University of Illinois at Urbana-Champaign Library.

Fludd does not associate this apparatus with the theater, but burning altar scenes are frequent enough to believe that this trick and such scenes may have shared techniques or, at least, a common origin. Fludd's method of creating a conflagration might even have been appropriate for such effects as "the Towne burning" in the background during Zenocrate's funeral in 2 *Tamburlaine* (2.2):[55]

> If then, a palace constructed in paper or wood or some perfumed combustible is placed there [on top of the altar], everything will burn. Thus for the destruction of Troy, the burning of Nero's Rome, the torching of Sardanalaus and its palace, and other displays of this kind, this device will be especially useful.[56]

Another means of producing such effects relied on alcohol. There is evidence for the use of alcohol in burning properties indoors as early as 1553 when the Revels Office bought "one pottle of aqauvite for the pageaunt of ma[r]ce and to burne in other properties."[57] The blue flame of alcohol is not very bright, however, and may not have been suitable in the amphitheaters. To produce fire effects for his indoor intermezzi, Sabbattini advised placing alcohol-soaked cloths on *periaktoi* and then lighting the cloths; but, he judiciously warns, this technique should be "avoided as much as possible on account of the danger sometimes attendant on it."[58]

Although fewer fire and lightning effects were called for in Jacobean and Caroline texts, the decrease cannot be explained solely by a rise in the number of hall theaters. Early indoor plays—especially those written in the 1560s and 1570s—contain numerous fire effects, an indication that the popularity of such conflagration scenes was determined by fashion as much as by the production venue. In 1572, for instance, a wax chandler made an expensive "device in counterfeting Thunder & Lightning" for a play by the Children of the Chapel at court.[59] Since a chandler and not a painter was responsible, we must assume that some kind of burning light was used indoors to represent lightning. But other indoor entertainments employed very conventionalized methods of representing fires. In 1566, Queen Elizabeth saw a play at Oxford at night in which a character ascended from hell with "flaming head, feet, arms."[60] Similar clothing "sprinkled with bloud & flames" is found in the dumb show before act 4 of *Gorboduc*, performed at the Inner Temple in 1561.[61] Perhaps costumes were flame-colored or decorated with strips of cloth that resembled flames when the actor moved. Such appears to be the method used in costuming Inigo Jones's fiery spirits for Jacobean masques.[62] In the late morality play *All for Money*, both Damnation and Judas have garments "painted with flames of fire," a technique that clearly afforded the troupe a flexible means of staging that would be appropriate in nearly any venue.[63]

In sum, the evidence we have indicates no substantially different use of property lights indoors or outdoors. The contrasts of darkness and light on the English Renaissance stage were first and foremost functions of the imagery in the spoken words and, hence, worked their effects most prominently in the imaginations of the spectators. Some of the lights brought onstage may never have been lit or may have produced their effect by conventional symbolism. It is all too easy to overestimate the allusive power of light used onstage by means of selective citations. Only half of Shakespeare's plays use any lights at all, and of those that do, the majority use lights simply as realistic detail.[64] Property lights were important technical considerations, but less because of the light they produced than because of the scenes they helped to set. Lights carried by the actors had the ability to participate in the concert of action, language, and theatrical environment by creating moods and, at times, by helping to show what, when, and even who was supposed to be onstage. And finally, the use of such property lights and special effects suggests that the stage conditions at the public and private theaters could not have been in such opposition as to oblige dramatists or actors to rewrite plays to fit different lighting systems.

10

ILLUMINATING THE SCENE
The Duchess of Malfi at the
Globe and Blackfriars

RECENT SCHOLARSHIP, in particular the Records of Early English Drama project, and the discoveries of the foundations of the Rose and Globe playhouses have provided us with a more complex view of early modern English theaters and staging than was true only some fifty years ago, when it was common to speak of "the Elizabethan theater." Following the lead of G. F. Reynolds in the 1940s, scholars have taken care not to create a generalized reconstruction of a "typical" playhouse and have instead sought to recognize differences among the early playhouses that Shakespeare and his contemporaries knew. All the same, we do well to recall that even at one playhouse, very different kinds of scenes were performed under its light and that some of these scenes may be said to have taken advantage of the prevailing illumination, some to disregard it, and others to call attention to a disparity between the pretended light of the scene and the real light in the theater. In short, there is a sense in which various actions onstage may have invited the audience to construe the prevailing illumination differently. Una Ellis-Fermor makes the charming observation that the decadent tone of many Jacobean dramas must have been well served by a sunset reflected in the sky above the outdoor amphitheaters, but in midsummer, those Jacobean tragedies would have been accompanied more often by glaring sunshine.[1]

As often as not, therefore, the natural light contributed little or nothing to any sense of illusion, even if it could occasionally help to clarify the staging of certain moments in the play. During nighttime scenes, for example, the daylight in the playhouse meant that the audience could clearly see actions that were supposed to be obscure to the characters onstage. As has been noted, the imaginary darkness of such plays as *A Midsummer Night's Dream* and *Othello* confuses the characters onstage, while we know precisely what is happening to them. *Macbeth* is one of the darkest plays of the period; scene after scene takes place at night or in the darkest corners of the palace. Despite its original production at the sunlit Globe, it is only at the very end of the play, when the sun breaks over Birnam Forest, colors are unfurled, and Macbeth takes up arms, that the nightmare come to an end. Far from attempting illusion, Shakespeare fashions the drama so that the stage light contrasts ironically with the action. J. L. Styan notes that when Ross comments on the gloomy omens in the sky after Duncan's murder—

> Thou seest the Heauens, as troubled with mans Act,
> Threatens his bloody Stage: byth' Clock 'tis Day,
> And yet darke Night strangles the trauailing Lampe:
> Is't Nights predominance, or the Dayes shame,
> That Darknesse does the face of Earth intombe,
> When liuing Light should kisse it? (F 930–35)

—Shakespeare goes out of his way to point out the daylight convention that permitted nighttime scenes on a sunlit stage.[2]

Still, Shakespeare goes further than simply calling attention to a discrepancy between the real light in the playhouse and the pretended light in the scene. Even at the beginning of the play, Macbeth is aware of what his villainy must look like in the light. While plotting the murder of Duncan, he vainly prays, "Let not Light see my black and deepe desires" (F 339). To an amphitheater audience, the "seeling night" that Macbeth hopes will veil murder and "Cancel" his duty did not exist. Macbeth would "Skarfe vp the tender Eye of pittifull Day" (F 1206), but as Ross reminds us, living light did indeed kiss the stage. As members of the audience, we see Macbeth's desires played out in broad daylight. Simon Forman saw *Macbeth* at the Globe in April 1611, but when the play was performed at court (probably at Hampton Court in August 1606), one doubts Ross's moving lines were cut because of different lighting arrangements. Shakespeare did not depend on the sun for the effect any more than he depended on nature to provide real thunder and lightning for the witches.

Compared to modern practice, early stage lighting enjoyed a more casual relationship with the drama. It was free to enhance aesthetic attitudes or not. There was no insistence that the light fit the mood of the play at every turn and no more expectation of logical consistency in the illumination than in the costuming or scenery. When the character of the illumination paralleled the scenic design, the actors might or might not point the correspondences out. But when the playhouse light and the scenic light were dissimilar, the actors were also free to exploit the discrepancy if that seemed profitable.

This multifarious exploitation of light notwithstanding, several scholars have attempted to assign plays to specific theaters on the basis of the luminary atmosphere of the plays themselves. In his admirable Revels Plays edition of *The Duchess of Malfi*, John Russell Brown argues that the scene with the "dead man's hand" (4.1) can have been effective only in a darkened theater and that the play must therefore have been written with the King's men's indoor Blackfriars playhouse in mind.[3] But the title page of the 1623 first edition states clearly that the play was "*[p]resented privately, at the Black-Friers; and publiquely at the Globe.*" Because Brown takes the lighting of this extraordinary scene to be critical to a proper understanding of its original staging and effect, I should like to examine the scene in relation to what we know of the illumination at both theaters and in the hope that a close look at the light shining on a specific scene will serve to balance the diagrammatic sketch of lighting we have been obliged to draw. Although I happen to think his interpretation of the facts is not the most plausible one, Brown nevertheless calls attention to an important, perhaps even crucial, point of comparison between the amphitheaters and hall playhouses—namely, their lighting. In assigning *The Duchess of Malfi* to Blackfriars on the basis of its stage light, Brown at least refers to an aspect of production that depends on the essential form of the playhouse.

For an example of the influence that stage lighting could exert on an audience's response to a play, we need look no further than Webster's other great tragedy, *The White Devil*, performed only a year or so before *The Duchess of Malfi*. When *The White Devil* was produced at an open-air playhouse (almost certainly the Red Bull) early in 1612, the play failed, not because the dramatist or actors were inept, but because the playhouse was dark and dreary—or so we have heard Webster claim. The play was acted "*in so dull a time of Winter,*" he complains, "*in so open and blacke a Theater, that it wanted (that which is the onely grace and setting out of Tragedy) a full and understanding Auditory.*"[4] Those who know London in the wintertime can sympathize with Webster, although it should be added that many plays did succeed in the winter despite outdoor performance. Still, Webster may himself have lived to see the play and his excuses for its failure at an open-air playhouse vindicated. According to the title page of the 1631 second edition, *The White Devil* was later revived and performed "diuers times" at the indoor Cockpit in Drury Lane, whose roof and artificial lights presumably afforded the play and its spectators more hospitable accommodations.

No one will doubt that playhouse conditions have a substantial, if not always so determining, effect on the audience's perception of a play. Insofar as the atmosphere in a playhouse may be said to influence a spectator's response, one naturally supposes that plays performed in the indoor and outdoor playhouses evoked responses that, all other things being equal, differed in proportion as the two theatrical environments differed. In assessing the distinctive contributions of the indoor and outdoor playhouses, however, it is difficult to keep other things equal. The success of *The White Devil* in the 1630s may have been due as much to changing literary fashions as to differences between the playhouse structures and their lighting systems. Or the actors and staging may simply have been better. With so many unknown quantities, a theatrical equation is not readily solved; one can never be sure whether Webster's gloomy picture of *The White Devil*'s premiere represents an accurate explanation of its failure or is the exaggeration of a disgruntled playwright. But in the case of *The Duchess of Malfi*, several of these indeterminate quantities are conveniently eliminated from consideration. For in examining the staging of the dead-man's-hand scene at the Globe and at Blackfriars, we are concerned with the same scene performed at about the same time by the same acting company.

In act 4, scene 1, of *The Duchess of Malfi*, the Duchess's brother Ferdinand begins his long-delayed punishment of her for remarrying. At the beginning of the scene, we see Ferdinand shortly before he is to visit the imprisoned Duchess. We learn that he has a request to make of her as a condition for their meeting, which he bids Bosola convey to her. Ferdinand retires, the Duchess enters, and Bosola informs her of the unusual request: it is that "neither Torch, nor Taper / Shine in your Chamber" during the interview because Ferdinand once "rashly made a solemne vowe / Neuer to see you more."[5] The Duchess agrees to the condition and orders, "Take hence the lights." Ferdinand reenters, and the darkness is established in an abruptly realistic touch when he is obliged to ask the Duchess, "Where are you?" Ferdinand then remarks, "This darkenes suites you well," and with ironic and sinister undertones continues:

> It had bin well,
> Could you haue liu'd thus alwayes: for indeed
> You were too much i' th' light. (I–I[v])

By this he alludes not only to the trick he is about to play but also to several closely interwoven connotations of "light"—her wantonness, her having been too freely exposed to other men, and even the efficacy of darkness to hide his own incestuous inclinations. There follows Ferdinand's offer of reconciliation; "here's a hand," he says, while in an apparently authorial stage direction, we read that he *"gives her a dead mans hand"* as his own. The Duchess dutifully kisses it, but when her lips feel how cold the hand is, she cries out, "Hah? lights: oh horrible"; whereupon Ferdinand, in one of Webster's most brutal lines, orders, "Let her haue lights enough."

Brown believes that the scene must be played in darkness so that the audience will experience the same shock the Duchess does when lights are brought back on and she sees the severed hand. He argues, rightly, that an audience might well laugh to see the Duchess holding a property hand while Ferdinand promises that he will "leaue this Ring with you, for a Loue-token: / And the hand, as sure as the ring." "What would be difficult, clumsy, and grotesque at the Globe," Brown concludes, "could be thrilling and sensitive in the darkened auditorium of the Blackfriars."[6]

But even if we agree that shocking the audience is a desideratum, are we positive that actual darkness could be achieved at the Blackfriars or, if it could, that darkness was the most likely means by which such a shock was produced? When he reenters, Ferdinand presumably carries the hand in his cloak sleeve to pretend it is his. Darkness would not be required to avoid giving the trick away to either the Duchess or the audience. And when he *"gives"* her his hand, need we imagine that he passes it to her, that is, actually hands it to her? It seems more probable that when she offers to kiss his hand, he simply extends his sleeve forward. She might then cross to him, kneel, take the hand in hers, and kiss it while he continues to hold the property hand through his sleeve as though it were his own. When she notices its coldness, he could then release it, letting her hold it a second or two in astonishment until in a paroxysm of horror she lets it fall to the ground. Richard Burbage, who created the role of Ferdinand, must certainly have possessed the talents to perform this literal sleight of hand in the Globe daylight. Indeed, as seen in bright light, the moment when Burbage let the hand go would have been substantially as shocking and a great deal more sudden and jarring than the corresponding reintroduction of light on the Blackfriars stage. If anything were clumsy (not to mention distracting), it would have been the rushing in of servants carrying torches and candles from the tiring-house at a time when our attention should be focused on the Duchess. I even wonder if the sudden bringing of torches into a darkened auditorium would not have temporarily blinded the audience at the very moment they needed most to see the severed hand. As it is, the stolid tone of Ferdinand's "Let her haue lights enough" hardly suggests lights were brought back on in enough of a hurry to startle the audience.

Surely the horror derived as much from the actors' reactions to the hand as from the hand itself—just as it does in such analogous public theater scenes as Benvolio's cutting off Faustus's head or Lavinia's entering to her brothers with her hands cut off in *Titus Andronicus*. To insist that the effect resided more in a blood-drenched stage property than in the actors' horrified responses (and, just as important in shocking an audience, in preparing the audience not to anticipate those responses) is to underestimate the sophistication of the audience and to overestimate the skills of the Jacobean property makers. It is to start once more down the quaint path that leads finally to little green lights twinkling on the Ghost's helmet in *Hamlet* while the startled faces of Horatio and the watch are invisible on a darkened stage.[7] The dead hand produced its gruesome effect primarily by the words and actions of the Duchess both before and after she kissed it, just as the Ghost in *Hamlet* frightened its original audience because it was seen to frighten the previously calm and unsuspecting Horatio and Hamlet. To produce the dead-hand scene illusionistically in darkness means that the audience can see neither the Duchess's initial shock nor her contrasting self-possession at the beginning of the scene; a little wax hand is made to carry almost the entire burden of this striking effect. If this kind of illusion in the lighting were actually required, one could argue as easily that the shadow Ferdinand throws in the outdoor gallery scene (5.2) required outdoor performance for an effective presentation.

In any case, the dead-man's-hand scene as originally staged in 1613 or 1614 need not have been blazingly lit at the Globe.[8] As shown in chapter 5, no strong sunlight could have illuminated the actors at any time. The stage was so well protected from the elements, in fact, that if ten windows lit the hall at Blackfriars, then, depending on the time of performance and the season of the year, it may occasionally have been possible to illuminate the Blackfriars stage with nearly as much natural light as the second Globe stage itself. Moreover, the lateness of the scene (act 4) in this long play (its first quarto reaches to 104 pages, nearly twice the normal length) would have put an open-air performance of the effect close to twilight in spring and autumn, assuming the King's men followed the practice of Lady Elizabeth's men in April 1614 at the Hope of beginning plays at 3 P.M.[9]

For that matter, Blackfriars hardly needed the special indoor "lighting device" Brown hypothesizes, either to produce darkness or to inspire Webster to write the scene. Blackfriars plays were given in the winter, and a wintertime performance of act 4, scene 1, would necessarily be played in twilight because Blackfriars plays apparently began no earlier than 2 or 3 P.M. We do not know the dates on which *The Duchess of Malfi* was first played, but Orazio Busino, in a report dated 7 February 1618 (28 January, English style), discusses *The Duchess of Malfi* as though it had recently been on the stage.[10] In advancing the theory that Webster fashioned the play with Blackfriars in mind, Brown hinges his argument on the presumed fact that the "auditorium could be darkened by covering its windows." But even with the windows wide open, little natural light could have illuminated the dead-hand effect at Blackfriars. Had the performance begun even as early as 2 P.M., I do not see how the effect could have taken place much before 4 P.M.—just the time of London's winter sunset. The diminution of light was unique neither to Blackfriars in particular nor to the indoor theaters in general. The early winter sunset managed the effect all by itself. Far from being darkened, the artificially lit Blackfriars stage would have appeared brighter in relation to the rest of the auditorium at the end of the play than when daylight flooded through the windows at the beginning. As the daylight waned, the apparent brightness onstage would have increased because the stage candles would have contributed a greater share of the total illumination. If one wanted to argue that

The Duchess of Malfi was written especially for Blackfriars, one might as well point to the suitability of artificial light to the increasingly "artificial" shows by which Ferdinand entertains the Duchess—the dead man's hand, the wax figures of Antonio and her children, and the masque of the madmen.[11] Not darkness, but artificial light suits the play toward its conclusion.

Brown cites no evidence for his assertion that the windows at Blackfriars could be covered. Apparently, he has inferred it from Dekker's reference to "clapt downe" windows in *The Seven Deadlie Sinns of London*. Certainly, it would have been possible to clap down window shutters, but Dekker makes it clear that when this was done, the windows were covered when the plays were "presently to be acted," that is, before the beginning of the performance. In that case, it would have been difficult to produce real darkness as property lights were carried offstage or as the time of the play was supposed to change from day to night, because some ten apprentices would need to open and close the shutters on cue in well-rehearsed unison for the effect to produce the response Brown posits. At any rate, it is unlikely that such a method of changing the amount of light would have been available to the King's men when they revived *The Duchess of Malfi* on 26 December 1630 in the newly remodeled Cockpit-in-Court, where performances were routinely given at night.[12] Even with the auditorium windows at Blackfriars covered, the stage would still have been lit by the playhouse candles. These lights might have been extinguished to darken the scene as well; but then the tireman would have had to lower and extinguish lights while the scene was in progress and relight and raise them sometime later. It is possible that the whole of act 4 was performed in darkness, but, as we have seen, no extant pre-Restoration playbook even hints that windows were covered or candles extinguished during the act breaks.

The only convenient way to decrease light (or to suggest that it was decreased) was to remove stage-property lights, and this is the method that Webster's dialogue tells us was used. To produce a significant change in light, however, would have required a large number of such property lights. For if some two or three dozen candles burned over the Blackfriars stage, then at least another dozen or so hand-held candles would have been required to produce a discernible fall or rise in the level of illumination as they were removed or brought back onstage. Brown adds a stage direction to his text indicating that Bosola removes the lights, but one doubts he could have removed and then quickly brought back on the large number of lights needed to shock the audience.

It is more probable that two or three lights were brought onstage when the Duchess entered and that darkness was indicated symbolically by their removal. Although darkness was usually suggested by the bringing in of lights rather than by their removal, property lights held close to the actors may have been able to indicate darkness more illusionistically by being extinguished, at least toward the ends of plays when the daylight had begun to fade. When Paris enters the graveyard in the last scene of *Romeo and Juliet*, for example, his page's torch is a conventional indication that the scene is presumed to take place at night. But immediately afterward, Paris tells his page, "[P]ut it out, for I would not be seene" (Q2 L2).[13] If the boy had held the torch close to Paris when they first entered, then its extinction soon afterward might have eliminated some of the highlights on Paris, at least in contrast to the entering Romeo and Balthasar—also carrying a torch—to whom Shakespeare wants the audience's attention directed. Similarly, if a few lights were brought on quickly in *The Duchess of Malfi* and held close to the dead man's hand, then a small increase in light on it is possible to imagine—not enough to jolt the audience, certainly, but enough to suggest that the previous dialogue was presumed to take place in darkness.

Whatever the case, the point is that both Paris and the Duchess need to be seen while they are supposed to be standing in the dark. Far from being grotesque in the light, one of the scene's most provocative moments would be obscured if the audience could not see the Duchess kiss the hand "affectionately" (11ᵛ). I should not be surprised if, instead of concealing the hand as his own, Burbage signaled somehow to the audience that the hand was indeed a dead man's hand. Her kiss would then be all the more ironic and degrading. In fact, the irony pervading Ferdinand's speeches suggests that Webster was less concerned with shocking the audience than with creating dramatic suspense, a growing anxiety in the audience that what they fear might happen will happen. Whether the point was shock or suspense, whether the darkness was only symbolic or was suggested by a slight diminution of light near the actors, the scene works best when played in enough light to allow the audience to see what is going on. As such, the scene was as effective outdoors as indoors.

I REGRET having to take issue with Professor Brown in discussing the lighting of this scene, not only because of the excellence of his edition, but also because he is the only editor of the play to venture a playhouse ascription based on specific technical evidence. Others have been happy to relegate the play to Blackfriars on the basis of what they take to be an "indoor" or "oppressive" atmosphere surrounding the play.[14] Indeed, there has been a tendency to assign bright, happy plays to the public theaters and dark, melancholy plays to the private theaters when no external evidence is available. Such assignments ignore all the countervailing evidence (the Globe's somber *Hamlet* and *Macbeth*, for example, or the popularity of such bright comedies as *Twelfth Night* and *The Comedy of Errors* indoors) and usually argue circularly that the nature of a playhouse's illumination must have been whatever would complement the mood of the play being assigned to it. While Brown gives *The Duchess of Malfi* to Blackfriars because of its "partially darkened stage," for instance, Frank Kermode calls Blackfriars the "natural home" of *The Tempest* because of the "brightly lit stage" there.[15] Their assessments are not necessarily contradictory—the Blackfriars stage could have been both bright and capable of being darkened. But it is clear that neither description can be taken as fact and that both scholars have selected only the presumed characteristics that fit their theories. External evidence for original Blackfriars production—thin enough for *The Duchess of Malfi* and nonexistent for *The Tempest*—has been stretched to fit less-than-definitive internal evidence.[16]

Whether or not Webster wrote *The Duchess of Malfi* specifically for Blackfriars, it is easy to see him offering it to the King's men in 1613 after the literally dismal failure of *The White Devil* at the *"open and blacke"* Red Bull in 1612. Besides being better actors than the Queen's men and able to attract more sophisticated audiences, the King's men would not have had to perform his new play under a gloomy winter sky. But if Brown is right and a dark theater was essential for a convincing presentation of *The Duchess of Malfi*, then Webster might have done better to have had it produced at the open and black Red Bull instead of the summertime Globe and artificially lit Blackfriars.

The literary historian might insist that a dramatist's creative faculties play a larger part in shaping a scene than do the necessities of physical production. The matter is sometimes difficult to settle, turning as it does on the usually unknowable intentions of the playwright. Still, in Webster's case, similarities between the dead-hand scene and a scene in *The White Devil* suggest that the darkness implied in both was inspired more by his personal vision than by his taking advantage of special lighting equipment.

For although Webster (and apparently his friend Thomas Dekker) had hoped that the premiere of *The White Devil* would take place under fair skies, Webster extinguishes stage-property lights in the play for many of the same reasons they are removed in his supposedly indoor *Duchess of Malfi*.[17] In act 1, scene 2, of *The White Devil*, Brachiano and Vittoria contrive to spend their first furtive night together. Like Bosola, Flamineo follows orders and arranges that no lights shine during their tryst. He tells the servants, "[T]is his [Brachiano's] pleasure / You put out all your torches and depart" (B2). When Brachiano enters, Vittoria (like the Duchess) is immediately told that darkness suits her actions; she hears (again like the Duchess) from her own brother that darkness hides her sin: "Come sister, darkenesse hides your blush" (B4v). She is reminded by her own family member (in this case by her mother) that she has been too "light," that is, wanton (C1v). The nocturnal "witch-craft" that deceives the Duchess (I1v) is the same "witch-craft" that lures Vittoria (C1v). And of course, darkness throughout underscores the illicit sexuality of the scene.

In act 4, scene 1, of *The Duchess of Malfi*, Ferdinand gives reasons for the removal of lights on similar grounds. And while the sexuality there is not overt and is easily overemphasized, it is nonetheless real.[18] What is more, Webster has taken care to link the darkness of the dead-hand scene with Ferdinand's deep involvement in his sister's sexuality. For it was when Ferdinand first discovered her marriage that he jealously made the vow never to see her again, which later provides the pretext for the darkness in act 4, scene 1. She had reminded him then of her youth and beauty, but her marriage, as he later admits, "drew a streame of gall, quite through my heart" (K3v). It was Ferdinand's "to[o] wilfull" and rash response to the Duchess's own sexual longings (G) that precipitates the darkness of the dead man's hand. Thus, when Ferdinand and the Duchess meet in her dark bedroom at night, and he wishes she could "haue liu'd thus alwayes," he alludes not only to the revenge he can exact in darkness but also to incipient sexual feelings he can express only in the darkness of a veritable torture chamber.

To be sure, the suitability of darkness to illicit love was a common rhetorical figure. When Shakespeare's Tarquin is about to ravish Lucrece, Tarquin puts out his torch, "For light and lust are deadlie enemies."[19] Similarly, the bed trick in *Measure for Measure* must be "ith' darke" to work (F 1814); Annabella in *'Tis Pity She's a Whore* blushes after spending the night with her brother only when daylight comes (2.1); and Arbaces in *A King and No King* nearly repeats Ferdinand's words when he tells who he believes to be his sister that if she consents to love him, "thy dwelling must be darke and close / Where I may neuer see thee."[20]

But while the rhetorical figure is hardly unique, Webster's use of it is, providing evidence that the darkness in the dead-hand scene was not introduced merely to seize an opportunity that the newly opened Blackfriars afforded. For in two separate plays, Webster is the only dramatist of the period to show us the removal of lights for scenes involving improper love. Webster has turned the figure-in-words into a figure-in-action, as H. T. Price describes Webster's persistent practice.[21] In both plays, the darkness protecting illicit love is signaled by the actual extinction of property lights, an indication, I think, that the effect in *The Duchess of Malfi* was not simply Webster's exploitation of a newly available indoor lighting device but rather a characteristic stage image that he knew would work as well at the Red Bull and Globe. A glance at the two plays shows that the network of light imagery in them is of a piece. A pervasive gloom strangles the heroine's light and cynically questions whether that light was not illusory all the while. Vittoria likens herself to a glittering jewel — "Through darkenesse Diamonds spred their ritchest light" (F2^v) — to which Flamineo later rejoins, "Glories, like glowe-wormes, a farre off shine bright / But lookt to neare, haue neither heat nor light" (H4^v–i). Likewise, the Duchess "staines [that is, eclipses] the time past: lights the time to come" (B4), even though Bosola must remind her, too, that "Glories (like glowe-wormes) a farre off, shine bright, / But look'd to neere, haue neither heate, nor light" (K). The very texture of the imagery points toward a single conception of the dramatic significance of light and darkness and calls into serious question any effort to see the plays as written with different playhouse atmospheres and lighting systems in mind.

With no compelling internal evidence to suggest that *The Duchess of Malfi* was composed with an eye toward Blackfriars production, we return finally to the only pertinent external evidence, the title page of the 1623 first edition. It gives honor of place to Blackfriars, but it does not follow that the King's men performed the play there as early as 1614. King's men's plays published in the early 1620s frequently mention the Blackfriars on their title pages, even though many of these plays are otherwise known as having premiered at the Globe. The title page of the 1619 first edition of *A King and No King* says the play was acted at the Globe (probably in 1611), but a second edition in 1625 mentions only the Blackfriars, implying a revival there sometime between 1619 and 1625. *Philaster* was published in 1620 as acted at the Globe, even though it is now usually dated to around 1609 and, on internal evidence, assigned to Blackfriars.[22] The second quarto of 1622 mentions both the Globe and Blackfriars, again suggesting an indoor revival around 1621. Or again, the 1622 first quarto of *Othello* names both the Globe and Blackfriars, but we know that *Othello* was performed some four years before the King's men even began acting at Blackfriars. The name of Blackfriars on a quarto published in 1623, then, proves nothing about where *The Duchess of Malfi* was performed ten years earlier. It remains possible that *The Duchess of Malfi* was premiered *"publiquely at the Globe"* and only eight or nine years later revived *"privatly, at the Black-Friers."*

I take act 4, scene 1, of *The Duchess of Malfi* to be a crucial instance of how we may use a knowledge of stage conditions to understand the performance and effect of an Elizabethan drama—crucial not only because of the importance of the scene in the play but also because the play itself stands just at the presumed shift from "public theater" to "private theater" sensibility, from exclusively natural to mixed natural and artificial illumination. I should like to suggest, moreover, that analyses of specific technical problems like lighting and acoustics may more profitably distinguish between the respective contributions of the amphitheaters and hall playhouses than can ambiguous comparisons of style and the social composition of the audience. The danger is that if we begin by assuming that performances at the indoor and outdoor playhouses differed significantly, then even the smallest shred of evidence pointing in that direction may be given too much weight. Were we not able to date *Othello*, for example, to before 1605, an attempt to identify its original playhouse might well have yielded the same conclusion as Brown's regarding *The Duchess of Malfi*. For in the last act of *Othello*, there is an important effect that, if it was intended as a lighting effect, would have been difficult to see at the Globe. When Othello enters Desdemona's bedroom *"with a light"* and compares it to her—"Put out the light, and then put out the light" (Q M)—one cannot imagine that either the candle or its extinction could have made much of an effect on the daylit Globe stage. May we conclude, then, that Shakespeare intended the audience to see a lonely candle burning in a darkened hall, poignantly signaling her chastity in a nasty world? Or are we to see it throwing out a feeble light on a bright, open-air stage? Was the scene presented illusionistically at Blackfriars with only Othello's flickering candle lighting the scene? In that case, the audience might have had difficulty seeing Desdemona's horrified reactions to Othello's accusations. Or can we rather believe, on the authority of the dead-hand scene, that Desdemona's death scene was performed in sufficient light at both playhouses and that the theatrical point resided more in poetry and acting than in lighting?

We possess no description of the original lighting of *The Duchess of Malfi*, but we do know that when the King's men performed *Othello* in the Elizabethan banqueting hall at Whitehall on 1 November 1604, the Revels Office went to some expense and trouble to provide a large number of lights. The office paid thirty shillings "for mendinge of yᵉ Old Brau[n]ches for A playe on Hallomas Night" and apparently purchased six new branches for the performance, as well.[23] Because Inigo Jones's lighting effects had not yet been introduced at court and because, in any case, Jones is not known to have aided in the production of professional plays at court until, perhaps, 1616,[24] I think we may assume that the nearly two hundred candles shining in the banqueting hall were not extinguished and relit as the play moved from day to night. And if a report of the King's men's performance of *Othello* at Oxford in September 1610 refers to an indoor venue (as it is likely to), then we may believe that such scenes were played in more than adequate light. We learn that the Oxford audience was deeply moved by Desdemona's death scene and especially by the expression on her face as she lay dead: "cum in lecto decumbens spectantium misericordiam ipso vultu imploraret."[25] That Desdemona aroused pity *ipso vultu*, "by her face alone," means that the audience could see even the smallest details clearly and that, if the play was indoors, darkness was not attempted by extinguishing the candles. The ability to see such details in nighttime scenes suggests, in fact, that the actors were not regularly obliged to alter their methods of staging as they moved from one playhouse to another. Some of the smallest indoor halls may have allowed the audience to enjoy subtler acting than was possible outdoors, but Hosley's reconstruction of the second Blackfriars shows that the majority of spectators there were nearly as far from the stage as those in the largest amphitheaters, where the audience could surround the actors. Hence, if the general illumination were good, audiences at both kinds of playhouse could discern about the same degree of refinement in the acting. The last act of *Othello*, like the dead-man's-hand scene in *The Duchess of Malfi*, could be performed outdoors and indoors, in the afternoon or at night, by daylight or candlelight.

In point of fact, the steady, overall illumination of the amphitheaters and halls, far from imposing a restriction on the actors and playwrights, meant that even in scenes of pretended darkness, the audience could see and respond to the visual media of the actors' craft. The King's men at Oxford, for instance, "moved the audience to tears, not only by their speech, but by their gestures as well."[26] Thus, as we read *The Duchess of Malfi* and come across severed hands and wax corpses, we must not forget the expressions and gestures of the actors that so deeply moved the original audiences. The largely ungovernable stage lighting of the era underscores the important but missing evidence of the acting and confirms indirectly that the staging at the indoor and outdoor playhouses may not have been so different in regard to an aspect of stage production that one might have assumed would define the principal difference between them.

Whereas modern lighting tends to be highly directional, emanating from two distinct positions to the front of the actor, early English lighting emanated from all around the actor, surrounding him with soft, indirect light. There was no impression of light focusing on the actor, no sense of the light exposing him to our view or the interpretive scheme of the lighting designer. The actors moved in the same light all Londoners moved in everyday. There was nothing theatrical or two-dimensional about it, nothing to suggest that the play created its own special light. Since the late eighteenth century, we have been pleased to call our actors "stars" in honor of the brilliant light they seem to radiate in our darkened theaters; Shakespeare called actors "shadows." Puck wonders "[i]f we shadowes haue offended" (*A Midsummer Night's Dream*, Q1 O3ᵛ), and to Macbeth the poor player that struts and frets his hour upon the stage is "but a walking Shadow" (F 2345). Picturing the playhouses he knew, it is easy to imagine why Shakespeare favored this image. The actors emanated no theatrical light of their own but rather acted in the shadows of the heavens or the indoor roof. "The best, in this kinde, are but shadowes," says Theseus of the drama (*A Midsummer Night's Dream*, Q1 H1ᵛ), by which he means shadows of reality—plays both once removed from the real world and at the same time illuminated and made understandable by it.

NOTES

INDEX

NOTES

1. Light on the Play

1. C. H. Herford and P. and E. Simpson, eds., *Ben Jonson*, 11 vols. (Oxford, 1925–52), 7: 514.

2. Stephen Greenblatt, *Renaissance Self-Fashioning* (Chicago, 1980), 4.

3. All Shakespeare citations are from Charlton Hinman, ed., *The First Folio of Shakespeare: The Norton Facsimile* (New York, 1968) or, except where noted, the appropriate quartos in Michael J. B. Allen and Kenneth Muir, eds., *Shakespeare's Plays in Quarto* (Berkeley, 1981). Folio references (F) are to "through line numbers," quarto references (Q) to signatures. On allusions to the heavens over the stage in *King Lear*, see William R. Elton, *King Lear and the Gods* (San Marino, 1968), 161–63.

4. *Othello* was performed under this ceiling 1 November 1604; see the Office of Works accounts in *Malone Society Collections* 10 (1975 [1977]): 20. Subsequent references to the *Malone Society Collections* series will be cited as *MSC*.

5. Andrew Gurr, *Playgoing in Shakespeare's London* (Cambridge, 1987), 205–51.

6. G. E. Bentley, *Shakespeare Survey* 1 (1948): 38–50, and recast with additional material in *Shakespeare and His Theatre* (Lincoln, Neb., 1964), 65–128.

7. Ann Jennalie Cook, *The Privileged Playgoers of Shakespeare's London* (Princeton, 1981); Gurr, *Playgoing*, 167.

8. T. J. King, *Shakespearean Staging: 1599–1642* (Cambridge, Mass., 1971), 2.

9. Clifford Leech, "The Dramatists' Independence," *Research Opportunities in Renaissance Drama* 10 (1967): 17–23; J. A. Lavin, "Shakespeare and the Second Blackfriars," *The Elizabethan Theatre* 3 (1973): 68–81.

10. John Marston, *The Malcontent* (London, 1604; fac. rpt. Menston, 1970), A4.

11. James Shirley, *Poems Etc.* (London, 1646), 154–55. Shirley had originally written the play for the indoor Werburgh Street theater, Dublin, which apparently was similar to the Blackfriars. Shirley's *The Court Secret* (London, 1653) was "prepared for the Scene at Black-Friers" but never acted, according to the title page. The printer of I.C.'s *The Two Merry Milkmaids* (London, 1620; fac. rpt. London, 1914) asserted that every playwright "must govern his Penne according to the Capacitie of the Stage he writes too, both in the Actor and the Auditor" (A1^v).

12. Richard Hosley, "Elizabethan Theatres and Audiences," *Research Opportunities in Renaissance Drama* 10 (1967): 13–14; and see Andrew Gurr, "Playing in Amphitheatres

and Playing in Hall Theatres," *The Elizabethan Theatre* 13 (1994): 47–62, for the limitations that the smaller stages in the hall playhouses may have imposed on scenes of battle and spectacle.

13. Prior to the uncovering of the Rose, the best reconstruction of amphitheater lighting was John Orrell's "Sunlight at the Globe," *Theatre Notebook* 38 (1984): 69–76, rpt. with additional material in *The Human Stage* (Cambridge, 1988), 88–102.

2. Tudor and Early Stuart Lighting Equipment

1. General background on lamps is found in F. W. Robins, *The Story of the Lamp (and the Candle)* (London, 1939). Early lighting instruments are best seen in Rupert Gentle and Rachel Feild, *Domestic Metalwork, 1640–1820*, rev. B. Gentle (Woodbridge, 1994), 114–218; Gabriel Henriot, *Encyclopédie du Luminare* (Paris, 1870), 1; and Ladislaus von Benesch, *Das Beleuchtungswesen* (Vienna, 1905), rpt. as *Old Lamps of Central Europe* (Rutland, Vt., 1962).

2. Nicola Sabbattini, *Pratica di fabricar scene e machine ne' teatri* (Ravenna, 1638; rpt. Rome, 1955), bk. 1, chap. 39, p. 55, trans. in A. M. Nagler, *A Source Book in Theatrical History* (New York, 1952), 88. Sabbattini's chapters on theatrical lighting were first printed in 1636.

3. Rushes were sometimes dipped in salad oil to make them burn, at least among the wealthy: privy-purse expenses of Henry VIII for 1529 list a bottle "of salet oyle and for Russhes to brenne wt. the said oyle"; see R. Goodwin-Smith, *English Domestic Metalwork* (1937; abridged ed. Leigh-on-Sea, 1973), 31.

4. Arthur Laing, *Lighting* (London, 1982), 43; Arthur H. Hayward, *Colonial Lighting* (1923; rpt. New York, 1962), 19.

5. John Stow, *Survey of London* (London, 1598), H6^v.

6. Stanley Wells, *Period Lighting* (London, 1975), 84; James Rogers, *A History of Agriculture and Prices in England*, 7 vols. (London, 1886–1902), 6: 652–53.

7. Caroline Spurgeon, *Shakespeare's Imagery and What It Tells Us* (Cambridge, 1935), 113.

8. Robert Greene, *Friar Bacon and Friar Bungay* (London, 1594), G1^v. Although there is no lamp in Greene's *Alphonsus, King of Aragon* (London, 1599; fac. rpt. London, 1926), it also features a brazen head "set in the middle of the place behind the Stage, out of which" the Elizabethan equivalent of stage hands are directed to "cast flames of fire" (F1^v).

9. Laing, *Lighting*, 36.

10. Thomas Middleton, *A Chaste Maid in Cheapside* (London, 1630; rpt. Menston, 1969), E1–E1^v.

11. G. Glen Gould, *Period Lighting Fixtures* (New York, 1928), 180–81.

12. Marston, *The Malcontent*, E1^v.

13. William O'Dea, *The Social History of Lighting* (New York, 1958), 3.

14. Gösta M. Bergman, *Lighting in the Theatre* (Stockholm, 1977), 54.

15. Walter Mountfort, *The Launching of the Mary* (MS, fac. printing Oxford, 1933), fol. 319b.

16. Randall Monier-Williams, *The Tallow Chandlers of London* (London, 1970), 1: 43. The word "stinkinge" is interlined and deleted.

17. *MSC* 13 (1986): 10.

18. John Dummelow, *The Wax Chandlers of London* (London, 1973), 12.

19. *MSC* 13: 141.

20. *MSC* 13: 10, 32, 51, 57, and passim.

21. Rogers, *A History of Agriculture and Prices*, 5: 398–400, 6: 652. In 1588, a statute regulating London victuals-prices set a pound of "Tallowe Candles made of wicke" at three halfpennies; in 1599, the price was increased to four pence. See *A Booke Conteining All Such Proclamations as were Published During the Reign of Q. Elizabeth* (London, 1618), folios 343–44.

22. Thomas Dekker and John Webster, *Westward Ho!* (London, 1607; fac. rpt. London, 1911), D.

23. John Webster, *The White Devil* (London, 1612; fac. rpt. London, 1970), E3^v.

24. Albert Feuillerat, ed., *Documents Relating to the Office of the Revels in the Time of Queen Elizabeth*, Materialen zur Kunde des älteren englischen Dramas 21 (Louvain, 1908): 296.

25. Stow, *Survey of London*, H6^v; Thomas Blount, *Glossographia* (London, 1656; rpt. London, 1670), s.v. "cresset": "an old word for a Lanthorn or burning beacon."

26. Stephen Spector, ed., *The N-Town Play*, Early English Text Society (Oxford, 1991), 1: 289; R. W. Ingram, "'To find the player,'" *The Elizabethan Theatre* 5 (1975): 35–36.

27. *MSC* 11 (1980 [1981]): 119–32.

28. John Webster, *The Duchess of Malfi* (London, 1623), E2, N1.

29. T. D., *The Bloody Banquet* (London, 1639; rpt. London, 1962), F1^v–F2. An eighteenth-century English dark lantern is pictured in Hayward, *Colonial Lighting*, pl. 43. The sinister connotations of dark lanterns continued well into the twentieth century when writers like Conan Doyle and Dorothy Sayers made use of them.

30. George Chapman, *Bussy D'Ambois* (London, 1607), I4–I4^v. On the taper as emblem, see Dieter Mehl, "Emblems in English Renaissance Drama," *Renaissance Drama* 2 (1969): 52.

31. Webster, *The White Devil*, K2–K2^v.

32. George Cavendish, *The Life and Death of Cardinal Wolsey* (MS c. 1558; printed London, 1959), 69.

33. Alan H. Nelson, *Early Cambridge Theatres* (Cambridge, 1994), 112.

34. R. A. Foakes and R. T. Rickert, eds., *Henslowe's Diary* (Cambridge, 1961), 319.

35. Sebastian Serly, *The First Booke of Architecture* (London, 1611), bk. 2, chap. 3, fol. 26^v.

36. Illustrations and descriptions of these globes are found in Frank L. Horton, "New Thoughts on Eighteenth-Century Lighting," *Antiques* 67.1 (1955): 56–57.

37. N. D. Shergold, *A History of the Spanish Stage* (Oxford, 1967), 204.

3. Early Lighting Systems

1. Glynne Wickham, *Early English Stages*, 3 vols. (New York, 1959–81), 2, pt. 1: 153–275.

2. Alexandra Johnston, "'All the World Was a Stage': Records of Early English Drama," in *The Theatre of Medieval Europe*, ed. E. Simon (Cambridge, 1991), 124.

3. Oscar Brownstein, "Why Didn't Burbage Lease the Beargarden? A Conjecture in Comparative Architecture," in *The First Public Playhouse: The Theatre in Shoreditch 1576–1598*, ed. H. Berry (Montreal, 1979), 81–96; Orrell, *The Human Stage*, 14–20.

4. Herbert Berry, *The Boar's Head Playhouse* (Washington, 1986), 111.

5. Johnston, "'All the World Was a Stage,'" 124. The Queen's men played in "the Colledge Churche yarde" in Gloucester in 1589–90; see *Records of Early English Drama: Cumberland, Westmorland, Gloucestershire*, ed. A. Douglas and P. Greenfield (Toronto, 1986), 311.

6. *Records of Early English Drama: Devon*, ed. J. Wasson (Toronto, 1987), 320.

7. Richard Hosley, "The Origins of the Shakespearean Playhouse," in *Shakespeare 400*, ed. J. C. McManaway (New York, 1964), 29–39; Richard Southern, *The Staging of Plays Before Shakespeare* (London, 1973), 257–535. Although Hosley and Southern overemphasized hall screens as forerunners of tiring-house facades (many hall stages were *not* placed against screens), they were among the first to stress indoor hall performances by professional actors; see Alan H. Nelson, "Hall Screens and Elizabethan Playhouses," in *The Development of Shakespeare's Theater*, ed. J. Astington (New York, 1992), 57–76.

8. Francis A. Yates, *The Theatre of the World* (London, 1969); Richard C. Kohler, "The Fortune Contract and Vitruvian Symmetry," *Shakespeare Studies* 6 (1970): 311; "Excavating Henslowe's Rose," *Shakespeare Quarterly* 40 (1989): 475–82; and "Vitruvian Proportions in Theater Design in the Sixteenth and Early Seventeenth Centuries in Italy and England," *Shakespeare Studies* 16 (1983): 265–325. See also John Orrell, "The Architecture of the Fortune Playhouse," *Shakespeare Survey* 47 (1994): 16. Skepticism regarding how thoroughly amphitheaters followed Vitruvius is voiced by S. P. Cerasano, "Raising a Playhouse from the Dust," *Shakespeare Quarterly* 40 (1989): 483–90.

9. A. C. Pickard-Cambridge, *The Dramatic Festivals of Athens*, 2nd ed. (Oxford, 1968), 64, 67; W. Beare, "Rome," in *The Oxford Companion to the Theatre*, ed. P. Hartnoll (London, 1967). Clifford Ashby, "Did the Greeks Really Get to the Theatre before Dawn — Three Days Running?" *Theatre Research International* 17 (1992): 2–7, emphasizes the paucity of evidence regarding performance times in Greek theaters.

10. Margarete Bieber, *The History of the Greek and Roman Theaters* (Princeton, 1961), 115, 119, 169, 171; Clifford Ashby, "The Siting of Greek Theatres," *Theatre Research International* 16 (1991): 181–201.

11. Bieber, *Greek and Roman Theaters*, 135, 147, 180.

12. Allardyce Nicoll, *The Development of the Theatre*, 5th ed. (London, 1966), 41, 43; James T. Allen, *Stage Antiquities of the Greeks and Romans* (1927; rpt. New York, 1963), 91. George C. Izenour, *Roofed Theaters of Classical Antiquity* (New Haven, 1992), reconstructs several small, completely roofed auditoriums, lit, he conjectures, by windows and lanterns projecting above the roofs.

13. Lucretius, *The Nature of Things*, trans. F. Copley (New York, 1977), 84–85.

14. Bieber, *Greek and Roman Theaters*, 179.

15. T. F. Ordish, *Early London Theatres* (London, 1899), 15–24; Wickham, *Early English Stages*, 2, pt. 1: 161–72.

16. Kathleen Kenyon, *The Roman Theatre of Verulamium* (n.p., 1963).

17. Jane A. Bakere, *The Cornish Ordinalia: A Critical Study* (Cardiff, 1980), 155–56. The plays of the *Ordinalia* seem to date from around 1375.

18. Bakere, *The Cornish Ordinalia*, 12–13.

19. Vitruvius, *The Ten Books on Architecture*, trans. M. H. Morgan (1914; rpt. New York, 1960), 138, 148.

20. Mary H. Marshall, "Theatre in the Middle Ages: Evidence from Dictionaries and Glosses," *Symposium* 4 (1950): 9, 21, 24–25.

21. Richard Southern, *The Medieval Theatre in the Round*, 2nd ed. (London, 1975), 56–58.

22. Southern, *The Medieval Theatre in the Round*, 117–20. The kinship between early English and French staging in summarized by Hardin Craig, *English Religious Drama* (Oxford, 1955), 138.

23. *Ten Books on Architecture by Leone Baptista Alberti*, trans. Cosimo Bartoli and James Leoni (1755; fac. rpt. London, 1955), 178. On neoclassical theater architecture, see Michael Anderson, "The Changing Scene: Plays and Playhouses in the Italian Renaissance," in *Theatre of the English and Italian Renaissance*, ed. J. R. Mulryne and M. Shewring (New York, 1991), 3–20.

24. Quoted by Robert Sarlos, "Development and Operation of the First Blackfriars," in *Studies in the Elizabethan Theatre*, ed. C. Prouty (Hamden, Conn., 1961), 167.

25. Yates, *The Theatre of the World*, 27–35.

26. Roy Strong, *Splendor at Court* (London, 1973), 70; Herford, Simpson, and Simpson, *Ben Jonson*, 11: 599.

27. Translated in D. F. Rowan, "'The Swan' Revisited," *Research Opportunities in Renaissance Drama* 10 (1967): 34.

28. Thomas Heywood, *An Apology for Actors* (London, 1612), D2–D3.

29. Foakes and Rickert, *Henslowe's Diary*, 320.

30. Kohler, "The Fortune Contract and Vitruvian Symmetry," 311.

31. L. B. Campbell, *Scenes and Machines on the English Stage During the Renaissance* (Cambridge, 1923), 20; Nicoll, *The Development of the Theatre*, 74–75.

32. T. E. Lawrenson, *The French Stage in the XVIIth Century* (Manchester, 1957), 12–13.

33. George R. Kernodle, *From Art to Theatre* (Chicago, 1944), 72–98.

34. Wickham, *Early English Stages*, 1: 70.

35. Wickham, *Early English Stages*, 1: 89.

36. Kernodle, *From Art to Theatre*, 94.

37. Raphael Holinshed, *Chronicles* (London, 1587), 3: 932.

38. Robert Withington, *English Pageantry* (1918; rpt. New York, 1963), 1: 186.

39. See Alan H. Nelson, *The Medieval English Stage* (Chicago, 1974), 78, 93, 114, 136, 148, 159.

40. For a summary, see Stanley J. Kahrl, "The Staging of Medieval English Plays," in *The Theatre of Medieval Europe*, 138–39.

41. W. W. Greg, ed., *Chester Play Studies* (London, 1935), 166. Rogers died in 1595.

42. Norman Davis, ed., *Non-Cycle Plays and Fragments* (London, 1970), xxxv.

43. Hardin Craig, ed., *Two Coventry Corpus Christi Plays* (London, 1957), 89, 99.

44. Wickham, *Early English Stages*, 1: 170; F. M. Salter, *Mediaeval Drama in Chester* (Toronto, 1955), 68–70.

45. A. C. Cawley, ed., *The Wakefield Pageants* (Manchester, 1958), xxv.

46. Craig, *Two Coventry Corpus Christi Plays*, 74.

47. R[obert] W[ilmot], et al., *Gismond of Salerne* (MS c. 1568; fac. printing London, 1912), fol. 9. In the printed version of 1592, which the title page says had been "[n]ewly reuiued and polished according to the decorum of these daies," Cupid only "commeth out of the heauens" (A2ᵛ). Perhaps the play was revived in a venue without descent machinery; or, as there is no record of later performance, "reuiued" may mean that Wilmot and his friends returned to working on the text after some kind of hiatus.

48. Feuillerat, *Elizabeth*, 296.

49. Greene, *Alphonsus, King of Aragon*, A3, 13.

50. Foakes and Rickert, *Henslowe's Diary*, 7.

51. Andrew Gurr, introduction to *Philaster*, by Francis Beaumont and John Fletcher (London, 1969), xxxvii.

52. Orrell, *The Human Stage*, 30–60.

53. See Bonner Mitchell, "Circumstance and Setting in the Earliest Italian Productions of Comedy," *Renaissance Drama* 4 (1971): 190.

54. Sydney Anglo, *Spectacle, Pageantry, and Early Tudor Policy* (Oxford, 1969), 159–61. I follow Anglo's transcriptions and translations of the 1520 sources throughout. For a reconstruction of the Calais theater, see Richard Hosley, "The Theatre and the Tradition of Playhouse Design," in *The First Public Playhouse*, 60–74.

55. Anglo, *Spectacle*, 217.

56. Calvete de Estrella, *El felícimo viaje del muy príncipe don Felipe* (Antwerp, 1552; rpt. Madrid, 1930), 2: 68. The following description is paraphrased from 67–69.

57. Thomas Heywood, *The Silver Age* (London, 1613), 14ᵛ. Presumably the play was produced at the Red Bull.

58. E. K. Chambers, *The Elizabethan Stage*, 4 vols. (1923; corr. ed. Oxford, 1951), 3: 78.

59. Bernard Beckerman, *Shakespeare at the Globe* (New York, 1962), 106; John Astington, "Descent Machinery in the Playhouses," *Medieval and Renaissance Drama in England* 2 (1985): 119–33.

60. Francis Grose, ed., *The Antiquarian Repertory* (London, 1807), 1: 313.

61. Anglo, *Spectacle*, 161.

62. The following description is based on Building and Revels Office accounts of May 1527, printed in Wickham, *Early English Stages*, 2, pt. 2: 212–20.

63. *Records of Early English Drama: Cambridge*, ed. Alan H. Nelson (Toronto, 1989), 1: 234.

64. Quoted by Wickham, *Early English Stages*, 1: 356.

65. W. Y. Durand, "*Palamon and Arcyte, Progne, Marcus Geminus*, and the Theatre in which They Were Acted, as Described by John Bereblock (1566)," *PMLA* 20 (1905): 505.

66. Felix Schelling, *Elizabethan Drama* (Boston and New York, 1908), 1: 107; W. J. Lawrence, *The Elizabethan Playhouse* (Stratford, 1913), 2: 13; and O'Dea, *The Social History of Lighting*, 155.

67. Wickham, *Early English Stages*, 1: 359.

68. Nelson, *Early Cambridge Theatres*, 111–13.

69. *Records of Early English Drama: Cambridge*, 1: 166.

70. *Records of Early English Drama: Cambridge*, 1: 152.

71. Royal Commission on Historical Monuments, *An Inventory of the Historical Monuments in the City of Cambridge* (London, 1959), 2: 209 and maps.

72. *Records of Early English Drama: Cambridge*, 1: 208.

73. *Records of Early English Drama: Cambridge*, 1: 357.

74. Royal Commission, *An Inventory of the Historical Monuments in the City of Cambridge*, 1, facing p. 84, and maps.

75. *Records of Early English Drama: Cambridge*, 1: 212.

76. G. C. Moore Smith, *College Plays Performed in the University of Cambridge* (Cambridge, 1923), 33.

77. G. E. Bentley, *The Jacobean and Caroline Stage*, 7 vols. (Oxford, 1941–68), 4: 529–30.

78. Bentley, *The Jacobean and Caroline Stage*, 5: 1263–64.

79. John M. Wasson, "The English Church as Theatrical Space," in *A New History of Early English Drama*, ed. J. Cox and D. Kastan (New York, 1997), 26.

80. *MSC* 8 (1974): 91–92.

81. E. K. Chambers, *The Mediaeval Stage* (Oxford, 1903), 2: 382.

82. *Records of Early English Drama: Norwich, 1540–1642*, ed. D. Galloway (Toronto, 1984), 52.

83. D. F. Rowan, "The Players and Playing Places of Norwich," in *The Development of Shakespeare's Theater*, 90.

84. T. W. Craik, *The Tudor Interlude* (Leicester, 1958); Southern, *The Staging of Plays Before Shakespeare*. Nelson, *Early Cambridge Theatres*, passim, demonstrates that Cambridge stages were not always set against hall screens, as assumed by Hosley and Southern.

85. John Heywood, *Johan Johan* (London, 1533; fac. rpt. London, 1972), A2ᵛ, B4ᵛ; Henry Medwall, *Nature* (n.d.; fac. rpt. London, 1908), G1.

86. John Heywood, *The Play of the Weather* (London, 1533; fac. rpt. London, 1914), A3.

87. *Records of Early English Drama: Cumberland, Westmorland, Gloucestershire*, 299. Andrew Gurr, *The Shakespearian Playing Companies* (Oxford, 1996), 181, 194, lists only a few payments by civic authorities for candles and torches for professional players.

88. John T. Murray, *English Dramatic Companies* (London, 1910), 2: 214.

89. *Records of Early English Drama: York*, ed. A. Johnston and M. Rogerson (Toronto, 1979), 449.

90. Sybil Rosenfeld, "Dramatic Companies in the Provinces in the 16th and Early 17th Centuries," *Theatre Notebook* 8 (1953): 58; Andrew Gurr, "The Loss of Records for Travelling Companies in Stuart Times," *Records of Early English Drama* 19.2 (1994): 11.

91. *Records of Early English Drama: Norwich, 1540–1642*, 71.

92. Murray, *English Dramatic Companies*, 2: 233.

93. *Records of Early English Drama: Norwich, 1540–1642*, 113. A "not" in this entry has been canceled, but Murray, *English Dramatic Companies*, 2: 338, retains it, which the sense seems to require.

94. *Records of Early English Drama: Chester*, ed. L. Clopper (Toronto, 1979), 292–93.

95. Bentley, *The Jacobean and Caroline Stage*, 1: 276.

96. Rosenfeld, "Dramatic Companies," 57.

97. Bentley, *The Jacobean and Caroline Stage*, 1: 312.

98. Chambers, *The Elizabethan Stage*, 4: 267.

99. *MSC* 2, pt. 3 (1931): 310.

100. Gervase Babington, *A very fruitful Exposition of the Commaundements by way of Questions and Answeres* (London, 1583), 317–18.

101. Chambers, *The Elizabethan Stage*, 4: 340.

102. Thomas Nash, *Nashes Lenton Stuffe* (London, 1599), A3.

103. *MSC* 5 (1960): 21–22.

104. Thomas Middleton, *Your Five Gallants* (London, [1608]), C2.

105. *The Letters of John Chamberlain*, ed. N. E. McClure (Philadelphia, 1939), 2: 159.

106. *The Diary of Samuel Pepys*, ed. Robert Latham and W. Matthews, 11 vols. (Berkeley, 1970–83), 1: 61.

107. Stephen Orgel and Roy Strong, eds., *Inigo Jones: The Theatre of the Stuart Court* (London, 1973), 1: 282.

4. Afternoon Performances at the Outdoor Playhouses

1. Pointed out by George R. Kernodle, "The Open Stage: Elizabethan or Existentialist?" *Shakespeare Survey* 12 (1959): 1. Bernard Beckerman, "Use and Management of the Elizabethan Stage," in *The Third Globe*, ed. C. W Hodges, S. Schoenbaum, and L. Leone (Detroit, 1981), 163, argues that

> actors lit by artificial light, when playing against a colorful façade that is either lit directly or that receives considerable spill light, tend to get lost. . . . In comparison, in natural light the background color is softer and does not interfere with a clear perception of the actor.

2. Edmond Malone, "An Historical Account of the Rise and Progress of the English Stage" (1790), rpt. in *The Plays and Poems of William Shakespeare* (Third Variorum), ed. James Boswell (London, 1821), 3: 109.

3. Quoted in Bentley, *The Jacobean and Caroline Stage*, 2: 694.

4. The best summary of performance times is in Gurr, *The Shakespearian Playing Companies*, 78–81.

5. C. W. Dugmore, "Canonical Hours," in *A Dictionary of Liturgy and Worship*, ed. J. Davies (New York, 1972). General background is in Horton Davies, *Worship and Theology in England from Cranmer to Hooker* (Princeton, 1970), 178, 204, and M. E. Cornford, "Ecclesiastical History: 1547–1563," in *The Victoria History of London*, ed. W. Page (London, 1909), 1: 295.

6. David Knowles, *The Monastic Order in England* (Cambridge, 1963), 715.

7. Charles Pendrill, *Old Parish Life in London* (London, 1937), 36.

8. Cornford, "Ecclesiastical History," 1: 295, 318. From 1582 onward, lectures were read in St. Margaret's Church in New Fish Street after evening prayer from 5 to 6 P.M. on Mondays and after 1591 on Sundays as well. Presumably, the evening prayer service there began at 3 or 4 P.M.

9. Reavley Gair, *The Children of Paul's* (Cambridge, 1982), 53.

10. Walter H. Frere, ed., *Visitation Articles and Injunctions of the Period of the Reformation* (London, 1910), 3: 303.

11. Ronald Bayne, "Religion," in *Shakespeare's England*, ed. S. Lee and C. T. Onions (Oxford, 1916), 1: 62; Chambers, *The Elizabethan Stage*, 1: 313.

12. Chambers, *The Elizabethan Stage*, 4: 268.

13. Chambers, *The Elizabethan Stage*, 4: 269.

14. Sunset times are drawn from Thomas Buckminster, *An Almanacke and Prognostication, for the yeere of Christes incarnation MD.XC.VIII* (London, 1598). These times check closely with modern figures in *Whitaker's Almanac* (London, 1994), taking into account the differences between old- and new-style calendars. England did not adopt the present Gregorian calendar until 1752. As a result, the equinoxes and solstices before that were ten days earlier than the dates on which they now fall. See W. W. Greg, "Old Style—New Style," in *Joseph Quincy Adams Memorial Studies*, ed. J. McManaway et al. (Washington, 1948), 563–569.

15. Gurr, "The Loss of Records," 11.

16. Richard Dutton, *Mastering the Revels: The Regulation and Censorship of English Renaissance Drama* (Iowa City, 1991). For relations among the Privy Council, the Corporation of the City of London, and the actors, see Carol Chillington Rutter's introduction to *Documents of the Rose Playhouse* (Manchester, 1984), 9–18, and Chambers, *The Elizabethan Stage*, 1: 269–307.

17. Virginia C. Gildersleeve, *Government Regulation of the Elizabethan Drama* (New York, 1908), 158.

18. *MSC* 1, pt. 1 (1907 [1908]): 53.

19. Chambers, *The Elizabethan Stage*, 4: 369.

20. Chambers, *The Elizabethan Stage*, 4: 285.

21. *MSC* 1, pt. 1: 54.

22. *MSC* 1, pt. 1: 63–64.

23. Raphael Holinshed, *Chronicles*, revised by John Hooker (London, 1577), 3: kkkkk6ᵛ.

24. John Stow, *The Annales of England* (London, 1592), Iiiiᵛ.

25. *MSC* 1, pt. 2 (1908): 164.

26. Gildersleeve, *Government Regulation*, 169–70. Also, the plague was widespread in 1583, perhaps forcing the players outside city regulation.

27. *MSC* 1, pt. 2: 169–70.

28. *MSC* 1, pt. 2: 172.

29. *MSC* 1, pt. 2: 174.

30. *MSC* 1, pt. 2: 187–88. Chambers, *The Elizabethan Stage*, 1: 314, confuses the date and location of the riot.

31. W. W. Greg, ed., *Henslowe's Diary* (London, 1904–8), 1: 220, 2: 51.

32. Foakes and Rickert, *Henslowe's Diary*, 19.

33. Foakes and Rickert, *Henslowe's Diary*, 19. The dates given in Henslowe's diary raise several problems; Greg distrusts many Sunday dates. Although a few are demonstrably wrong, we cannot disregard such important evidence as the diary contains. For a summary of the difficulties, see Foakes and Rickert, *Henslowe's Diary*, xxvi–xxviii.

34. Gildersleeve, *Government Regulation*, 181.

35. Chambers, *The Elizabethan Stage*, 4: 312–13.

36. See Wickham, *Early English Stages*, 2, pt. 1: 194; Chambers, *The Elizabethan Stage*, 4: 268; and *MSC* 2, pt. 3: 310.

37. *MSC* 1, pt. 1: 74.

38. Wickham, *Early English Stages*, 2, pt. 2: 95–101; see also T. S. Graves, *The Court and the London Theatres* (1913; rpt. New York, 1967), 32. O. L. Brownstein, "A Record of London Inn Playhouses from c. 1565–1590," *Shakespeare Quarterly* 22 (1971): 22, assumes the actors occupied large rooms in the Cross Keys and Bull, but Chambers, *The Elizabethan Stage*, 2: 527, doubts the inns had any indoor rooms large enough for plays.

39. *Records of Early English Drama: Norwich, 1540–1642*, 71, and see David Galloway,

"Records of Early English Drama in the Provinces," *The Elizabethan Theatre* 7 (1980): 97–98.

40. Berry, *The Boar's Head Playhouse*, 16–17. Berry cautions that the Boar's Head involved in the 1557 account might possibly be a different inn from the one converted to a more permanent theater in 1597.

41. Chambers, *The Elizabethan Stage*, 4: 369. Because records of Elizabethan fencing matches do not include the Cross Keys or the Bull, Brownstein, "A Record of London Inn Playhouses," 23, suggests that these inns may have had only indoor performance venues.

42. L[eslie] S[tephens], "Flecknoe, Richard," *DNB* (1963–64).

43. Murray, *English Dramatic Companies*, 1: 30; E. K. Chambers, *William Shakespeare: A Study of Facts and Problems* (Oxford, 1930), 2: 323; Chambers, *The Elizabethan Stage*, 2: 412, 413, 442; Andrew Gurr, *The Shakespearean Stage*, 3rd ed. (Cambridge, 1992), 42; Bentley, *The Jacobean and Caroline Stage*, 1: 163, 2: 677, 7: 37, 100.

44. Webster, *The White Devil*, A2; Ben Jonson, *Poetaster* (London, 1602), F3ᵛ.

45. Brownstein, "A Record of London Inn Playhouses," 21–22.

46. Printed in *The Plays and Poems of William Shakespeare*, 21: 414.

47. Chambers, *The Elizabethan Stage*, 2: 543; Thomas Platter, *Beschreibung der Reisen*, ed. R. Keiser (Basel, 1968), 2: 791. Later in the diary, Platter omits the "etwann," saying that plays were acted every day "umb 2 uhren nache mittag" (792).

48. Because Platter went to the theater directly from lunch, the fact that it took a gallant in Sir John Davies's *Epigrammes and Elegies* (Middleborough, [1590]), D1, one hour to go from the playhouse to supper may indicate more than just a quick trip for Platter.

49. See Bentley, *The Jacobean and Caroline Stage*, 4: 875, 6: 33.

50. Malone, "An Historical Account," in *The Plays and Poems of William Shakespeare*, 3: 144.

51. I[ohn] D[avies], *Epigrammes and Elegies*, D1.

52. J. P. Collier, *Annals of the Stage* (1831; rpt. London, 1879), 3: 180.

53. *Histriomastix, or The Player Whipt* (London, 1610; fac. rpt. London, 1912), B4ᵛ–C1.

54. Thomas Cranley, *Amanda, or The Reformed Whore* (London, 1635), F3.

55. Thomas Dekker, *The Guls Horne-booke* (London, 1609), D3ᵛ.

56. Bentley, *The Jacobean and Caroline Stage*, 4: 875.

57. Gurr, *The Shakespearian Playing Companies*, 79.

58. See, e.g., T[homas?] G[offe?], *The Careless Shepherdess* (London, 1656), B4ᵛ.

59. Foakes and Rickert, *Henslowe's Diary*, 86.

60. T. S. Graves, "Night Scenes in the Elizabethan Theatre," *Englische Studien* 47 (1913): 67. Graves does not mention that in 1617, Orazio Busino records that a trick was played on him in the "evening" at a playhouse that has regularly been identified as the Fortune, although Bentley, *The Jacobean and Caroline Stage*, 6: 151–52, shows that this is an unverified nineteenth-century identification.

61. Foakes and Rickert, *Henslowe's Diary*, 88.

62. Gurr, "The Loss of Records," 2–18, shows that before 1603, Elizabeth's 1559 proclamation generally allotted touring companies the largest room in town; after 1603, when the proclamation was not renewed, provincial cities increasingly disallowed performances or relegated the actors to local inns.

63. Marvin Rosenberg, "Public Night Performances in Shakespeare's Time," *Theatre Notebook* 8 (1953): 44–45.

64. *MSC* 4 (1956): 60; Chambers, *The Elizabethan Stage*, 4: 320.

65. Gurr, "The Loss of Records," 12–15.

66. Albert Cohn, *Shakespeare in Germany* (London, 1865), pl. 2.

67. Alfred Hart, "The Time Allotted for Representation of Elizabethan and Jacobean Plays," *Review of English Studies* 8 (1932): 402.

68. David Klein, "Time Allotted for an Elizabethan Performance," *Shakespeare Quarterly* 18 (1967): 434–38.

69. Chambers, *The Elizabethan Stage*, 2: 345.

70. Gurr, *The Shakespearian Playing Companies*, 82.

71. Herford, Simpson, and Simpson, *Ben Jonson*, 5: 15.

72. H. A. Rennert, *The Spanish Stage in the Time of Lope de Vega* (1909; rpt. New York, 1963), 111. However, fines were levied against performances extending past dusk (which, for most of the year, is later in Madrid than in London); see E. Wilson and D. Moir, *A Literary History of Spain: The Golden Age Drama* (London, 1971), 34–35.

73. J. H. Brazell, *London Weather*, Meteorological Office Publication 783 (London, 1968), 172.

74. See H. H. Lamb, *The Changing Climate* (1966; rpt. London, 1972), 5–12; and Brazell, *London Weather*, appendix 1.

75. C. Walter Hodges, *Shakespeare's Theatre* (London, 1964), 64.

76. Bentley, *The Jacobean and Caroline Stage*, 6: 136.

77. Dekker, *The Guls Horne-booke*, E4^v. Dekker's chapter on playhouses is a composite description of both public and private playhouses with the scene shifting vaguely back and forth. At the point in question, Dekker seems to be discussing amphitheaters.

78. N. C. Bawcutt, ed. *The Control and Censorship of Caroline Drama: The Records of Sir Henry Herbert, Master of the Revels 1623–73* (Oxford, 1996), 166.

5. Illumination of the Outdoor Playhouses

1. Richard Hosley, "The Playhouses," in *The Revels History of Drama in English*, ed. T. W. Craik et al. (London, 1975), 3: 136–74.

2. Janet Leongard, "An Elizabethan Lawsuit: John Brayne, his Carpenter, and the Building of the Red Lion Theatre," *Shakespeare Quarterly* 34 (1983): 309.

3. Richard Hosley, "The Playhouse and the Stage," in *A New Companion to Shakespeare Studies*, ed. K. Muir and S. Schoenbaum (Cambridge, 1971), 30.

4. Details of the Rose's remains are conveniently summarized by Julian M. C. Bow-

sher and Simon Blatherwick, "The Structure of the Rose," in *New Issues in the Recon-struction of Shakespeare's Theatre*, ed. F. Hildy (New York, 1990), 55–78.

5. Berry, *The Boar's Head Playhouse*, 139, 164.

6. Orrell, *The Human Stage*, 81–87. But Andrew Gurr, "The Bare Island," *Shakespeare Survey* 47 (1994): 37, points out that rainwater falling off a roof whose gable end faced the yard would not produce the visible erosion line parallel to the front of the Rose stage.

7. Bentley, *The Jacobean and Caroline Stage*, 6: 183.

8. Richard Hosley, "Stage Superstructures of the First Globe and the Swan," in *The Development of Shakespeare's Theater*, 128–137. Hosley is supported by Stuart E. Baker, "Turrets and Tiring Houses on the Elizabethan Public Stage," *Theatre Notebook* 49 (1995): 134–51, who argues that "integrated" stage covers (i.e., with the rear of the roof con-nected to the galleries and the front of the roof supported by pillars) would be mechani-cally unstable.

9. Richard Hosley, "A Reconstruction of the Fortune Playhouse, Part 1," *The Eliza-bethan Theatre* 6 (1978): 1–20.

10. W. W. Greg, *Henslowe Papers* (London, 1907), 26.

11. Hosley's assumptions also force him to posit an unmentioned third door giving ac-cess to the tiring-house and lords' rooms, even though Thomas Platter implies that spec-tators who ultimately arrived in the yard, galleries, and lords' rooms all initially entered at the same door.

12. Alan Young, "The Orientation of the Elizabethan Stage," *Theatre Notebook* 33 (1979): 80–85.

13. Vitruvius, *The Ten Books on Architecture*, 138.

14. See Wickham, *Early English Stages*, 1: 37.

15. Dekker, *The Guls Horne-booke*, E2^v.

16. John Orrell, "Beyond the Rose: Design Problems for the Globe Reconstruction," in *New Issues in the Reconstruction of Shakespeare's Theatre*, 110.

17. C. Walter Hodges, "Reconstructing the Rose," in *New Issues in the Reconstruction of Shakespeare's Theatre*, 79–94.

18. Glynne Wickham, "'Heavens,' Machinery, and Pillars in the Theatre and Other Early Playhouses," in *The First Public Playhouse*, ed. H. Berry (Montreal, 1979), 1–15.

19. Berry, *The Boar's Head Playhouse*, 108, 127.

20. Bowsher and Blatherwick, "The Structure of the Rose," in *New Issues in the Re-construction of Shakespeare's Theatre*, 71.

21. Berry, *The Boar's Head Playhouse*, 109, 111.

22. Greg, *Henslowe Papers*, 5.

23. A. M. Nagler, *Shakespeare's Stage*, trans. R. Manheim (New Haven, 1958), 24–25.

24. Chambers, *The Elizabethan Stage*, 2: 466–67.

25. C. Walter Hodges, *Shakespeare's Second Globe: The Missing Monument* (London, 1973), 61–73.

26. Hodges, *Shakespeare's Second Globe*, 73–76.

27. Bentley, *The Jacobean and Caroline Stage*, 6: 273.

28. Richard Hosley, "The Second Globe," *Theatre Notebook* 29 (1975): 141–42.

29. Hodges, *Shakespeare's Second Globe*, 75; Richard Southern, "On Reconstructing a Practicable Elizabethan Playhouse," *Shakespeare Survey* 12 (1959): 30. Southern's estimate of the purpose of these windows is confirmed by the similar slot windows in the Jones playhouse (see fig. 29).

30. Greg, *Henslowe Papers*, 5.

31. Baker, "Turrets and Tiring Houses," 143.

32. Richard H. Palmer, *The Lighting Art* (Englewood Cliffs, 1985), 15.

33. Foakes and Rickert, *Henslowe's Diary*, 6–7. John Ronayne, "Totus Mundus agit Histrionum," in *Shakespeare's Globe Rebuilt*, ed. J. Mulryne and M. Shewring (Cambridge, 1997), 122–43, argues that Elizabethan decorative style implies brightly painted playhouse interiors.

34. Foakes and Rickert, *Henslowe's Diary*, 309–10.

35. Estimates are based on figures derived from the Department of Scientific and Industrial Research Technical Paper No. 17, *Seasonal Variations of Daylight Illumination* (London, 1935), 3–7, and R. G. Hopkinson, *Architectural Physics: Lighting* (London, 1963), 50–88.

36. *A Warning for Fair Women* (London, 1599; fac. rpt. London, 1912), A3. Chambers cites other references to black hangings in *The Elizabethan Stage*, 3: 79.

37. The following discussion of the perception of light is based on C. A. Padgham and J. E. Saunders, *The Perception of Light and Colour* (New York, 1975), 37–60, and Matthew Luckiesh and Frank Moss, *The Science of Seeing* (New York, 1937).

38. I use photographs taken in August 1995, when no artificial lights were used; the stage cover was temporary and lacked the gable now in place, which further reduces frank sunshine in the yard.

39. That is, since Stanley McCandless's influential *A Method of Lighting the Stage* (New York, 1932).

40. Luckiesh and Moss, *The Science of Seeing*, 335.

41. For example, Bertolt Brecht, *Schriften zum Theater* (Frankfurt, 1957), 260–61; Antonin Artaud, *The Theatre and Its Double*, trans. M. C. Richards (New York, 1958), 96; and Jerzy Grotowski, *Towards a Poor Theatre* (New York, 1968), 20, call for the illumination of the entire theater largely on the authority of Elizabethan stage practice.

42. J. L. Styan, *Shakespeare's Stagecraft* (Cambridge, 1967), 42–44.

43. Cyril Tourneur, *The Atheist's Tragedy* (London, 1611), 12^V.

44. William Haughton, *Englishmen for My Money* (London, 1616; fac. rpt. London, 1912), G1–G1^V.

45. Styan, *Shakespeare's Stagecraft*, 42.

46. Most praise for acting, for example, was based on truth to nature; see Daniel Seltzer, "The Actors and Staging," in *A New Companion to Shakespeare Studies*, 36, and Gurr, *The Shakespearean Stage*, 100.

47. See "The Dialogues of Leone di Somi," qtd. in Nicoll, *The Development of the Theatre*, 275, and M. St. Claire Byrne, "Stage Lighting," in *The Oxford Companion to the Theatre*, 567. Di Somi also called for some of the first "mood" lighting on record. He preferred brilliant light on the scene until "the first unhappy incident occurred," when he extinguished most of the light near the stage (274).

48. Chambers, *The Elizabethan Stage*, 2: 543. Hart, "Time Allotted," 410; T. S. Graves, "Notes on Elizabethan Theatres," *Studies in Philology* 103 (1916): 112; William Poel qtd. in Robert Speaight, *William Poel and the Elizabethan Revival* (London, 1954), 132; and Lawrence, *The Elizabethan Playhouse*, 2: 13, concur and propose that torches, candles, or cressets were used outdoors. Michael Hattaway, *Elizabethan Popular Theatre* (London, 1982), 56, is even more emphatic: "Lighting was necessary," he states, "and may have been used for theatrical effects in the public playhouses."

49. Herford, Simpson, and Simpson, *Ben Jonson*, 7: 88.

50. *MSC* 2, pt. 2 (1923): 153–54.

51. See I. von Roeder-Baumbach and H. G. Evers, *Versieringen bij Blijde Inkomsten* (Antwerp, 1949). In Spain itself, large torches routinely graced daytime performances of outdoor *autos*; see Nagler, *A Source Book in Theatrical History*, 67.

52. Kernodle, *From Art to Theatre*, 116–29; W. M. H. Hummelen, "Types and Methods of the Dutch Rhetoricians' Theatre," in *The Third Globe*, 164–80.

53. W. J. Lawrence, "Night Performances in the Elizabethan Theatres," *Englische Studien* 48 (1915): 219. I quote from Collier, *Annals*, 1: 144.

54. Greg, *Henslowe Papers*, 84.

55. Berry, *The Boar's Head Playhouse*, 173. Here, Mago's "cressett lights" refers not to the sturdy iron utensils but to the woven frales placed in them.

56. Stow, *Survey of London*, H6^v.

57. See Gurr, *Playgoing*, 20.

58. Bentley, *The Jacobean and Caroline Stage*, 6: 106.

59. Keith Brown, "More light, more light," *Essays in Criticism* 34 (1984): 1–13. In reply, Andrew Gurr, "'Lights, Ho!' (I)," *Essays in Criticism* 34 (1984): 271–77, pointed out Brown's lack of evidence and suggested that if poor light was a problem, the companies' response was to move indoors; while John Orrell, "'Lights, Ho!' (II)," *Essays in Criticism* 34 (1984): 278–82, agreed that cressets would have been regularly required in winter.

60. Luckiesh and Moss, *The Science of Seeing*, 86, 387–93.

61. Luckiesh and Moss, *The Science of Seeing*, 336.

62. Padgham and Saunders, *The Perception of Light and Colour*, 41.

63. Wickham, *Early English Stages*, 2, pt. 1: 194.

64. Wilfred T. Jewkes, *Act Division in Elizabethan and Jacobean Plays* (Hamden, Conn., 1958), 100–101; Richard Hosley, "Was There a Music-Room in Shakespeare's Globe?" *Shakespeare Survey* 13 (1960): 117.

65. Lawrence, "Night Performances," 228, citing Edmund Howe's additions to John Stow's *Annales of England* (London, 1631), Iiii^v.

66. We must question, therefore, whether Robert Fludd's *Theatrum Orbis* is a picture of the second Globe, as Francis Yates claims in *The Theatre of the World*. Fludd shows direct sunlight covering the back wall and most of the "stage" floor, an impossibility at the second Globe judging by Hollar's view of the hut. For similar reasons, we may discount I. A. Shapiro's alternate suggestion in "Robert Fludd's Stage-Illustration," *Shakespeare Studies* 2 (1966): 192–209, that it portrays the Blackfriars.

6. Daylight in the Indoor Playhouses

1. Bentley, *The Jacobean and Caroline Stage*, 2: 694.
2. See, for example, L. B. Wright, "The Britain That Shakespeare Knew," *National Geographic* 125 (1967): 651, and Irwin Smith, *Shakespeare's Blackfriars Playhouse* (New York, 1964), 259.
3. Harold N. Hillebrand, *The Child Actors* (Urbana, Ill., 1926), 123.
4. Gair, *The Children of Paul's*, 53. Because Westcott bequeathed ten shillings to the keeper of the gate (presumably the gates to the churchyard), Gair assumes that the performances sometimes continued after dusk, when the gates were normally closed (56), although a 1608 sermon by the puritan divine William Crashawe suggests that plays were extended in the other direction when he describing evening prayers as "cut shorter to make roome" for plays (166).
5. Chambers, *The Elizabethan Stage*, 4: 320.
6. John Day, *The Isle of Gulls* (London, 1606; fac. rpt. London, 1936), A3.
7. MSC 1, pt. 1: 91–92.
8. In 1602, German tourists were delighted by a one-hour concert before a Children of the Chapel play at Blackfriars (Bentley, *The Jacobean and Caroline Stage*, 6: 33).
9. John Earle, *Microcosmographie* (London, 1628), E7ᵛ.
10. Bawcutt, *The Control and Censorship of Caroline Drama*, 182. Presumably, the King's men had moved from the Globe by 19 and 21 October 1633, the dates of the canceled performances.
11. Mildmay went to Blackfriars before supper on 25 April 1632, 25 November 1635, 27 October 1638, and 15 May 1640; "this after Noone" on 28 April 1635; and "dined . . . & wento the fryers blacke to a play" on 3 November 1637 (Bentley, *The Jacobean and Caroline Stage*, 2: 677–78).
12. J. Q. Adams, *Shakespearean Playhouses* (Boston, 1917), 232–33; Bentley, *The Jacobean and Caroline Stage*, 6: 34–36. Bawcutt, *The Control and Censorship of Caroline Drama*, 174–75, 188, adds two instances of the queen's visits to Blackfriars unknown to Adams and Bentley.
13. J. Q. Adams, ed., *The Dramatic Records of Sir Henry Herbert* (New Haven, 1912), 76–77. Occasional afternoon rehearsals at court also necessitated a Blackfriars cancellation. On 16 March 1632, for example, the King's men were paid for "the rehersall of one [play] at the Cockpitt by which meanes they lost their afternoone at the House" (MSC 2, pt. 3: 360).

14. Although the queen's attendance at Blackfriars in 1636 and 1638 is noted in extant King's men's bills, her presence is not confirmed by Herbert's corresponding accounts, a fact not mentioned by Adams or Bentley. No venues are cited for 1636, and Blackfriars is specifically excluded from the 1638 warrant that assigns all plays that season to Hampton Court, Richmond, and Whitehall; see the warrants in *MSC* 2, pt. 3: 382 and 388–89. Gurr, *The Shakespearian Playing Companies*, 80, doubts that all these performances were at night.

15. T. S. Graves, "The 'Act Time' in Elizabethan Theatres," *Studies in Philology* 12 (1915): 110, and I. Smith, *Shakespeare's Blackfriars Playhouse*, 259, cite references to "night" in various Blackfriars plays as proof of nighttime performances.

16. Chambers, *The Elizabethan Stage*, 2: 369. However, there is a record of one surreptitious night performance at Whitefriars by sixteen "apprentices"; see D. F. McKenzie's introduction to *The Hog Hath Lost His Pearl* (London, 1972), vi–vii. When the Whitefriars lease expired in 1615, Philip Rosseter, the lutanist, fitted up a hall in the Blackfriars district, to which puritan neighbors objected on the grounds that it was a "greevous Disturbaunce to the Devine service of God" (*MSC* 4: 60).

17. Bentley, *The Jacobean and Caroline Stage*, 2: 676–77.

18. G[offe?], *The Careless Shepherdess*, B4^v. It is thought the praeludium was written for a revival about 1638.

19. Bentley, *The Jacobean and Caroline Stage*, 6: 106.

20. This estimate of the number of candles is based on prices in Rogers, *A History of Agriculture and Prices*, 5: 398–400, 6: 652.

21. Bentley, *The Jacobean and Caroline Stage*, 6: 97, 100, 104, 112. There is also reason to believe that the occupants in 1639, Queen Henrietta's men, did not make regular summer tours; see Murray, *English Dramatic Companies*, 1: 269.

22. John Astington, "*The Wits* Illustration, 1662," *Theatre Notebook* 47 (1993): 122–40, argues that the illustration is a collage drawn from various iconographic sources, some Continental, but not based on a particular theater, however much it may reflect theatrical practice before the 1660s.

23. Thomas Dekker, *The Seven Deadlie Sinns of London* (London, 1606), D2.

24. Bawcutt, *The Control and Censorship of Caroline Drama*, 199.

25. The description of the hall at Hampton Court is based on the Royal Commission on Historical Monuments, *An Inventory of the Historical Monuments in Middlesex* (London, 1937), 34–35, except that I use the dimensions in Alvin Kernan, *Shakespeare, the King's Playwright* (New Haven, 1995), 209. The present window glass dates from the nineteenth century.

26. This description of the Middle Temple hall is based on the Royal Commission on Historical Monuments, *An Inventory of the Historical Monuments in London* (London, 1929), 4: 148. G. P. V. Akrigg, in "*Twelfth Night* at the Middle Temple," *Shakespeare Quarterly* 9 (1958): 422–24, has suggested that Feste's indication of more than one bay window in Malvolio's "mad" scene implies that *Twelfth Night* had its premiere at the Middle Temple rather than at the Tudor hall in Whitehall with its single oriel window. I doubt that

we can be so precise in the matter; when he wrote the play, Shakespeare surely knew that it would also be performed at the Globe, which had no bay windows.

27. Adams, *Shakespearean Playhouses*, 95.

28. I. Smith, *Shakespeare's Blackfriars Playhouse*, 11–15, 98–100.

29. MSC 2, pt. 1 (1913 [1914]): 61.

30. Hillebrand, *The Child Actors*, 183.

31. Hosley, "The Playhouses," 3: 202.

32. Chambers, *The Elizabethan Stage*, 2: 516.

33. Reproduced in Adams, *Shakespearean Playhouses*, 313.

34. A. W. Clapham, "The Topography of the Carmelite Priory of London," *Journal of the British Archological Association* 16 (1910): 15–16.

35. Geoffrey Webb, *Architecture in Britain: The Middle Ages* (Harmondsworth, 1956), 65, 212.

36. W. A. Hinnebusch, *The Early English Friars Preachers* (Rome, 1951), 158–61.

37. For the agreement between English and neoclassical precedent on steeply angled interior light, see Per Palme, *The Triumph of Peace* (Uppsala, 1956), 176–201.

38. Thomas Fuller, *The Holy State* (Cambridge, 1642), Y4. The only definite theatrical exception to Fuller's precepts was the Trinity Hall, sporadically rented by actors from 1557 to 1568. This hall was only thirty-five by fifteen feet, with a large, high window opposite the gallery but no windows in the sidewalls. See C. T. Prouty, "An Early Elizabethan Playhouse," *Shakespeare Survey* 6 (1953): 64–75.

39. MSC 10: 19.

40. See D. F. Rowan's "The Cockpit-in-Court," *The Elizabethan Theatre* 1 (1969): 89–102; "A Neglected Jones/Webb Theatre Project," *The Elizabethan Theatre* 2 (1970): 60–73; and "The English Playhouse: 1595–1630," *Renaissance Drama* 4 (1971): 37–51.

41. See John Orrell's "Inigo Jones at the Cockpit," *Shakespeare Survey* 30 (1977): 157; *The Theatres of Inigo Jones and John Webb* (Cambridge, 1985), 39–77; and his and Andrew Gurr's *Rebuilding Shakespeare's Globe* (London, 1989), 129–48.

42. The vertical placement of the galleries in the private theaters is a matter of pure conjecture. Most interest has focused on the second Blackfriars. I. Smith, *Shakespeare's Blackfriars Playhouse*, 307, puts the galleries on the floor of the hall with none on the stage; D. F. Rowan, "The Tiring-House Wall and the Galleries in the Second Blackfriars," *Theatre Notebook* 26 (1972): 101–4, puts them on the level of the stage all around the theater on the authority of the Jones playhouse drawings; Richard Hosley, "A Reconstruction of the Second Blackfriars," *The Elizabethan Theatre* 1 (1969): 74–78, compromises and has the galleries to each side of the stage rest on the stage platform itself while the galleries in the auditorium rest on the floor of the hall. Because Orrell persuasively argues that the private theater auditoriums were U-shaped and that their pit floors ascended in wedge-shaped steps, galleries would presumably be positioned at least as high as the stage (*The Human Stage*, 193–203).

43. See C. W. Wallace, *The Evolution of the English Drama*, Schriften der Deutschen Shakespeare-Gesellschaft (Berlin, 1912), 4: 175, and Hillebrand, *The Child Actors*, 183.

44. MSC 2, pt. 2: 223 and passim. Nelson, *Early Cambridge Theatres*, 52, 56–58, suggests that "haircloths" were sometimes placed over windows to protect their glass lights.

45. Orrell, *The Theatres of Inigo Jones and John Webb*, 95–100.

46. R. A. Foakes, *Illustrations of the English Stage: 1580–1642* (Stanford, 1985), 70–71, identifies the wall facing the pond (and the viewer) in Danckert's painting as corresponding to the stage-right wall in Webb's plan.

47. Pre-Restoration Office of Works accounts for the Cockpit-in-Court are cited from Bentley, *The Jacobean and Caroline Stage*, 6: 272–73.

48. Restoration Office of Works citations are from Eleanore Boswell, *The Restoration Court Stage* (1932; rpt. New York, 1966), 240–41.

49. John Astington, "The Whitehall Cockpit," *English Literary Renaissance* 12 (1982): 312–13.

50. Reproduced in London County Council, *Survey of London*, 44 vols. (London, 1900–1994), 14: pl. 9.

51. Orrell, *The Human Stage*, 30–48.

52. Palme, *The Triumph of Peace*, 215.

53. Palme, *The Triumph of Peace*, 200–224.

54. See Nathaniel Lloyd, *A History of the English House* (New York, 1931), 117–19, 327–32, for a pictorial history of English windows.

55. Palme, *The Triumph of Peace*, 207.

56. See Hillebrand, *The Child Actors*, 183. Terminology is confusing: shutters were often called "windows," while wooden window frames inserted in masonry were usually called "casements"; see L. F. Salzman, *Building in England Down to 1540* (Oxford, 1952), 255–58.

57. Bentley, *The Jacobean and Caroline Stage*, 4: 529, 5: 1263–64.

58. Herford, Simpson, and Simpson, *Ben Jonson*, 8: 407. Palme (*The Triumph of Peace*, 221) rehearses a long, unconvincing chain of obscure associations to show that "slyding" means "sloping," as in the translation of *Fenestre bastarde* in Randle Cotgrave's *Dictionarie* (London, 1611): "a sloping window (as in some shops) yeelding a false light." I take these sliding windows to refer to sliding window shutters or, perhaps, to the sliding scenes themselves, which by the Restoration were called shutters. Similarly, "false Lights" may refer to boarded-up windowpanes, but Jonson may be inveighing against artificial lights near the scenes or to awnings or canopies of some kind, which are equated with false lights in *Women Beware Women* (1653; rpt. Berkeley, 1969), 47.

59. W. J. Lawrence, "The Elizabethan Nocturnal," in *Pre-Restoration Stage Studies* (Cambridge, Mass., 1927), 122–45. K. Brown, "More light, more light," 1–13, correctly dismisses Lawrence's theories.

60. Bentley, *The Jacobean and Caroline Stage*, 6: 294.

61. Thomas Dekker, *Worke for Armorours* (London, 1609), B1–B1^v.

62. *MSC* 6 (1961 [1962]): 47.

63. Gregorio Leti, *Il Cardinalismo di Santa Chiesa; or The History of the Cardinals of the Roman Church* (London, 1670), 91.

64. The calculation of daylight indoors is explained by Hopkinson, *Architectural Physics*, 50–88.

65. Hopkinson, *Architectural Physics*, 19.

7. Theatrical Lighting at Court

1. Cited in Orgel and Strong, *Inigo Jones*, 1: 284.

2. Chambers, *The Elizabethan Stage*, 1: 225.

3. *MSC* 2, pt. 3: 354–55; Bawcutt, *The Control and Censorship of Caroline Drama*, 199.

4. Bawcutt, *The Control and Censorship of Caroline Drama*, 135–217.

5. Other multiple performances were on 22 February 1596, 6 January 1601, 14 February 1602, 20 February 1604, and 6 February 1634; see the court calendars in Chambers, *The Elizabethan Stage*, 4: appendix A, and Bentley, *The Jacobean and Caroline Stage*, 7: appendix C.

6. Kernan, *Shakespeare, the King's Playwright*, xvii, assigns *A Midsummer Night's Dream* to the afternoon, but Dudley Carleton puts it at night; see Chambers, *William Shakespeare*, 2: 329.

7. Orrell, *The Human Stage*, 107.

8. *MSC* 10: xvii.

9. *MSC* 10: 36.

10. Feuillerat, *Elizabeth*, 216, 218. Feuillerat prints eleven accounts and miscellaneous records covering 1571 to 1588. Jacobean and Caroline accounts are printed in *MSC* 13. Although the authenticity of the 1604–5 and 1611–12 accounts has been questioned, they are now generally regarded as genuine.

11. Feuillerat, *Elizabeth*, 237, 159, 196; also 295, 353, and 380. Jacobean and Caroline accounts also list numerous entries for ropes and rods to hang the branches; see *MSC* 13: 27, 32, 38, 43, 50.

12. Feuillerat, *Elizabeth*, 159, 237.

13. Feuillerat, *Elizabeth*, 353, 368.

14. Feuillerat, *Elizabeth*, 309, 327, 338.

15. *MSC* 13: 50, 57.

16. Orgel and Strong, *Inigo Jones*, 1: 282.

17. Feuillerat, *Elizabeth*, 274; *MSC* 13: 51.

18. Feuillerat, *Elizabeth*, 203, 327.

19. Wickham, *Early English Stages*, 2, pt. 2: 213.

20. *MSC* 13: 10, 11, 127.

21. Feuillerat, *Elizabeth*, 159. For use above the spectators, Sabbattini (*Pratica di fabricar*, bk. 1, chap. 38, p. 54) recommends chandeliers that support only three candles.

22. MSC 13: 10.

23. MSC 13: 50.

24. MSC 13: 83.

25. Orrell, *The Human Stage*, 109.

26. Feuillerat, *Elizabeth*, 176, 202.

27. MSC 13: 10.

28. MSC 13: 51.

29. Bentley, *The Jacobean and Caroline Stage*, 6: 286.

30. Feuillerat, *Elizabeth*, 325.

31. Feuillerat, *Elizabeth*, 237, 228, 202, 216.

32. Morton Paterson, "The Stagecraft of the Revels Office during the Reign of Elizabeth," in *Studies in the Elizabethan Theatre*, 46, gives a brief account of court lighting in which this interpretation of "hats" plays the major part. He takes the association of hats with funnels and pipes to imply a ventilation system for lanterns; but the usual Elizabethan term for the top of a lantern was "nozzle." In 1560–61, for example, Trinity College, Cambridge, purchased a "greate nosell for the stage lanthorne." See Nelson, *Early Cambridge Theatres*, 112, who suggests this nozzle was a socket to hold a candle; but it more likely refers to the funnel-shaped lid of a large lantern with multiple candles.

33. Feuillerat, *Elizabeth*, 202, 210, 176; MSC 13: 50.

34. MSC 13: 98, 122, 58.

35. Feuillerat, *Elizabeth*, 327.

36. Feuillerat, *Elizabeth*, 176, 202, 237, 327, 353, 300, 368.

37. Feuillerat, *Elizabeth*, 209, 208, 206. The masque was canceled because of the "tediousness" of the play that night.

38. MSC 13: 52, 58, 64, 70, 84, 105, 111, 116, 123, 134, 141.

39. Orgel and Strong, *Inigo Jones*, 2: 464.

40. MSC 12 (1983): 45, 63.

41. Bawcutt, *The Control and Censorship of Caroline Drama*, 187.

42. See Scott McMillin, "Jonson's Early Entertainments," *Renaissance Drama* 1 (1968): 155.

43. E. Boswell, *The Restoration Court Stage*, 92.

44. J. R. Elliot and J. Buttrey, "The Royal Plays at Christ Church 1636: A New Document," *Theatre Research International* 10 (1985): 104.

45. See E. Boswell, *The Restoration Court Stage*, 95.

46. Herford, Simpson, and Simpson, *Ben Jonson*, 10: 419; Bentley, *The Jacobean and Caroline Stage*, 5: 1228; E. K. Chambers, *Aurelian Townshend's Poems and Masks* (Oxford, 1912), 83.

47. Herford, Simpson, and Simpson, *Ben Jonson*, 7: 186, 314.

48. John Nichols, *The Progresses . . . of James the First* (London, 1828), 2: 742.

49. Serly, *The First Booke of Architecture*, bk. 2, chap. 3, fol. 25. Serlio's treatise appeared in Paris in 1545 and in a Dutch edition, from which the English translation was made.

50. Herford, Simpson, and Simpson, *Ben Jonson*, 7: 346.

51. Herford, Simpson, and Simpson, *Ben Jonson*, 7: 155.

52. Orgel and Strong, *Inigo Jones*, 1: 126–27.

53. Allardyce Nicoll, *Stuart Masques and the Renaissance Stage* (London, 1938), 129; C. F. Bell, "The Artificial Lighting of the Court Stage," in *Ben Jonson*, 10: 413–20.

54. Bell, "The Artificial Lighting of the Court Stage," 10: 420.

55. *MSC* 13: 114–15.

56. Feuillerat, *Elizabeth*, table 2, l. 36; Orrell, *The Theatres of Inigo Jones and John Webb*, 24–25; Foakes, *Illustrations of the English Stage*, 61. Office of Works accounts sometimes mention oil—in one case clearly for plays at Somerset House (*MSC* 10: 54)—but this oil seems to be intended for lubrication. Some descriptions of court masques mention burning lamps as properties, for example, for the 1561 *Masque of Wise and Foolish Virgins* (Chambers, *The Elizabethan Stage*, 1: 159); Jonson's masques also call for occasional property lamps, but they may not always have been lit.

57. See E. Boswell, *The Restoration Court Stage*, 163, 268.

58. Feuillerat, *Elizabeth*, table 2.

59. Francis Bacon, *The Essays or Covnsels, Civill and Morall: of Francis Lo. Verdam* (London, 1639), 224–25.

60. Nicoll, *The Development of the Theatre*, 275.

61. Serly, *The First Booke of Architecture*, bk. 2, chap. 3, fol. 26; Donald Mullin, "Lighting on the Eighteenth-Century London Stage: A Reconsideration," *Theatre Notebook* 34 (1980): 84.

62. Herford, Simpson, and Simpson, *Ben Jonson*, 6: 314.

63. Herford, Simpson, and Simpson, *Ben Jonson*, 6: 257–58.

64. Herford, Simpson, and Simpson, *Ben Jonson*, 6: 171.

65. George Chapman, *The Memorable Maske* (London, 1613), A2.

66. Bruce Allsopp, ed., *Inigo Jones on Palladio* (Newcastle on Tyne, 1970), 1: 1. As early as 1514, Baldassare Peruzzi had also placed his lights "di dentro che servono alla prospettiva"—that is, within or inside the perspective scene; see Giorgio Vasari, *Le Vite de' più eccellenti pittori scultori e architettori* (1550; rpt. Milan, 1963), 4: 266.

67. Herford, Simpson, and Simpson, *Ben Jonson*, 6: 425; Chambers, *Aurelian Townshend's Poems and Masks*, 83.

68. Orgel and Strong, *Inigo Jones*, 1: 194.

69. Nicoll, *Stuart Masques*, 73.

70. W. A. Armstrong, "Ben Jonson and Jacobean Stagecraft," in *Jacobean Theatre*, ed. J. R. Brown and B. Harris (1960; rpt. New York, 1967), 51; Herford, Simpson, and Simpson, *Ben Jonson*, 8: 405.

71. This less-abstract movement of light coincides with Jones's growing interest in large perspective scenes, described well by Orrell, *The Human Stage*, 225–52.

72. See Kenneth Richards, "Changeable Scenery for Plays on the Caroline Stage," *Theatre Notebook* 23 (1968): 20; John Freehafer, "Perspective Scenery and the Caroline Playhouses," *Theatre Notebook* 27 (1973): 102–4; and T. J. King, "*Hannibal and Scipio* (1637): How 'The Places Sometimes Changed,'" *Theatre Notebook* 29 (1975): 20–22.

73. Orrell, *The Theatres of Inigo Jones and John Webb*, 11–12.

8. Artificial Light in the Indoor Playhouses

1. Francis Beaumont and John Fletcher, *Comedies and Tragedies* (London, 1647), Bbbbbb3ᵛ.

2. Herford, Simpson, and Simpson, *Ben Jonson*, 8: 370–71.

3. An agreement between Samuel Daniel and the Queen's Revels children specifies the company will perform only "Six Monethes in euerie yeare" (Hillebrand, *The Child Actors*, 335).

4. J. Issacs, *Production and Stage-Management at the Blackfriars Theatre* (London, 1933), 4.

5. Thomas Middleton, *Michaelmas Term* (London, 1607), A3.

6. Bentley, *The Jacobean and Caroline Stage*, 1: 312.

7. Chambers, *The Elizabethan Stage*, 3: 282.

8. John Marston, *What You Will* (London, 1607), A2–A3.

9. Bentley, *The Jacobean and Caroline Stage*, 4: 629–30. The title page puts the premiere in 1625, but this date was apparently old-style, given the play's allusions to Lent and the coronation of Charles I (27 March 1626).

10. Herford, Simpson, and Simpson, *Ben Jonson*, 6: 280.

11. Orgel and Strong, *Inigo Jones*, 1: 282. Stressing that candles should be lit as quickly as possible to prevent the spectators from becoming restless, Sabbattini (*Pratica di fabricar*, bk. 1, chap. 41, p. 56) also recommended that the candles not be lit until the audience was seated and the performance about to begin.

12. The provenance of these plays is unclear: they are pre-Restoration in style but bear traces of Restoration revision. There is no record of them before their publication, and a dedicatory epistle to the publisher intimates they were never performed.

13. Francis Lenton, *The Young Gallant's Whirligig* (London, 1629), C4ᵛ.

14. George Wither, *Faire-Virtue* (London, 1622), F4ᵛ.

15. *The Overburian Characters*, ed. W. J. Paylor (Oxford, 1936), 60.

16. See Henry Fitz-Geoffrey, "Notes from Blackfriars" (1617), in which a stage sitter sees a rival "drop / out of the *Tyring-house*" (Bentley, *The Jacobean and Caroline Stage*, 6: 44); and Francis Beaumont's *The Knight of the Burning Pestle* (London, 1613), B1ᵛ, acted at Blackfriars around 1607, where the citizen's wife must climb up onto the stage because there are no stairs leading up from the pit.

17. W. A. Armstrong, *The Elizabethan Private Theatres* (London, 1958), 13.

18. *OED*, s.v. "sconce" (*sb.*³): "A small fort or earthwork; esp. one built to defend a fort, pass, castle-gate, etc., or erected as a counterfort."

19. Emmett L. Avery, *The London Stage, 1700–1729: A Critical Introduction* (Carbondale, 1968), xlviii.

20. See J. J. Elson, ed., *The Wits, or Sport upon Sport* (Ithaca, 1932), 426.

21. Astington, "*The Wits* Illustration, 1662," 122–40.

22. I. C., *The Two Merry Milkmaids*, O1–O1^v.

23. G[offe], *The Careless Shepherdess*, cited in G. E. Bentley, *The Seventeenth-Century Stage* (Chicago, 1968), 33.

24. Sabbattini, *Pratica di fabricar*, bk. 1, chap. 41, p. 57, trans. in Nagler, *A Source Book in Theatrical History*, 90.

25. Mullin, "Lighting on the Eighteenth-Century London Stage," 74.

26. For example, Dublin theaters of the eighteenth century were lit "with tallow candles, stuck into tin circles hanging from the middle of the stage, which were every now and then snuffed by some performer" (Charles B. Hogan, *The London Stage, 1776–1800: A Critical Introduction* [Carbondale, 1968], lxv).

27. Bentley, *The Jacobean and Caroline Stage*, 6: 105–6. Cunningham did not say where he found the manuscript, and its whereabouts are unknown today.

28. "To my friend, Master John Fletcher, upon his 'Faithful Shepherdess'" (c. 1609), *The Works of Francis Beaumont and John Fletcher*, ed. A. H. Bullen (London, 1908), 3: 12.

29. *The Diary of Samuel Pepys*, 8: 55.

30. Recent reconstructions estimate its outside dimensions as 50 by 112 feet; see Donald C. Mullin, "The Theatre Royal, Bridges Street: A Conjectural Restoration," *Educational Theatre Journal* 19 (1967): 25–28; and Richard Leacroft, *The Development of the English Playhouse* (Ithaca, 1973), 83.

31. Bentley, *The Jacobean and Caroline Stage*, 6: 88, 92.

32. Bentley, *The Jacobean and Caroline Stage*, 6: 97, 100, 104, 112.

33. Murray, *English Dramatic Companies*, 1: 269; Gurr, *The Shakespearian Playing Companies*, 433–34.

34. MSC 1, pts. 4 and 5 (1911): 365.

35. Hillebrand, *The Child Actors*, 224, although the chronicler of Otto of Hesse-Cassel's trip to London in 1611 says that the boys at Whitefriars played "nur bei lichtern"; Chambers, *The Elizabethan Stage*, 2: 369.

36. Pertinent Office of Works accounts for the Cockpit-in-Court are from MSC 10: 40–44; Revels Office accounts are from MSC 13: 110, 126, and 133.

37. Restoration Office of Works citations are from E. Boswell, *The Restoration Court Stage*, 15–16, 240–41.

38. Bergman, *Lighting in the Theatre*, 26.

39. Wither, *Faire-Virtue*, F4^v.

40. John Heywood, *A dialogue conteinyng the nomber in effect of all the prouerbes In the englishe tongue* (London, 1546), B2.

41. Andrew Gurr, *Shakespeare's Hats* (Rome, 1993). Hats also served the practical function of intercepting tallow and wax dripping from overhead, both on stage and in everyday rooms.

42. See Palmer, *The Lighting Art*, 21, for the calculation of the effect of glare on visibility.

43. Denis Diderot, *Oeuvres Complètes* (Paris, 1980), 10: 435.

44. Thomas Campbell, *Life of Mrs Siddons* (London, 1834), 2: 38.

45. Chambers, *William Shakespeare*, 2: 319–35, lists recorded performances of the company.

46. Gurr, "Playing in Amphitheatres," 47–62.

47. Sabbattini, *Pratica di fabricar*, L3–L3ᵛ.

48. *The Works of John Dryden*, ed. J. H. Smith and D. MacMillan (Berkeley, 1962), 8: 103. The earliest stage direction calling for the extinction of playhouse candles is in Shadwell's 1674 adaptation of *The Tempest* (Montague Summers, *Restoration Theatre* [London, 1934], 191, 194, 275).

49. Thomas Heywood, 2 *Iron Age* (London, 1632), D4ᵛ; Richard Brome, *A Mad Couple Well Matched* (London, 1653), F6ᵛ. The provenance of both plays is somewhat cloudy. Brome's play might possibly have been written for Salisbury Court a year or so earlier. Heywood's play was later revived at the Cockpit in Drury Lane, after which it was published. Thus, its stage direction might possibly also reflect the use of pantomime indoors to suggest night. See Alan C. Dessen, *Recovering Shakespeare's Theatrical Vocabulary* (Cambridge, 1995), 139 ff., for a thorough discussion of "as if" stage directions, including ones indicating imagined darkness.

50. Herford, Simpson, and Simpson, *Ben Jonson*, 5: 445. Lawrence, *Pre-Restoration Stage Studies*, 229, lists a half-dozen allusions to mists and fogs in dialogue and two stage directions calling for damp and mist, but none is identified with imaginary darkness.

51. Francis Beaumont and John Fletcher, *The Maid's Tragedy* (London, 1619), C1. The title page gives Blackfriars as the site of production, probably in the 1610–11 winter season. The play was also performed at court, 1612–13 (Chambers, *The Elizabethan Stage*, 3: 224). The only known production of *Catiline* was at court on 9 November 1634.

52. Herford, Simpson, and Simpson, *Ben Jonson*, 5: 445.

9. Property Lights and Special Effects

1. W. J. Lawrence's essays "Light and Darkness in the Elizabethan Theatre," in *The Elizabethan Playhouse*, 2: 1–22, and "Characteristics of Platform Stage Spectacle," in *Pre-Restoration Stage Studies*, 251–76, recount the major effects with a wealth of examples. Lee Mitchell, "Shakespeare's Lighting Effects," *Speech Monographs* 15 (1948): 72–84, centers on the lighting effects and classifies them by chronographic, symbolic, ceremonial, and metaphoric functions—categories that I have slightly altered for my own purposes. Brownell Salomon, "Visual and Aural Signs in the Performed English Renaissance Play," *Renaissance Drama* 5 (1972): 163–64, follows in Mitchell's footsteps with a semiological view of property lights in non-Shakespearean drama. Alan C. Dessen, *Elizabethan Stage Conventions and Modern Interpreters* (Cambridge, 1984), 70–83, demonstrates the complexity of transferring Renaissance lighting conventions to the modern stage.

2. Armstrong, *The Elizabethan Private Theatres*, 12; and Henry Chettle, *The Tragedy of Hoffman* (London, 1631), H.

3. Foakes and Rickert, *Henslowe's Diary*, 207.

4. R. A. Foakes, "Tragedy at the Children's Theatres after 1600," *The Elizabethan Theatre* 2 (1970): 52, sees an early children's theater influence in the play.

5. Marston, *What You Will*, H1^v.

6. Robert Armin, *The History of the Two Maids of More-clack* (London, 1609), A1^v. Later, in a welcoming ceremony, lords and ladies parade over the stage "so many as may be" (H2^v). Such indefinite and "permissive" stage directions (usually without lights) are common and associated with authorial, rather than playhouse, intentions; see W. W. Greg, *The Shakespeare First Folio* (Oxford, 1955), 135–38.

7. Similarly in John Marston's *Antonio's Revenge* (London, 1602), a funeral procession includes *"two mourners with torches, two with streamers; Castilio & Forobosco, with torches"* (C3).

8. Peter Arnott, *Greek Scenic Conventions in the Fifth Century B.C.* (London, 1962), 121, finds that darkness was indicated at the daylit Theater of Dionysos in Athens by a burning lamp in *Iphigeneia in Aulis* and by choruses carrying lighted torches in the *Rhesus* and the *Ekklesiazusae*. He notes that the convention was reputed to be common in Middle Comedy. As a corollary to this convention, a standard sight gag in ancient comedy was singeing fellow actors; the scholiast on *Lysistrata* 1218 plausibly concludes that "it is vulgar to come on stage with a lamp and burn somebody."

9. Lawrence, *The Elizabethan Playhouse*, 1: 6–7, 2: 2–3.

10. Harley Granville-Parker, *Prefaces to Shakespeare* (Princeton, 1946), 1: 472.

11. In *Richard III*, in a similar scene with a soldier in a tent dreaming of ghosts, Richard notes that "[t]he Lights burne blew," that is, dim (F 3642). Both effects would be difficult to produce at the outdoor amphitheaters.

12. Dessen, *Recovering Shakespeare's Theatrical Vocabulary*, 166.

13. Dessen, *Recovering Shakespeare's Theatrical Vocabulary*, 35.

14. *Tragedy of Alphonsus, Emperor of Germany* (London, 1654), B. Similarly, in Marston's *Antonio's Revenge*, Antonio follows the tapers discussed above in his nightgown and nightcap. In assigning plays to Blackfriars and the Cockpit in Drury Lane, I follow T. J. King in citing plays whose stage directions probably reflect actual stage practice there; see King's "Staging of Plays at the Phoenix in Drury Lane," *Theatre Notebook* 19 (1965): 149–50, and his review article of I. Smith's *Shakespeare's Blackfriars Playhouse* in *Renaissance Drama* 9 (1966): 297–99.

15. An eyewitness description of English actors in Germany around 1626 recounts the scene with slightly different emphasis. Real moonshine is never considered, but a red and yellow paper moon and one made of rotten wood that glows in the dark are. The mechanicals conclude that the most "natural" method is a lantern "hung on a butcher's skewer, which one of us will carry and move along with it a little every quarter hour"; see Ernest Brennecke, *Shakespeare in Germany* (Chicago, 1964), 65.

16. Foakes and Rickert, *Henslowe's Diary*, 319–20.

17. Allan Holaday, "Heywood's *Troia Britannica* and the *Ages*," *JEGP* 14 (1946): 437.

18. [1] *Troublesome Reign of John* (1591; rpt. London, 1911), G2ᵛ.

19. Chambers, *The Elizabethan Stage*, 4: 23.

20. Thomas Wright, *A History of Domestic Manners and Sentiments in England During the Middle Ages* (London, 1862), 454–55.

21. Kernodle, *From Art to Theatre*, 142.

22. Salter, *Mediaeval Drama in Chester*, 17.

23. Hardin Craig, "The London Cordwainers' Pageant," *PMLA* 25 (1917): 606.

24. Chambers, *The Mediaeval Stage*, 2: 399.

25. [George Peele,] *The Battle of Alcazar* (London, 1594), F. In *Two Elizabethan Stage Abridgments* (London, 1922), 117, W. W. Greg argued that the text of *The Battle of Alcazar* was a cut version for the provinces (which might well have included indoor performances), while the "plot," which does not specifically mention the blazing star, reflects practice at the Rose. However, David Bradley, *From Text to Performance in the Elizabethan Theatre* (Cambridge, 1992), convincingly shows that differences between the plot and text were not caused by different performance venues but rather by the process of preparing the play for the stage. Still, another Rose play, *Captain Thomas Stukeley* (London, 1605; fac. rpt. London, 1911), K, performed around 1596, uses a blazing star in a very similar dumb show.

26. William Rowley, *The Birth of Merlin* (London, 1662), F4–F4ᵛ.

27. Jewkes, *Act Division in Elizabethan and Jacobean Plays*, 309.

28. John Bate, *The Mysteries of Nature and Art* (London, 1635), P4ᵛ.

29. Thomas Dekker and John Webster, *Northward Ho!* (London, 1607; fac. rpt. London, 1914), F3ᵛ–F4.

30. John Marston, *Parasitaster, or The Fawn* (London, 1606), B.

31. Inga-Stina Ewbank, "A Note on 'The Revenger's Tragedy,'" *Notes and Queries* 200 (1955): 98–99.

32. Chambers, *The Elizabethan Stage*, 3: 110.

33. See also D. L. Frost, *The School of Shakespeare* (Cambridge, 1968), 259–60.

34. Thomas Goffe, *The Courageous Turk* (London, 1632), H; and Bentley, *The Jacobean and Caroline Stage*, 4: 506.

35. Chambers, *The Elizabethan Stage*, 3: 342–43; Madeleine Doran, ed., *If You Know Not Me* (1606; rpt. London, 1934), 1: xii–xv, 2: xi, E2ᵛ.

36. Bentley, *The Jacobean and Caroline Stage*, 1: 109, 2: 695; and John Fletcher, *Rollo, Duke of Normandy; or The Bloody Brother*, ed. J. D. Jump (London, 1636; fac. rpt. London, 1948), 67.

37. Bentley, *The Jacobean and Caroline Stage*, 2: 695.

38. W. W. Greg, ed., *Dramatic Documents from the Elizabethan Playhouses* (Oxford, 1931), 1: 310. Greg dates the manuscript to around 1600.

39. Continental effects were sometimes more sophisticated. For a 1539 play (and *intermedii*) in the great courtyard of the Medici palace at Florence, for example, Aristotile de San Gallo created a sun, approximately two feet high, made of a crystal ball filled with water behind which two torches shone. Over the courtyard was stretched an artificial sky of blue cloth, from which also hung lights. The sun was controlled by a winch (*arganetto*) that drew the sun along an arc, so that the sun rose to the zenith by the middle of the comedy and sank in the west by the end. Giorgio Vasari claimed it "looked like a veritable sun" (*Le Vite de' più eccellenti pittori scultori e architettori*, 5: 475).

40. See Filippo Pigafetta's first-hand account in Nagler, *A Source Book in Theatrical History*, 81–86.

41. Chambers, *The Elizabethan Stage*, 2: 455.

42. John Ford, *The Broken Heart* (London, 1633), D2.

43. Christopher Marlowe, *The Tragical History of Doctor Faustus* (London, 1616), H2.

44. John Melton, *Astrologaster* (London, 1620), E4.

45. Dekker, *Worke for Armorours*, F4.

46. Serly, *The First Booke of Architecture*, bk. 2, chap. 3, fol. 26v.

47. *A Warning for Fair Women*, A2v.

48. *The Poems of Richard Lovelace*, ed. C. Wilkinson (Oxford, 1930), 67. The play itself has not survived.

49. L. B. Campbell, *Scenes and Machines*, 64–65, 157, describes the classical method of painting lightning on *periaktoi* (which could be spun) or on planks (which could be dropped from the heavens) and a seventeenth-century Italian method of cutting a board lengthwise in a zigzag pattern and then placing candles behind while the rift between the two sections of the board was opened and closed.

50. Robert Wilson, *The Cobler's Prophecy* (1594; rpt. London, 1914), G1v–G2. The provenance of the play is unclear; Chambers, *The Elizabethan Stage*, 3: 516, suggests a courtly venue.

51. Beaumont and Fletcher, *Comedies and Tragedies*, Hhhh1.

52. R. C. Bald, *Bibliographical Studies in the Beaumont and Fletcher Folio* (London, 1938), 78; Chambers, *The Elizabethan Stage*, 3: 228.

53. Thomas Middleton, *A Game at Chess* (MS c. 1624; fac. printing London, 1990), fol. 43b. In James Shirley's *St. Patrick for Ireland* (London, 1640)—written for the Dublin stage—an altar is discovered, lights and incense prepared, and a "flame behinde the Altar" ignites (C4v).

54. Robert Fludd, *Utriusque cosmi maioris scilicet et minoris metaphysica, physica atqve technica historia*, Tomus Primus, Tractatus Secundus: *De naturae simia seu technica macrocosmi historia* (Oppenheim, 1618), 477. My translation.

55. Christopher Marlowe, 2 *Tamburlaine* (London, 1590), H2.

56. Fludd, *Utriusque*, 477–78.

57. Albert Feuillerat, ed., *Documents Relating to the Revels at Court in the Time of King Edward VI and Queen Mary* (Louvain, 1914), 110.

58. Sabbattini, *Pratica di fabricar*, bk. 2, chap. 11, trans. in Barnard Hewitt, *The Renaissance Stage* (Coral Gables, 1958), 111.

59. Feuillerat, *Elizabeth*, 142.

60. Durand, "*Palamon and Arcyte*," 514.

61. Thomas Sackville and Thomas Norton, *Gorboduc* (London, 1565), C5.

62. Note the costume designs for Thomas Campion's *Lords' Masque*, 1613. The earl of Salisbury paid twenty-two shillings "for cutting 42 flames and coulleringe them" for his headpiece; see Orgel and Strong, *Inigo Jones*, 1: 242 and pl. 81 (see also William Davenant, *The Temple of Love*, 1635).

63. T. Lupton, *All for Money* (1578; rpt. London, 1910), Bij and Eij.

64. Frances Teague, *Shakespeare's Speaking Properties* (Lewisburg, 1991), 19–20, 158–93.

10. Illuminating the Scene: *The Duchess of Malfi* at the Globe and Blackfriars

1. Una Ellis-Fermor, *The Jacobean Drama*, 4th ed., rev. (1961; rpt. New York, 1964), 275.

2. Styan, *Shakespeare's Stagecraft*, 42–44.

3. John Russell Brown, ed., *The Duchess of Malfi*, by John Webster (London, 1964), xxiii.

4. All subsequent citations are from the 1612 edition.

5. All subsequent citations are from the 1623 edition.

6. J. Brown, *The Duchess of Malfi*, xxiii.

7. On the absurdities resulting from too much illusion in the illumination of Shakespearean revivals, see G. Wilson Knight, *Shakespearean Production* (Evanston, Ill., 1964), 63–65. Martin White, *Renaissance Drama in Action* (London, 1998), 151, argues that, at Blackfriars, the audience would be as surprised as the Duchess is by the dead man's hand, while at the Globe, the audience would experience the scene from Ferdinand's point of view.

8. The date of the original production can be fixed at 1613 or 1614 because the play incorporates material not published until late 1612 and because its cast list includes William Ostler, who died in December 1614. In suggesting that the play could work as well at the Globe as at Blackfriars, I am aware that the Globe fire on 29 June 1613 cut short the first of the two Globe seasons in which the play could have premiered and perhaps delayed the beginning of the second until the new theater was finished. See Bentley, *The Jacobean and Caroline Stage*, 6: 182.

9. We know that the play was cut, but the most frequently mentioned constraint—early sunsets—does not support a theory that the playhouse windows were covered.

10. Chambers, *The Elizabethan Stage*, 3: 511. Marion Lomax, *Stage Images and Traditions* (Cambridge, 1987), 147, in an insightful comparison of *The White Devil* and *The Duchess of Malfi*, concludes that the reference to Ostler in the cast list implies a De-

cember 1614 performance of the latter play. This is possible, perhaps even likely, but the December date provides only a *terminus ad quem* for the premiere.

11. I do not include in this list the light that Antonio believes he sees over the Duchess's grave in act 5, scene 3. J. Brown (*The Duchess of Malfi*, xxxv) takes this hallucination to be a special lighting effect that would have to be "cut for performance at the Globe," although he can hardly believe the dead-man's-hand scene was also cut there. It is questionable whether there is any light at all, but if one were required I imagine a torch held by the Duchess's ghost would have done as well at the Globe as at Blackfriars. Lomax (*Stage Images and Traditions*, 146) draws my attention to Arthur C. Kirsch's view (*Jacobean Dramatic Perspectives* [Charlottesville, 1972], 111) that "in the last acts of *The Duchess*, the artificial and the natural become interchangeable."

12. MSC 13: 108.

13. Dessen, *Elizabethan Stage Conventions*, 78, discusses a similar effect in *Macbeth* 3.3.19, where one of Banquo's murderers mistakenly puts out his light.

14. See, for example, M. L. Wine, ed., *Drama of the English Renaissance* (New York, 1969), 498; and E. M. Brennan, ed., *The Duchess of Malfi*, by John Webster, New Mermaid ed. (London, 1964), 114–15, who, disregarding the many scenes of pretended darkness in public theater plays, believes Bosola's mistaken killing of Antonio in act 5, scene 4, was due to the weak light "provided by candles or lanterns which the speakers held." Ellis-Fermor, *The Jacobean Drama*, 43, remarks that Bosola's last speech could not be spoken in an outdoor theater "with that almost inaudible faintness which the implied musical notation demands." She does not insist on a Blackfriars premiere, but, in any case, one doubts John Lowin threw away these lines to inaudibility at the Globe.

15. Frank Kermode, ed., *The Tempest*, [New] Arden Shakespeare (Cambridge, Mass., 1958), 151–52.

16. Andrew Gurr, "*The Tempest*'s Tempest at Blackfriars," *Shakespeare Survey* 41 (1989): 91–102, points to the break between acts 4 and 5 (Prospero exits and then immediately reenters) as confirming Blackfriars provenance for *The Tempest*.

17. Dekker wished *The White Devil* a "*Faire and Fortunate Day*" in a dedication to his own play, *If This Be Not a Good Play* (London, 1612), A3ᵛ.

18. For a reasonable account of it, see J. R. Mulryne, "*The White Devil* and *The Duchess of Malfi*," *Stratford-upon-Avon Studies* 1 (1960), rpt. in *Jacobean Theatre*, 223. Clifford Leech, "'Three Times *Ho* and a Brace of Widows': Some Plays for the Private Theatre," *The Elizabethan Theatre* 3 (1973): 32, points out that the Duchess transcends the prejudice against remarriage in private theater drama. The sympathetic treatment of Antonio's rise in fortune also seems out of character for a play written expressly for a private theater "coterie."

19. William Shakespeare, *The Rape of Lucrece* (London, 1594; fac. rpt. London, 1890), F.

20. Francis Beaumont and John Fletcher, *A King and No King* (London, 1619), 13ᵛ.

21. H. T. Price, "The Function of Imagery in Webster," *PMLA* 20 (1955), rpt. in *Elizabethan Drama*, ed. R. J. Kaufmann (London, 1961), 225–49.

22. See Andrew Gurr's introduction to the Revels edition of Beaumont and Fletcher's *Philaster*, xxxv–xliv, for a balanced assessment of the influence of the Blackfriars on the King's men's repertory and this play.

23. *MSC* 13: 10.

24. Orrell, *The Theatres of Inigo Jones and John Webb*, 11.

25. Geoffrey Tillotson, "*Othello* and *The Alchemist* at Oxford in 1610," *TLS*, 20 July 1933, 494.

26. Tillotson, "*Othello* and *The Alchemist* at Oxford," 494.

INDEX

R. B. Graves is an associate professor and the director of the Ph.D. program in theater at the University of Illinois, Urbana-Champaign. His research includes articles on early modern and Irish theater and (with A. J. Kim) a book on contemporary Korean drama.